P9-DUX-807

ALSO BY ELIZABETH D. SAMET

No Man's Land: Preparing for War and Peace in Post-9/11 America

Soldier's Heart: Reading Literature Through Peace and War at West Point

Willing Obedience: Citizens, Soldiers, and the Progress of Consent in America, 1776–1898

EDITED BY ELIZABETH D. SAMET

World War II Memoirs: The Pacific Theater

The Annotated Memoirs of Ulysses S. Grant

Leadership: Essential Writings by Our Greatest Thinkers

LOOKING
FOR THE
GOOD WAR

LOOKING
THE
GOOD WAR

AMERICAN AMNESIA

AND THE VIOLENT

PURSUIT OF HAPPINESS

ELIZABETH D.
SAMET

FARRAR, STRAUS AND GIROUX
NEW YORK

FARRAR, STRAUS AND GIROUX   NEW YORK

LOOKING FOR THE GOOD WAR

AMERICAN AMNESIA
AND THE VIOLENT
PURSUIT OF HAPPINESS

ELIZABETH D. SAMET

Farrar, Straus and Giroux
120 Broadway, New York 10271

Grateful acknowledgment is made for permission to reprint an excerpt from
"The Good War": An Oral History of World War Two, copyright © 1984 by Studs
Terkel. Reprinted by permission of The New Press. www.thenewpress.com.

Library of Congress Cataloging-in-Publication Data
Names: Samet, Elizabeth D., author.
Title: Looking for the good war : American amnesia and the violent pursuit
    of happiness / Elizabeth D. Samet.
Other titles: American amnesia and the violent pursuit of happiness
Description: First edition. | New York : Farrar, Straus and Giroux, 2021.
Identifiers: LCCN 2021028289 | ISBN 9780374219925 (hardcover)
Subjects: LCSH: World War, 1939–1945—United States—Influence.
    World War, 1939–1945—Social aspects—United States. | Collective
    memory—United States. | Memory—Social aspects—United States. |
    War and society—United States.
Classification: LCC D744.7.U6 S26 2021 | DDC 940.53/73—dc23
LC record available at https://lccn.loc.gov/2021028289

Our books may be purchased in bulk for promotional, educational, or
business use. Please contact your local bookseller or the Macmillan
Corporate and Premium Sales Department at 1-800-221-7945, extension
5442, or by email at MacmillanSpecialMarkets@macmillan.com.

www.fsgbooks.com
www.twitter.com/fsgbooks • www.facebook.com/fsgbooks

10   9   8   7   6   5   4   3   2   1

In memory of my father,

Theodore S. Samet

(1924–2020)

Staff Sergeant
126th Army Airways Communications System Squadron
Pacific Theater
World War II

War would only be a remedy for a people always seeking glory.
    —Alexis de Tocqueville, *Democracy in America*, part 2 (1840)

Some insisting on the plumbing, and some on saving the world: these being the two great American specialties.
    —D. H. Lawrence, foreword to *Studies in Classic American Literature* (1923)

Yes—what the American public always wants is a tragedy with a happy ending.
    —William Dean Howells on the failed dramatization of Edith Wharton's tragic novel *The House of Mirth*; quoted in Wharton, *A Backward Glance: An Autobiography* (1934)

Sentimentality is a failure of feeling.
    —Wallace Stevens, from the *Adagia* (1957)

So you're unhappy. Relax. There's no law says you got to be happy. Look at me. I'm not happy. But I get my kicks. Gee, how could anybody stand it if they didn't get their kicks?
    —Pat (Mary Astor), *Act of Violence* (1948), dir. Fred Zinnemann

CONTENTS

LOOKING FOR THE GOOD WAR

PROLOGUE: Is This Trip *Really* Necessary?

> Quotation marks have been added, not as a matter of caprice or editorial comment, but simply because the adjective "good" mated to the noun "war" is so incongruous.
>
> —Studs Terkel, note to *"The Good War": An Oral History of World War Two* (1984)

During World War II, American automobile owners were required to affix gas-rationing stickers to their windshields. Drivers were classified by occupation (A, B, C, etc.), each authorized a certain number of gallons per week. The backs of many of these stickers posed a pointed question to the man or woman at the wheel: "Is This Trip *Really* Necessary?" Designed to train civilian attention on an unseen war being fought far away, the sticker became at once a badge of sacrifice and a practical necessity. It would soon become a valuable black-market commodity. In May 1942, to save fuel and tires, a number of states also introduced a thirty-five-mile-per-hour speed limit: Victory Speed. As the literary critic and combat veteran Paul Fussell proposed in his angry, provocative 1989 book *Wartime: Understanding and Behavior in the Second World War,* the resulting "inconvenience" served to remind Americans that there was "a war on." That the public should need reminding; that there was in fact a robust black

market (chiefly in beef and gasoline), operated, as John Steinbeck noted in a 1943 newspaper article, not by "little crooks,
but the best people"; that the government felt the need to
launch an unprecedented propaganda campaign to motivate
civilians and soldiers alike—all these facts suggest the degree
to which the goodness, idealism, and unanimity we today
reflexively associate with World War II were not as readily
apparent to Americans at the time.

John H. Abbott was a conscientious objector assigned by
the authorities to a series of stateside public works details until he refused even this duty. Convicted in 1943 for failing
to remain in a public-service camp, he served two years in a
federal prison. Years after the war, in an interview with Studs
Terkel, Abbott recalled a prank he and some of his fellow
COs used to play: "These gasoline stickers for rationing that
you had on your windshield had a little note on it: Is this trip
really necessary? We'd scratch out 'trip' and write 'war': Is
this war really necessary?" One can disagree with Abbott—in
other words, one can, as I do, believe that the United States'
involvement in the war was necessary—yet still question the
way that participation has been remembered in the wake of
wars considerably less galvanizing and unifying. Has the prevailing memory of the "Good War," shaped as it has been by
nostalgia, sentimentality, and jingoism, done more harm than
good to Americans' sense of themselves and their country's
place in the world? Has the meaning of American force been
perverted by a strident, self-congratulatory insistence that a
war extraordinary in certain aspects was, in fact, unique in
all? Has the desire to divorce that war from history—to interpret victory as proof of America's exceptionalism—blinded
us to our own tragic contingency? Finally, has the repeated
insistence by so many on the country's absolute unity behind
the war effort effectively exacerbated ongoing social and political divisions?

These are some of the questions motivating this book. More than seventy-five years on, World War II remembrance continues to distort the country's past and thus to obstruct the realization of a more expansive future. But that belief hasn't prevented me from asking myself while writing this book, "Is this trip *really* necessary?" Such is the sacral force of war's mythology, especially that of World War II—the good war that served as prologue to three-quarters of a century of misbegotten ones—that I embarked on this project with some trepidation, even as I perceived the need to explore the ways in which retrospective interpretations of the Second World War, the last American military action about which there is anything like a positive consensus, have shaped our thinking about American identity and, in particular, about American violence abroad and at home.

Myths grant life and take it away, give birth to nations and tear them apart. All the countries that fought World War II developed particular narratives about this cataclysmic event. Several—France and Germany most conspicuously, perhaps—have already undergone serial, substantive revisions to their initial versions. There has always been a double edge to the American mythology surrounding World War II: for a long time now, it has simultaneously fortified and diminished the United States. In this book I set out to explore the ways in which the meaning and memory of World War II have evolved and periodically intersected with those of the other wars that have punctuated American history: Korea, Vietnam, and the Gulf War; our more recent wars; and, retrospectively, the Civil War. These conflicts, about which Americans tend to feel far more ambivalence, lie as close as World War II does to the heart of national identity, even if we prefer to think otherwise. Such trips into the past really are necessary if we are to see our way toward a viable future.

INTRODUCTION: One War at a Time

We crossed the Belgian border and went for Mons at 4 o'clock in the afternoon on September 2, 1944 . . . When the first tank crossed the border it stopped. The general was riding behind it . . . and he got out and the first thing he did was urinate. That is the kind of a commander he was, and that is what he thought of World War II . . .

"If we'd got here nine days sooner," I said, "it would have been the thirtieth anniversary of the British retreat from Mons."

"Who cares?" one of the guys said.

"Nobody cares," I said, "but you don't have to get sore about it."

"Nobody's sore about it," he said. "Just let's fight one war at a time."

"I don't want to fight any of them," I said. "I'll give you both of them."

—W. C. Heinz, war correspondent,
"The Retreat at Mons," *True* (1950)

World War II transformed the way Americans understood the country and its role in the world. The United States, so isolated only a few years before, would take a leading role in reconfiguring the world order, most conspicuously at first by means of its economic and physical-security assistance to Europe. A new set of assumptions found official political as well as unofficial cultural expression. In 1945, the United States was a power as dominant, its vanquished enemies as inhumane, as any the world had seen. The depravity against which Americans had fought, most clearly evidenced by the Nazi death camps, ultimately came to gild the unprecedentedly intense and indiscriminate violence that achieved victory. Miraculously, the deadliest conflict in human history became something inherently virtuous. To interpret the war in this way required a selective memory. "If the character of Hitler and his paladins gave to the Allied side a moral justification unusual in warfare," argues the philosopher and veteran J. Glenn Gray, "the Western nations have no reason to forget their share of responsibility for Hitler's coming to power or their dubious common cause with the Russian dictator." But forgetting was the order of the postwar day, and every American exercise of military force since World War II, at least in the eyes of its architects, has inherited that war's moral justification and been understood as its offspring: motivated by its memory, prosecuted in its shadow, inevitably measured against it. As the latest expeditions in Iraq and Afghanistan reveal, the United States continues to struggle beneath the burden of its last good war.

We continue to search in vain for a heroic plot comparable to the one woven out of our experience in World War II, a war into which the American GI was pulled belatedly, yet out of which he marched a heroic liberator armed by destiny. Force, when exercised by the United States, seemed to have acquired an innate, exceptional goodness. In the summer of 1941, on the eve of our entrance into the war, the archetype of the reluctant American warrior was given an old-fashioned showcase in *Sergeant York*, the top-grossing film of the year, which recruited a hero from World War I for overtly propagandist aims. The film documents Alvin York's gradual conversion from Christian pacifist and conscientious objector to calmly efficient infantryman and eventual recipient of the Medal of Honor.

The GI of the European—but generally not the Pacific—Theater would become a legend largely through identification with several iconic acts preserved in photographs and newsreels: giving chocolate bars to hungry European children, being kissed by grateful Frenchwomen (and sometimes, to his consternation, by men), having his hair adorned with a flower by his liberated Italian host. William I. Hitchcock's *The Bitter Road to Freedom: The Human Cost of Allied Victory in World War II Europe* offers a sobering chronicle of European perspectives on their "liberation." The travel writer Norman Lewis, who served as a British intelligence officer attached to the U.S. Fifth Army during the invasion of Italy, recorded a scene in his diary, later published as *Naples '44*, of shock and despair as he made his way through a series of towns on the way to Naples: "We made slow progress through shattered streets, past landslides of rubble from bombed buildings. People stood in their doorways, faces the colour of pumice, to wave mechanically to the victors, the apathetic Fascist salute of last week having been converted into the apathetic V-sign of today, but on the whole the civilian mood seemed one of stunned indifference." (Similar scenes can be found in many eyewitness accounts.) But a recognition that the totality of the war's devastation made pure gratitude an impossibility—that ambivalence could signify something other than ingratitude—is inconsistent with the myth of our deliverance of Europe.

World War II left behind the dangerous and seemingly indestructible fantasy that our military intervention will naturally produce (an often underappreciated) good. Each succeeding conflict has led to the reprise and reinvention of the Good War's mythology in order to justify or otherwise explain uses of American power. The idea of war's nobility, and the attendant rhetoric of religiosity and chivalry, was in truth far more characteristic of Alvin York's war than of World War II. But the origins of the high-flown language later associated with the Second World War can be found in General Dwight D. Eisenhower's D-Day radio address to the troops. "You are about to embark upon the Great Crusade, toward which we have striven these many months. The eyes of the world are upon you," Eisenhower exhorted his audience. "The hopes and prayers of liberty-loving people everywhere march with you. In company with our brave Allies and brothers-in-arms on other Fronts, you will bring about the destruction of the German war machine, the elimination of Nazi tyranny over the oppressed peoples of Europe, and security for ourselves in a free world." Eisenhower's speech, harmonizing with those of Churchill and Roosevelt, supplied a sense of one grand unifying cause that seems to us in retrospect always to have been there but was in truth far more elusive. The title of Eisenhower's 1948 memoir, *Crusade in Europe*, harked back to this speech.

World War II was in crucial ways an exceptional war: a struggle against the unremitting brutality of totalitarianism, albeit one that America joined late, and only in response to direct attack. The Roosevelt administration's own inclinations and sympathies notwithstanding, the proximate cause for the country's entrance into the conflict was not proactive, but reactive: the attack on Pearl Harbor, not a quest to liberate the world's oppressed peoples. As the journalist Martha Gellhorn wrote in *Collier's* in 1945 after visiting the Nazi concentration camp at Dachau, "We are not entirely guiltless, we the Allies, because it took us twelve years to open the gates of Dachau. We were blind and unbelieving and slow, and that we can never be again." As much as we would later make of our role in liberating the camps, their liberation, even after our entrance into the war, was never a priority. The Roosevelt administration first learned of Hitler's Final Solution as early as the summer of 1942, but as late as January 1944, Secretary of the Treasury Henry Morgenthau Jr. presented to the president his department's "Report to the Secretary on the Acquiescence of This Government in the Murder of the Jews." It was only then that Roosevelt created the War Refugee Board, which was entrusted with developing a plan "for (a) the rescue, transportation, maintenance, and relief of the victims of enemy oppression, and (b) the establishment of havens of temporary refuge for such victims." Frank Capra's *Why We Fight* (1942–45), the widely circulated propaganda films created, as Capra recalled in interviews with George Stevens Jr. at the American Film Institute in the 1970s, in response to Army Chief of Staff General George C. Marshall's desire for "a series of films that will tell these boys why they are fighting," made no mention of the Nazi program for exterminating the Jews.

Fussell was blunt on the subject of ideology: "The war seemed so devoid of ideological content that little could be said about its positive purposes that made political or intellectual sense, especially after the Soviet Union joined the great crusade against what until then had been stigmatized as totalitarianism." Fussell's position may be extreme, but it sheds some light on the perspective of the soldier on the ground, where the mandate of near-term survival left as little room for the long view in this war as it has done in virtually every other. Even a soldier as committed to big ideas as J. Glenn Gray—he received his doctorate in philosophy and his army induction notice on the same day—found it impossible to tell a hermit he met on an Italian hilltop "what World War II was all about" even as he marked the "bitter, hateful . . . heritage the Nazis" left in their wake. Such reflections make plain the fundamental ambiguities and contradictions the mythmakers smoothed over when they transformed the consequences of victorious force—the liberation of Europe from fascism and Asia from the imperial abuses of Japan chief among them— into an animating sense of purpose.

The year 1945 began a new chapter in the ongoing narrative of American exceptionalism. Charting the evolution of the term in *The New American Exceptionalism*, the literary critic Donald E. Pease calls attention to the remarkable elasticity of this national "fantasy" and to the violence in which our national "victory culture" has been rooted from the start. As Pease notes, the Cold War energized the concept of exceptionalism, but the idea, if not the term, had been in place since colonial days. Ever since John Winthrop, on his way to the Massachusetts Bay Colony in 1630, alluded to his future home "as a city upon a hill" toward which "the eyes of all people" would be directed, the notion of exceptionalism has inspired yet also distorted American cultural and political thought. In language similar to Winthrop's, Eisenhower's speech called attention to this sense of national mission. Because it unfolded on a global stage, World War II galvanized a faith that America was different, special, unique in the history of nations. American force had likewise come to be understood as exceptional force, an assumption helping to guide foreign policy in the decades that followed and contributing not a little to the overheated rhetoric surrounding our twenty-first-century wars, which have been so deeply indebted to the visceral, volatile motive of vengeance. American violence, as distinguished from that enacted by other nations, took on a special luster that combined righteous might and comic-book exuberance with native decency and a sense of fair play.

Geography has long been at the heart of the myth of the United States. Winthrop devised his rhetoric en route to a haven long distant from Europe. The continent's vast expanse—and the social and economic opportunities it made possible—was central to Benjamin Franklin's thoughts on the colonial experiment and later to the shrewd French observer Alexis de Tocqueville's understanding of the nature of American exceptionalism, which was for him primarily geographical. The fact that the continental United States had not experienced war's destruction since 1865 confirmed twentieth-century mystical ideas about national destiny and influenced American attitudes about the use of force elsewhere. Victory in World War II seemed somehow the ultimate revelation of all these formative mysteries. Lewis H. Lapham alluded to this phenomenon in 1979, in an often-quoted *Harper's* article: "The continental United States had escaped the plague of war, and so it was easy enough for the heirs to believe that they had been anointed by God." Postwar foreign policy, Lapham proposed, became "a game of transcendental poker, in which the ruthless self-interest of a commercial democracy . . . got mixed up with dreams, sermons, and the transmigration of souls."

A faith that violence had been unleashed in the name of American liberty and decency disguised the fact that the bare essence of war itself has remained largely unchanged since its mythic Western origins at Troy. Indeed, its violence has grown only more indiscriminate and encompassing. "The true hero, the true subject, the center of the *Iliad* is force," the French philosopher Simone Weil argued soon after the fall of France in 1940. This is the opening claim of her treatise *L'Iliade ou le poème de la force*, which was published in the Marseilles literary magazine *Cahiers du Sud* in 1940–41, and in an English translation by Mary McCarthy in *Politics* in November 1945, in the immediate aftermath of the war. Weil defined force as "that x that turns anybody who is subjected to it into a *thing*. Exercised to the limit, it turns man into a thing in the most literal sense: it makes a corpse out of him." No cause, however noble, could alter the nature of that force—even if technology amplified it to a heretofore inconceivable scale—and Weil discerned a fundamental continuity between the seemingly alien world of Homer and that of 1940s Europe:

> Force employed by man, force that enslaves man, force before which man's flesh shrinks away. In this work, at all times, the human spirit is shown as modified by its relations with force, as swept away, blinded, by the very force it imagined it could handle, as deformed by the weight of the force it submits to. For those dreamers who considered that force, thanks to progress, would soon be a thing of the past, the *Iliad* could appear as an historical document; for others, whose powers of recognition are more acute and who perceive force, today as yesterday, at the very center of human history, the *Iliad* is the purest and the loveliest of mirrors.

Allied victory would shatter that crystalline mirror for all but the most stubborn witnesses of force. The always inglorious work of war gradually became sanctified by virtue of its having been waged against regimes of unequivocal maleficence. In the process, war, the inherently violent thing itself—rather than the causes force might serve—became the subject of nostalgic remembrance and heroic celebration.

In this book I explore many attitudes toward the war as they evolved over the decades: individual and corporate, some expressed directly but others obliquely, full-throated patriotic fairy tales and remorseless satire. In addition to the eyewitness reportage of Gellhorn, Ernie Pyle, A. J. Liebling, John Hersey, and others, I examine the work of later journalists, historians, and commentators, including Reinhold Niebuhr,

Studs Terkel, James Baldwin, Joan Didion, Stephen Ambrose, and Tom Brokaw. I explore the postwar fiction of Ross Macdonald, Dorothy B. Hughes, David Goodis, and others, together with Hollywood films, the latter as collaborative expressions—involving not only screenwriters, directors, and actors, but also studio executives concerned chiefly with the marketability of their products—of a very different way of telling the World War II story. I am especially concerned with those observers who express doubt or confusion, ask questions, or otherwise complicate our picture of the war, for they illuminate at once the power and perils of mythmaking. Their work suggests that there are many other ways to understand and to tell the national story. Immune to the American horror of ambiguity as some kind of Old World con, these thinkers largely lack the "national vanity" Tocqueville attributed to us:

> All free nations are vainglorious, but national pride is not displayed by all in the same manner. The Americans, in their intercourse with strangers, appear impatient of the smallest censure and insatiable of praise. The most slender eulogy is acceptable to them; the most exalted seldom contents them; they unceasingly harass you to extort praise, and if you resist their entreaties, they fall to praising themselves. It would seem as if, doubting their own merit, they wished to have it constantly exhibited before their eyes. Their vanity is not only greedy, but restless and jealous; it will grant nothing, while it demands everything, but is ready to beg and to quarrel at the same time.

It is Tocqueville to whom the champions of American exceptionalism like to trace their doctrine. But those champions tend to read him selectively; they forget not only that the chief source of exceptionalism as he saw it was national geography (largely protected by oceans and rich in resources) but also that the generally admiring Tocqueville was attuned to potential fault lines in the great experiment he was witnessing. It is his fascinated ambivalence they have conveniently forgotten.

The most potent and highly polished version of the World War II myth, which crystallized in the celebration of the Greatest Generation in the late 1990s, arose during and in the aftermath of the war's fiftieth-anniversary commemorations. Its emphasis on a set of superior national virtues—generosity, decency, love of freedom—concealed a fundamental chauvinism. Its chief evangelists were the historian Stephen Ambrose, the journalist Tom Brokaw, and in certain respects the filmmaker Steven Spielberg. Today, in a young century defined by renewed confusion about why we go to war and how we get out of it, World War II endures for many as testament to the redemptive capacity of American violence. Long axiomatic, World War II's goodness—and the greatness of the generation that fought it—has survived subsequent questions about the atomic bomb's necessity and condemnations of the firebombing of German and Japanese cities. It withstood, and gathered strength from, a gradual erosion of American confidence in the latter half of the twentieth century, when a series of misguided military adventures failed to achieve anything like victory.

In the 2015 preface to his incisive book *The Best War Ever: America and World War II*, originally published in 1994, the historian Michael C. C. Adams proposed that the "widely accepted version" of the "Good War" was "fading or being put aside . . . as seemingly less relevant to the situation facing us in the second decade of the twenty-first century." I don't think that's the case. In fact, the hold exerted by the Good War remains strong, one of the few national stories still available to both major political parties in a deeply partisan nation. It was especially attractive to the retrograde preoccupation with greatness that characterized the Donald Trump presidency and its commitment to the doctrine of America First. The appropriation of this term, originally the name of the committee of isolationists and fascist sympathizers who opposed our entry into World War II, is a symptom of American amnesia. Not even the Trump administration, for which nothing seemed sacred and everything appeared a target for disruption, dared to dismantle the myth of the Greatest Generation. Indeed, in June 2019, Trump engaged in what has become a presidential ritual—the D-Day anniversary speech in Normandy—with unaccustomed piety and restraint.

After the Allied victory in 1945, a Manichaean worldview, masterfully articulated in the rhetoric of Churchill and Roosevelt, outlived its propagandist purpose and the existential desperation that produced it to shape the Cold War. It required a paradoxical about-face: the USSR, mistrusted before the war, our ally during the conflict, became the new enemy, recognized as a totalitarian regime that outpaced even Nazi evil. It was a reversal so complete that in 1985, President Ronald Reagan claimed to be speaking for "most Americans" when he declared that the American volunteers (some of them communists) who fought against Franco's fascists in the Spanish Civil War were in fact "fighting on the wrong side." In a prime example of tortured cold warrior logic that same year, Reagan joined the German chancellor Helmut Kohl in a wreath-laying ceremony at a German war cemetery at Bitburg, home to the graves of SS as well as Wehrmacht troops. On this occasion, Reagan proclaimed that the buried soldiers were "victims of Nazism just as surely as the victims of the concentration camps."

Reagan's tendency to miss the "key point," was, as Joan Didion suggests in a 1989 essay on the Reagan White House,

"In the Realm of the Fisher King," one of his defining char-
acteristics. He was a man who engaged the "big picture," not
the crucial detail. It was the way he understood the Cold
War: "The Soviet Union appeared to Ronald Reagan as an
abstraction, a place where people were helpless to resist 'communism,' the inanimate evil which, as he . . . put it . . . had
'tried to invade our industry' and been 'fought' and eventually
'licked.' This was a construct," Didion continues, "in which
the actual citizens of the Soviet Union could be seen to have
been," like Hollywood during the Red Scare, "'invaded'—in
need only of liberation. The liberating force might be the appearance of a Shane-like character, someone to 'lick' the evil,
or it might be just the sweet light of reason. 'A people free
to choose will always choose peace,' as President Reagan told
students at Moscow State University in May of 1988."

After 1989, once the specter of communism officially
stopped haunting us, the war myth would be invoked with
renewed energy. George H. W. Bush's service as a navy pilot
in World War II invested him with a certain authority during
the Gulf War, a credibility that perhaps predisposed the nation to support it and, as the former CIA analyst Patrick Ed-
dington suggests, subsequently blinded the public to not only
the abandonment of the Shiites and Kurds who had risen up
against Saddam Hussein at America's urging but also Bush's
indifference to the Gulf War syndrome suffered by many
veterans and the longer-term consequences of our military
intervention in the Middle East. Before the war began, Bush
himself framed the problem by explicitly comparing Saddam
Hussein's regime to Hitler's: Iraqi forces "have committed
outrageous acts of barbarism," he claimed, a degree of "brutality that I don't believe Adolf Hitler ever participated in."

That this war would redeem Vietnam for Bush also became clear: "Prior to ordering our forces into battle," he told
the nation in his announcement of Operation Desert Storm,

I instructed our military commanders to take every necessary step to prevail as quickly as possible, and with the
greatest degree of protection possible for American and
allied service men and women. I've told the American
people before that this will not be another Vietnam, and
I repeat this here tonight. Our troops will have the best
possible support in the entire world, and they will not
be asked to fight with one hand tied behind their back.
I'm hopeful that this fighting will not go on for long and
that casualties will be held to an absolute minimum.

It is impossible to fight one war at a time. After the war, Bush
proved far more interested in the metaphorical "Vietnam syndrome" than he was in the actual syndrome affecting Gulf
War veterans: "By God," he proclaimed in the wake of Desert Storm, "we've kicked the Vietnam syndrome once and
for all." Vietnam constituted the most serious threat to the
World War II mythology; victory in Iraq allowed us to hear
once again the positive, life-affirming signals still pulsing
from Bush's own first war. This was the culmination of Reagan's revisionist work.

In the wake of the attacks of September 11, 2001, the case
for war was once again made through analogy with Hitlerian
evil. George W. Bush, Secretary of Defense Donald Rumsfeld, and others used a vocabulary inherited from World War
II to shape the post-9/11 dispensation. The coinage *Islamo-
fascism* yoked an amorphous new enemy with an old one that
was easy to picture. Bush hailed American soldiers as liberators and described the enemy as an "axis of evil," a phrase
that evoked the Axis Powers. Analogies to Pearl Harbor appeared everywhere, stoking a desire for vengeance that, at
least initially, generated support for the war and a great deal
of show-patriotism. In *Cultures of War*, the historian John
Dower, whose work has immeasurably complicated and

enriched our understanding of the war in the Pacific, illuminates the ways in which, after 9/11, Pearl Harbor became a
"code" for righteous American vengeance and "everlasting
remembrance." As public opinion turned against the Iraq
War, Rumsfeld revived the specter of Hitler to justify its con-
tinuance. Typical of Rumsfeld's rhetoric was a 2006 speech
to the American Legion in which, in an argument about ap-
peasement, he likened the world situation at the beginning of
the twenty-first century to that of the 1930s:

> It was a time when a certain amount of cynicism and
> moral confusion set in among Western democracies,
> when those who warned about a coming crisis, the rise
> of fascism and Nazism were ridiculed or ignored. In-
> deed, in the decades before World War II, a great many
> argued that the fascist threat was exaggerated or that
> it was someone else's problem. Some nations tried to
> negotiate a separate peace, even as the enemy made
> its deadly ambitions crystal clear. It was, as Winston
> Churchill observed, a bit like feeding a crocodile, hop-
> ing it would eat you last.

Rumsfeld went on to suggest that the world was facing "similar challenges in efforts to confront the rising threat of a new
type of fascism." As early as 1946, George Orwell pointed
out that the word *fascism* had lost its specificity and had become a term that could be indiscriminately applied to any
enemy. At the beginning of the twenty-first century, history
offered no more useful word for an administration facing increasing opposition to its seemingly unending military campaigns. Trump, whose foreign policy seemed to be guided by
anachronistic isolationism combined with good measures of
caprice, greed, and contempt, also returned to World War II,
albeit in unconventional fashion, to justify his October 2019

abandonment of the Kurds to their Turkish enemies. The Kurds, he explained, "didn't help us in the Second World War. They didn't help us with Normandy, as an example." Pundits who called attention to the fact that Kurds did fight on the Allied side missed the larger point: World War II, eighty years in the past, could still be invoked as a kind of loyalty test.

This book explores various incarnations of—and alternatives to—a versatile, durable myth that still serves as a dangerous lodestone in American culture. The first chapter anatomizes its most influential version, that of the Good War and the Greatest Generation. There are many competing narratives of the war and always have been, and the second chapter looks back at the deeply ambivalent attitudes expressed toward World War II while it was being fought. My third and fourth chapters explore postwar reinterpretations, some crafted in response to successive conflicts, while the final chapter explores the powerful and particular connection between the country's most significant foreign war and its monumental domestic conflict, the Civil War.

There have been several significant anatomies of the World War II mythos over the years. The historian John Bodnar offers an overview of strands of the myth in The "Good War" in American Memory, in which, he explains, "the sweet sounds of valor ultimately eclipsed the painful cries of loss." Bodnar's book illuminates various costs of American sentimentalizing of the war and suppression of alternative perspectives. He does not trace the consequences for foreign policy. Richard Drinnon's Facing West: The Metaphysics of Indian-Hating and Empire-Building and the literary critic Richard Slotkin's Gunfighter Nation: The Myth of the Frontier in Twentieth-Century America have addressed World War II within a broader national history and specifically in connection with the idea of the frontier, while further complicating our understanding of war, violence, and memory, but both books were written before the turn of the century. In his recent book *Total Mobilization: World War II and American Literature* Roy Scranton interprets our postwar attitudes toward projections of American power as the product of a reverence for the figure of the "trauma hero" and an undue deference to the veteran's special, exclusive knowledge of war. That reverence, he argues, has been instrumental in concealing some of the war's fundamental "contradictions," and it led to a corresponding neglect of those literary responses that exposed them.

Recent alternative military histories have also illuminated aspects of wartime life that had been largely eclipsed by sentimental remembrance. These books include Mary Louise Roberts's *What Soldiers Do: Sex and the American GI in World War II France*, which explores the destructive behavior of American soldiers in France, and Aaron Hiltner's *Taking Leave, Taking Liberties: American Troops on the World War II Home Front*, which documents the war's unleashing of violence at home in the form of "uncontrolled and aggressive troops," most conspicuously on the streets of "liberty ports" and army-post towns. "Nationwide," Hiltner explains, "the papers filled with lurid stories of criminal activity perpetrated by soldiers and sailors." Such work helps to remind us of the dangers of preferring myth at a moment when nostalgia for a good war, a greatest generation, and a simpler time remains as seductive as ever.

The ambiguities of Korea (the "forgotten" war that, technically, has yet to end), the mendacity and failure of Vietnam, the transitory triumph of the First Gulf War, the ultimate confusion of a seemingly unending war against what has come to be called global extremism, and, in the last few years, the prospective dissolution of the postwar liberal world order under the Trumpian mandate of America First: all these events have invoked, reflected, and renewed the mythical status of World War II. Each generation has found a new use for the Good War. Nostalgia for the war years remains a bulwark against doubt and disillusion, a great golden age to which we can always retreat to remember who we were and might be again, seeking safety through violent conflict because once we thought we found it there, retaining a faith in the American capacity for exceptional violence. Victory in the twentieth century's second global conflict transformed the world and at the same time condemned the United States to a futile quest for another just as good, just as definitive, just as transformational. Wars never can do the work of redemption, even when their causes meet generally agreed-upon criteria for justice.

1

AGE OF GOLD

I think this is the greatest generation any society has
ever produced.

—Tom Brokaw, interviewed on *Meet the Press* during the
fiftieth-anniversary D-Day commemoration

Giants of Decency

The most enduring and tenacious iteration of America's World
War II myth was burnished to perfection during and soon after the war's fiftieth anniversary. Its celebrants sounded several
keynotes, which I enumerate here in the style of the six rules
for writing that appear toward the end of "Politics and the English Language," George Orwell's essay on the connection between "the decay of language" and the "political chaos" of the
mid-twentieth century, which appeared in *Horizon* in 1946:

1. The United States went to war to liberate the
   world from fascism and tyranny.
2. All Americans were absolutely united in their
   commitment to the war effort.
3. Everyone on the home front made tremendous
   sacrifices.
4. Americans are liberators who fight decently, reluctantly, only when they must.

5. World War II was a foreign tragedy with a happy
   American ending.
6. Everyone has always agreed on points 1–5.

We reflexively invoke this dogma even when we know, at
some level, beneath the righteous passion, that it cannot be
entirely true. This is the tale that continues to dominate the
popular imagination and the politician's rhetoric. It appeals
to our national vanity, confirms the New World's superiority
to the Old, and validates modernity and the machine. To do
all these things, however, the myth must bend history to its
purposes.

Its first tenet, conflating the consequences of our intervention with the causes Americans believed they were fighting
for, ignores the timing and proximate catalyst of our entry
into the war (the attack on Pearl Harbor). The second—often
used in recent years to underscore (and shame) our indifference to wars fought by a small cadre of volunteer professionals
while the home front preserves a sense of normalcy—ignores
both the reluctance that survived even Pearl Harbor in some
quarters as well as the diversity of motives, including cynical
opportunism, at work among supporters of the war. The third
exaggerates the economic sacrifices of a country that the war
actually brought back to work for the first time after years of
economic depression. The fourth makes American violence
a special case, its brutality almost miraculously mitigated by
national temperament. The fifth insists that war, at least when
we prosecute it, is not a tragedy but a comedy, in the rich literary sense of comedy as a plot that ultimately restores order
to chaos, sorts out the winners and the losers, enlarges the circle of justice, and thereby declares victory. It is a symptom of
what Reinhold Niebuhr recognized in the 1950s as an American tendency to regard tragedy, like feudalism and fascism, as
European. This tenet also passes over one of the most crucial

senses in which World War II was sui generis: its scale and mode of destruction. In the firebombing of German and Japanese cities and, finally, in the explosion of atom bombs over Hiroshima and Nagasaki, war became not simply exceptional destruction but prospective global annihilation. John Hersey documented this transformation with precision in *Hiroshima*. Hersey, as Nicholas Lemann noted in *The New Yorker* in 2019, found his calling "during the Second World War, which he was early in coming to understand primarily as a great catastrophe rather than an inspiring American triumph. He went to the scene, he tirelessly looked where most journalists didn't, and he found ways of writing about what he saw that gave his journalism an enduring power." Hersey's vision has not won out, however; those who have seen fit to question the myth have never succeeded in dislodging its longest tendrils.

The sixth and final tenet involves a special kind of amnesia, akin to what Martha Gellhorn called, in describing the revisionist history of the Vietnam War crafted by the Reagan administration, a "collective forgetting of nations." Against this collective amnesia, the dissenter often announces him- or herself as the first to awaken to the truth. Witness Paul Fussell's declaration in the preface to *Wartime*, published in 1989: "For the past fifty years the Allied war has been sanitized and romanticized almost beyond recognition by the sentimental, the loony patriotic, the ignorant, and the bloodthirsty." Fussell sought "to balance the scales." Thirty years on, the scales still need balancing, but that balancing act entails dispelling the notion that everyone has somehow been in agreement all along. In truth, there have been contrarian voices from the start, but we have been reluctant to reckon with the stakes of their critiques. I'm talking here not about the cranks and the conspiracists, nor about those who imagine we would have been somehow better off remaining neutral, but rather about those thinkers, writers, and artists who seem able to resist the twin seductions of sentimentality and certitude, who find in coolness and ambivalence a way of understanding their country that shows its true worth to better effect than the "garrulous patriotism" Tocqueville long ago attributed to Americans.

As the epigraph to this chapter intimates, the very mention of World War II encourages emotional, hyperbolic, unprovable claims. This is but one manifestation of the phenomenon Tocqueville observed: "If I say to an American that the country he lives in is a fine one, 'Ay,' he replies, 'there is not its equal in the world.'" John Bodnar calls Tom Brokaw's coinage "the quintessential expression of the American myth of World War II." As Brokaw himself acknowledges, much of the groundwork for his celebration was laid by the historian Stephen Ambrose, who marked the war's fiftieth anniversary with *Band of Brothers* (1992) and *D-Day: June 6, 1944* (1994), his breakthrough bestseller. He subsequently added to his body of work on the war with *Citizen Soldiers* (1997), *The Victors: Eisenhower and His Boys* (1998), and *The Wild Blue: The Men and Boys Who Flew the B-24s over Germany 1944–45* (2001).

As Richard Goldstein noted in a *New York Times* obituary for Ambrose in 2002, these books "fueled a national fascination with the generation that fought World War II." Ambrose himself explained that they "flowed" from his "association with Eisenhower," about whom he had earlier written a multivolume biography, and from his own emotions about the GIs. "I was ten years old when the war ended," he said. "I thought the returning veterans were giants who had saved the world from barbarism. I still think so. I remain a hero worshiper." Throughout his books, that youthful adoration tends to overwhelm the historian's mandate to report complex realities. On a number of occasions Ambrose declared, "I want to tell all the things that are right about America."

This mission, which is as uninstructive as telling only the things that are wrong, was in large measure a reaction to the widespread disillusionment and disaffection following the Vietnam War. As Benjamin Schwarz notes in his review of Ambrose's *The Good Fight: How World War II Was Won*, a children's book, "Ambrose's version of events retroactively imposes an elevated meaning on the American side of the war." It is, Schwarz concludes, "a pious interpretation."

Ambrose carefully sculpted his stories, all of which share a worshipful tone and largely ignore contradictions or complexities that prove disruptive to a sentimental account of American decency and goodness. He promulgated a fantasy that American soldiers somehow preserved a boyish innocence amid the slaughter required to save "the world from barbarism." In *Band of Brothers*—eventually turned into an HBO miniseries, executive-produced by Steven Spielberg and Tom Hanks—Ambrose shrewdly zeroed in on the story of a single company: E (or Easy) Company, 506th Parachute Infantry Regiment, 101st Airborne Division. This narrow focus distilled an unwieldy epic of global disaster into an intimate tale of individual "giants," in this case members of "an elite unit" of paratroopers, who, Ambrose claims, were "special in their values . . . idealists, eager to merge themselves into a group fighting for a cause, actively seeking an outfit with which they could identify, join, be a part of, relate to as a family." Bodnar notes the degree to which this triumphant narrative ignores any mourning for the dead. It also elides the brutalizing effects of violence.

A very different picture of volunteerism emerges from Alvin Kernan's description of a group of early-1941 naval recruits in his memoir *Crossing the Line: A Bluejacket's Odyssey in World War II*. Kernan, who later became a professor of English, joined the navy after confronting bleak economic prospects at home in rural Wyoming. He enlisted with about a hundred others in Cheyenne: "We were . . . kids who couldn't get jobs. Here and there were men in their twenties, jobless workers at the end of their rope, or incorrigible 'fuck-ups' who had gotten into some kind of trouble at home once too often and had been given the ancient choice by the judge of going to jail or joining one of the services." Kernan continues, "Most of us were from small towns, often from broken families, notable for bad teeth and worse complexions, the marginal American products of more than ten years of the hardest of times." As he reflects on the experience of basic training, Kernan sees a group of children learning a deadly trade:

> We were children still—astonishingly stoical, self-reliant, tough children, but children still—and, like all children, fascinated with killing. The guns drew us like magnets . . . Stands of boarding cutlasses still stood as ornaments next to the cases of rifles, but so innocent were we that we thought boarding enemy vessels—just like Errol Flynn in the movies set on the Spanish Main—was still a part of naval warfare and were disappointed . . . with only a murderous sixteen-inch bayonet.

Such men, Kernan goes on to recount, fought no less valiantly than the men of Easy Company, but their motivations were hardly lofty, their experience less than ennobling.

Ambrose's paratroopers appear to be motivated by a heady combination of patriotism and fraternity. As the extensive social science literature on combat motivation suggests, idealism and cohesion are both important to a citizen army, but the first quality largely recedes into the background during actual combat. Even cohesion—fighting and sacrificing for one's "buddy"—might often more accurately be described as something else: peer pressure, perhaps; honor, sometimes; but often cruelty, shame, guilt, or a lack of other options. As Charles Glass notes in his book *The Deserters: A Hidden History of World War II*, there were far fewer deserters in the Pacific Theater than in Europe, largely because there was nowhere to run. Because the unimpeachable patriotism of the GI is crucial to Ambrose's vision, he takes issue with the argument made by the Civil War historian James McPherson in his 1997 book *For Cause and Comrades* that World War II GIs were in fact less invested in an ideological cause than were their Civil War predecessors. According to a 2003 analysis of soldier motivation conducted by the U.S. Army's Strategic Studies Institute, soldiers fighting as part of the all-volunteer force in the post-9/11 wars in Iraq and Afghanistan were also more likely than the GIs of World War II to be motivated by ideological commitments.

Volunteerism is a tricky subject in the era of a draft, when the threat of conscription hangs over the decision to enlist. The federal government first passed a conscription act in 1863, in the midst of the Civil War. A man could serve, pay $300, or hire a substitute to take his place. Inhabitants of New York City responded with a draft riot in which a white mob killed almost a hundred people and burned down the Colored Orphan Asylum. In an unpublished letter on the constitutionality of the draft, Abraham Lincoln mused that men enter military service through a "voluntary weighing of motives," among them "patriotism, political bias, ambition, personal courage, love of adventure, want of employment, and convenience, or the opposites of some of these." Anyone who wanted to avoid "the horrors of the draft," he wryly noted, could quite easily do so by volunteering.

Franklin D. Roosevelt signed the Selective Training and Service Act into law on September 16, 1940. It was the first peacetime draft in U.S. history. Approximately sixty percent

of World War II servicemen were draftees. Of those, roughly
ten percent were engaged in combat; as Glass documents,
most of the almost fifty thousand deserters came from that
ten percent. Those who voluntarily enlisted were at least
able to exert some choice over their branch of service. This
calculation doesn't negate their potential patriotism, but it
does make them practical human beings with real hopes and
fears, rather than superhuman giants. "Those who showed
the greatest sympathy to deserters," notes Glass, "were other
frontline soldiers. They had, at one time or another, felt the
temptation to opt out of the war through desertion, shooting
themselves in the foot or lagging behind when ordered forward. It was a rare infantryman who attempted to prevent his
comrades from leaving the line." Arriving on Saipan in 1944,
when it was periodically raided by Japanese planes, the airman and poet John Ciardi caught sight of a shell-shocked soldier sitting alone next to a shelter with all his equipment and
a supply of K rations. The figure never moved, and Ciardi recorded the episode with generosity in his diary, published as
Saipan in 1988: "It's a pitiable case of pure panic . . . He just
sits. It may of course be a stunt . . . but I doubt it . . . Someone
that is in immediate charge of him has sense enough to leave
him alone, but what he really needs is some competent psy-
chiatry . . . He's certainly no good here—a weird, unwashed
bundle of panic hugging the sandbags, and who knows what
churns inside of him."

Ambrose's vision of idealistic liberators is more easily sustained by a group of self-selecting paratroopers than it would
have been by a study of resigned or reluctant conscripts, or
of prudently patriotic enlistees. To make his case in *Citizen
Soldiers*, Ambrose is forced to interpret the very laconism of
GIs as confirmation of a purity of motive. When he can't find
evidence for the kind of idealism that McPherson, for example, unearths in the letters of Civil War soldiers, Ambrose

rationalizes that GIs were simply "embarrassed by patriotic bombast," unlike their less self-conscious nineteenth-century predecessors: "They knew they were fighting for decency and democracy and they were proud of it and motivated by it. They just didn't talk or write about it."

John Hersey's *Into the Valley: Marines at Guadalcanal* offers a more nuanced, less stable interpretation of American attitudes. In his preface to a new edition in 1989, published just three years before Ambrose's *Band of Brothers*, Hersey reflected on the inherent falseness of his own wartime thinking. He had written in the first edition: "Courage is largely the desire to show other men that you have it." Decades later, Hersey revised his analysis:

> What we think of as "courage" can range . . . from pure self-sacrifice for the sake of others to the release of a deep and gross bloodlust; it could embrace the cool steadfastness of David facing Goliath, . . . the costly sulking anger of Achilles, the implicit love of others of Horatio at the bridge, the idiotic fervor of . . . the Light Brigade—and, alas, the telegenic viciousness, so popular in recent years with violence-besotted American viewers, of a Rambo.

The *Rambo* franchise, which began with *First Blood* in 1982, marked a significant turning point in pop-culture representations of Vietnam and, more generally, of American violence abroad. This proved to be a cause for alarm to careful observers of war cultures, Hersey and Martha Gellhorn among them.

Writing in the late 1980s, Hersey enriched his perspective on the "complex" and mysterious nature of the "bravery" displayed by the U.S. Marines on Guadalcanal. In 1942, as a naïve novice reporter, he had asked a group of marines,

"Today, here in this valley, what are you fighting for?" The marines respond with an embarrassed silence; they won't even look at Hersey. Finally, one breaks the silence: "Jesus, what I'd give for a piece of blueberry pie." Of course Hersey knows that's not quite what he means: "When they say they are fighting for these things," he explains, "they mean that they are fighting . . . 'to get the goddam thing over and get home.'" Hersey admits that the reason "sounds less dynamic than the Axis slogans. But home seems to most marines a pretty good thing to be fighting for . . . where the good things are—the generosity, the good pay, the comforts, the democracy, the pie." Hersey's marines lack ideological zeal. Had an officer told them they could go into the valley or go home, "they would have said the hell with the valley." He praises such "rational and mature" motivations as far healthier than the zeal of the fanatic. It's homely, human, and rooted mostly in the tangible and material; it is the furthest thing from the lofty, almost saintly devotion of Ambrose's soldiers. Hersey proposes that the choice of pie over self-sacrifice embodies the "lifesaving skepticism and irony embedded in the confused courage of men bred to free choice." That skepticism and irony, Hersey suggests, more than any faith, is what helped gain an Allied victory.

Empirical evidence for the absence of ideological motivation among World War II GIs comes from *The American Soldier*, a pathbreaking, multivolume study conducted by the sociologist Samuel A. Stouffer and others in the 1940s. It was sponsored by the army and based on survey research. Stouffer found evidence for "a minimum of idealism or heroics." And the predominant element in these episodes turned out to be "the close solidarity of the combat group." As the study's authors explain, the only consensus among Americans "both in and out of the Army . . . lies simply in the undebatable assumptions that the Japanese attack on Pearl Harbor meant war, and that once in the war the United States had to win . . . Beyond this basic unanimity . . . beyond acceptance of the war as a necessity forced upon the United States by an aggressor, there was little support of attempts to give the war meaning in terms of principles and causes involved, and little apparent desire for such formulations."

The military sociologist Charles C. Moskos would later sum up Stouffer's most important discovery about the World War II GI as follows: "The findings revealed a profoundly nonideological soldier." The GI fought, but not because he necessarily understood or "believed in the stated purposes of the war." Moskos's own study of the Vietnam era army led him to conclude that even though the comparative "ideological conformity of World War II" led to an underemphasis of "ideological factors in the combat studies" of the time, those factors had only an indirect influence. Moskos's research led him to conclude that "latent ideology is an important though indirect variable on combat motivation." As the antiwar movement gathered steam in the late 1960s, soldiers' attitudes began to change; nevertheless, it was not the "moral-political" but practical antiwar arguments that actually did the work of shifting public opinion. In other words, Moskos concludes, soldiers did not "become less patriotic" after 1969; they "reflected a basic change in the national perspective toward the Vietnam War."

Building on the pioneering work of Stouffer and his colleagues in understanding the American soldier in combat, Moskos demystified the phenomenon of cohesive combat units that inspires Ambrose's *Band of Brothers*: "Rather than viewing soldiers' primary groups as some kind of semi-mystical bond of comradeship, they can be better understood as pragmatic and situational responses. This is not to deny the existence of strong interpersonal ties within combat squads," Moskos writes in *Soldiers and Sociology*, "but only to reinterpret them as derivative from the very private war each individual is fighting for his own survival." In the "Hobbesian" world of war, basic survival becomes the order of the day. While American soldiers in Vietnam "had a general aversion to overt ideological symbols and patriotic appeals," Moskos suggests that at least in the early years of the conflict, these ties of expediency were complemented by "underlying value commitments" and by "a belief . . . in the worthwhileness of American society."

There is little room for such subtleties in Ambrose's myth. The ideal of eager volunteerism, rather than the reality of conscription, also bolsters the narrative of *D-Day*, which closes with Eisenhower's observation, made on Omaha Beach in 1964: "It just shows what free men will do rather than be slaves." While necessarily more sweeping in scope than the portrait of Easy Company in *Band of Brothers*, Ambrose's *D-Day*, published two years later, likewise hinges on defining the GI as a warrior for democracy. The complex amalgamation of political, sociological, environmental, and personal factors that determine the outcome of war is submerged in misty legend. Attempting to dramatize the citizen-soldier's individual fighting spirit in *D-Day*, the story drifts into bathos, nowhere more dramatically than in the prologue, which introduces readers to the first British and American officers killed during the landings. After telling the story of these two "citizen-soldiers" who acquitted themselves bravely on the beaches, Ambrose declares, "If Hitler had seen Den Brotheridge and Bob Mathias in action at the beginning of D-Day, he might have had second thoughts." This is less historical analysis than comic-book thought bubble. It is also a particularly American way of thinking and talking about war. One might compare Theodore Roosevelt's rhetoric, which makes war seem like an especially bloody football game. It survives in Ronald Reagan's 1984 D-Day speech, written by Peggy Noonan, who came up with the line "These are the boys of Pointe du Hoc," which Noonan admitted in her memoir to stealing from Roger Kahn's sentimental remembrance of baseball's Brooklyn Dodgers, *The Boys of Summer.* "These are the boys of Pointe du Hoc," Reagan had proclaimed on the beach at Normandy, where the Rangers sat together in front of him: "These are the men who took the cliffs. These are the champions who helped free a continent. These are the heroes who helped end a war."

Political scientists tend to attribute the fact that democracies generally win wars—Stephen Biddle and Stephen Long call it "democracy's apparent effectiveness bonus"—to various factors encouraged within democratic society, among them a reluctance to go to war in the first place and a corresponding need for consent. As Dan Reiter and Allan C. Stam argue in their classic study *Democracies at War,* once at war, a democracy's emphasis on individuality seems to enhance performance on the battlefield. The advantage, they propose, is not to be found in superior economies or in some sense of supranational obligation to other democracies—the high-flown rhetoric of politicians notwithstanding—but rather in the people's political will and the democratic citizen's "qualities of better initiative and leadership."

Despite the Allies' ultimate success and the celebration of the "citizen-soldier," the aptitude of citizen armies for combat remains a subject of debate. One of the first and most influential books on the combat performance of amateurs (as opposed to career professionals) in World War II, S.L.A. Marshall's *Men Against Fire* has itself been under fire almost since its publication in 1947. Marshall concluded that fewer than one in four U.S. infantry soldiers fired their weapons at the enemy. Marshall's dubious research methods and boundless capacity for self-promotion have prompted many to discredit his findings, but others at the time voiced similar concerns about the apparent reluctance among citizen-soldiers to use deadly force. The army itself recognized a problem at the time and traced it, in part, to the fact that the lowest-scoring recruits on the Army General Classification Test tended to be assigned to the infantry. In a 2013 study, *The Combat Soldier: Infantry Tactics and Cohesion in the Twentieth and Twenty-First Centuries*, the British sociologist Anthony King finds certain conclusions about "the underperformance of the citizen soldier" during the Second World War "broadly sustainable." He suggests that objective assessments are especially difficult given the power of "national mythologies and contemporary nostalgia."

Armies tend to solve the problem of inertia in citizen-soldiers on the battlefield, King explains, by appealing to social ties and commonalities. Among the chief motivations—not readily disentangled—are masculinity, honor (or personal reputation), and a frequently racialized patriotism or nationalism. King goes on to explain that a professional army largely replaces these volatile motives with a cohesion based on technical proficiency and the particular sense of honor that accompanies membership in a professional organization. Although King may underestimate the persistence of more traditional white masculine concepts of honor in the armed services today, especially in combat units, he persuasively contends that while "citizen soldiers need political motivation . . . to fight effectively," such motivation did not replace small-unit cohesion in the twentieth century but rather "defined, justified, and augmented the mutual obligations between the members of the platoon."

An episode from John Ciardi's diary gives personal expression to the sociologists' observations about combat motivation. In December 1944 Ciardi saw the film *A Guy Named Joe*: "All about how to die in an airplane, but too noble." There's "no music" in the air, he adds, just a series of lifesaving equipment checks. One flies, he explains, "for one reason only—that wherever one race sets out to take over the rest for private exploitation somebody has to live crazily enough to stop it." Having such a reason won't make the insane sane, and it gilds nothing: "I resent the Hollywood touch," Ciardi notes before going on to describe a dismembered Japanese pilot "smoking like a charred roast. There aren't enough speeches or parades in the world to make it pretty. There's not enough of anything in the world to justify it, except necessity." No cause, for Ciardi, can turn the violence into something inherently beautiful or noble. Living "crazily" is not the same thing as living nobly.

Ambrose tries to circumvent all of this in *Band of Brothers* by focusing on an elite unit that underwent extensive precombat training. He routinely emphasizes the paratroopers' status as amateurs: they are citizen-soldiers with a sense of patriotic mission who "had not soured . . . on their country" despite the hard times of the Depression. But because it is so difficult to prove the presence of idealism in these laconic GIs, cause must ultimately recede before the dynamic of social cohesion. The title of Ambrose's book—and the epigraph that provides its Shakespearean source—signals the primacy of fraternal honor as a motivator: "From this day to the ending of the World, / . . . we in it shall be remembered / . . . we band of brothers." This radically abbreviated excerpt comes from Shakespeare's history play *Henry V*, specifically from the titular king's rousing speech before the Battle of Agincourt, where his outnumbered and demoralized army is about to join battle with a French force defending home ground. Henry has just overheard a loyal noble wishing for a few more soldiers with which to fight the French:

> If we are marked to die, we are enow
> To do our country loss; and if to live,
> The fewer men, the greater share of honour.
> God's will! I pray thee, wish not one man more.
>   . . .
> Rather proclaim it, Westmoreland, through my host,
> That he which hath no stomach to this fight,
> Let him depart; his passport shall be made
> And crowns for convoy put into his purse:
> We would not die in that man's company
> That fears his fellowship to die with us.
> This day is called the feast of Crispian:
> He that outlives this day, and comes safe home,
> Will stand a tip-toe when this day is named,
> And rouse him at the name of Crispian.
> He that shall live this day, and see old age,
> Will yearly on the vigil feast his neighbours,
> And say "To-morrow is Saint Crispian":
> Then will he strip his sleeve and show his scars,
> And say "These wounds I had on Crispin's day."
> Old men forget; yet all shall be forgot,
> But he'll remember with advantages
> What feats he did that day . . .
>   . . .
> And Crispin Crispian shall ne'er go by,
> From this day to the ending of the world,
> But we in it shall be remembered;
> We few, we happy few, we band of brothers;
> For he to-day that sheds his blood with me
> Shall be my brother; be he ne'er so vile,

This day shall gentle his condition:
And gentlemen in England now a-bed
Shall think themselves accursed they were not here,
And hold their manhoods cheap whiles any speaks
That fought with us upon Saint Crispin's day.

The definition of honor articulated here has its roots in a Renaissance medievalism that idealizes the past rather than reflects some precise historical sense of honor in warfare. Like Ambrose (albeit for different reasons), Shakespeare is conjuring a mythic past. Honor belongs to the nobleman, but any soldier who sheds his blood will acquire a kind of nobility that makes him an honorary "brother" to the king himself. It is an honor rooted entirely in the performance of battlefield courage, the glorification of which, as the historian Eugen Weber noted years ago in his essay "The Ups and Downs of Honor," too often conceals "ugly motives and ugly deeds." The cause for which these men fight is murky at best and largely mysterious to the bulk of the army.

Ambrose pays scant attention to any of this. His title and epigraph initiate a collision—not for the last time in his tapestry—between dreams of medieval chivalry and the realities of a twentieth-century democracy at war. Only a superficial reading of Shakespeare can sustain the analogy between the very different worlds of Henry V and the American GI. In the resulting incoherence, violence achieves a positive value. As Samuel Johnson suggested in the eighteenth century, a military life "has the dignity of danger. Mankind reverence those who have got over fear, which is so general a weakness." Because the dignity of danger licenses conquest and oppression as often as it does justice and liberation, its celebration can never be allowed to eclipse the end if we are to see violence for what it is. Alert to the ways in which danger seems to confer dignity, J. Glenn Gray resisted the

temptation to turn the "confraternity of danger and exposure" into something grand and noble in his 1959 book *The
Warriors: Reflections on Men in Battle*, rooted in his own firsthand observations, where he suggested that each soldier is "of
interest" to his fellow "only as a center of force, a wielder
of weapons, a means of security and survival." The "links"
between soldiers, "passionate" though they may be, are in-
escapably "utilitarian and narrow."

Shakespeare is alert to the weak ties of cause in *Henry V.*
The king's Agincourt speech follows a heated argument
with one of his subjects over the justice of his cause and the
king's own self-pitying soliloquy on the burdens of his office. Seeking to gauge the morale of his men by circulating
among them in disguise on the eve of battle, Henry encounters three unhappy soldiers who would much rather be back
in England, just as Hersey's marines would have preferred
home to Guadalcanal. The first man does not participate in
the debate, while the second seems resigned to following the
king unquestioningly. If the "cause be wrong," he explains,
"our obedience to the king wipes the crime of it out of us."
But the third soldier, Williams, refuses to grant the justice of
the king's cause so easily, even though his misery does not
impel him to disobedience. Informing the disguised monarch
that if his cause is not just, the king will have "a heavy reckoning to make" because of the many who will suffer for it, he
tallies up a grisly butcher's bill: "All those legs and arms and
heads, chopped off in a battle, shall join together at the latter
day and cry all, 'We died at such a place'—some swearing,
some crying for a surgeon, some upon their wives left poor
behind them, some upon the debts they owe, some upon their
children rawly left. I am afeard there are few die well that
die in a battle; for how can they charitably dispose of any
thing, when blood is their argument?" Small wonder, then,
that Henry appeals to his soldiers' masculinity—"gentlemen

in England" will "hold their manhoods cheap," he tells them—and to their desire for a kind of glory and fame usually reserved for aristocrats and kings. He proclaims, "For he to-day that sheds his blood with me / Shall be my brother; be he ne'er so vile."

Real-life World War II generals like George Patton and Britain's Bernard Montgomery were quick to recognize the practical value of Henry V's rhetoric; both incorporated parts of it into their own speeches to soldiers. Signally, they were not drawn to the sentimental "band of brothers" motif, nor did they appeal to some lofty sense of honor. They knew that Henry's power, like their own, lay to a large degree in shaming men. Montgomery, newly arrived in North Africa in 1942 after a series of British losses to Erwin Rommel's Afrika Korps, echoed Henry's defiant offer to transfer anyone who didn't want to be there: "I will tolerate no bellyaching. If anyone objects to doing what he is told, then he can get out of it: and at once. I want that made very clear right down through the Eighth Army." Patton, speaking to the Third Army in 1944, echoed Henry V's appeal to his soldiers' concern for their reputations: "You may be thankful that twenty years from now, when you are sitting by the fireplace with your grandson on your knee and he asks you what you did in the great World War II, you won't have to shift him to the other knee, cough, and say, 'Well, your granddaddy shoveled shit in Louisiana.' No, sir, you can look him straight in the eye and say, 'Son, your granddaddy rode with the Great Third Army and a son-of-a-goddamned-bitch named Georgie Patton!'"

The Agincourt speech's special connection to World War II also owes to Laurence Olivier's 1944 film version, made in wartime England at the behest of the British Ministry of Information—its battle scenes filmed in Ireland—and released not long after D-Day. Olivier's Henry was less ambiguous than the one invoked by the generals. The film historian David Thomson, who saw Olivier's *Henry V* as a young boy in Britain, recalled:

> No matter that the wretched French had to stand in for the Germans, *Henry V* was a self-bestowed flag of honor in approaching victory in late 1944 . . .
>
> I can only remember the complete assurance with which victory came to the British, and the breathtaking idea that "history" might be as immediate as the rush of arrows in the air . . .
>
> So the Olivier *Henry V* is not just a matter of taking pride in one's country, but of discovering the medium.

Olivier's masterful *Henry V* massaged its source to suit the propagandistic moment. The voices of dissent that populate the play and the sharp memory of the civil insurrection enacted in the first three installments of Shakespeare's English history cycle—*Richard II* and the first and second parts of *Henry IV*—largely disappear on the screen. In the preceding play (*2 Henry IV*), Henry's father, Henry IV, advises his son to "busy giddy minds / With foreign quarrels." Picking a fight with France accomplished just that, supplanting division with unity, promoting cooperation where there once was deadly internecine strife. The play redirects the violent impulses that tore open the country in a civil war outward onto France, but it has moments of subversive discontent and a certain ambient unease ignored by many readers—as the king himself so ardently hopes they will be by his subjects—searching for a message of patriotic unity. As a result, the speech has long been a favorite of high school football teams and military units alike, yet most of the young men and women who memorize or recite it for inspirational purposes have little or no sense of its literary or historical context.

Neither, it seems, did Ambrose, who, as a writer of history, not a football coach or dramatist, theoretically had a different threshold of responsibility. As he makes clear in the introduction to *The Victors*, Ambrose's first memories of World War II were those of a child: he went to the movies with his brothers to see newsreels and played war "constantly: 'Japs' vs. marines, GIs vs. 'Krauts.'" This enthusiasm, leading him to see war as a game rather than a global bloodbath, finds in Shakespeare's "band of brothers" a conceit perfectly suited to his childhood memories as well as to his agenda as a mature storyteller. Here is his initial description of Easy Company in *Band of Brothers*:

> Each of the 140 men and seven officers who formed the original company followed a different route to its birthplace, Camp Toccoa, Georgia, but they had some things in common. They were young, born since the Great War. They were white, because the U.S. Army in World War II was segregated. With three exceptions, they were unmarried. Most had been hunters and athletes in high school.

The whiteness of the band is mentioned only in passing, just one item in a catalogue. Institutional segregation is a simple fact of their lives, together with youth, high school, and hunting, the latter pursuit recalling the old American ideal of the frontiersman-as-soldier, rural American self-sufficiency translating naturally into battlefield aptitude, as it did for Hollywood's Sergeant York, who shoots men in battle just the way he shot turkeys at home. Anthony King, the sociologist, notes the degree to which racial exclusivity implicitly strengthened the bond among white soldiers: "US soldiers may not have understood the conflict as part of an ethno-national mission as their German opponents often did, but their front-line solidarity was based on ethnic presumptions." Cultural presumptions and prejudices, some bolstered by law and regulation, reinforcing the masculine bonds of white units, included widely held convictions about the inferior courage and intelligence of African Americans, the disloy-alty of Japanese Americans, and the rightful subordination of women of all races to the needs of men. In chapter 4, I will explore the ways in which racial and other divides fractured the sense of unity we project onto the period.

By means of emphasis and convenient omission, Ambrose preserves his focus on unity, not division; right, not wrong; liberation, not subjugation. Paradoxically, given that he makes so much of American idealism, he often subordinates a consideration of causes altogether to a veneration for the magnificence of the army itself. The creation of that army, rather than the victory it made possible, becomes "the great achievement of the American people and system," just as the nation's "greatest nineteenth-century achievement" had been, according to Ambrose, "the creation of the Army of the Potomac" rather than the end it eventually secured—the abolition of chattel slavery. The conclusion of *Citizen Soldiers* signals the triumph of sentimentality in Ambrose's narrative and a peculiar amnesia about origins and causes (a char-acteristic shared with so much writing about the American Civil War, a phenomenon I explore in chapter 5). This in-clination is especially apparent in a 1998 afterword in which Ambrose—chronicling an unlikely postwar friendship be-tween two erstwhile enemies: Murray Shapiro, an American, and Hans Herbst, a German—attempts to show that the GIs "liberated the Germans" from Nazism. Like many other sol-diers, Ambrose writes, Shapiro and Herbst have "learned to forgive." That capacity for forgiveness and the reconciliation of former enemies becomes the ultimate testament to American greatness. "The American soldier can take a great deal of credit for making that conversation possible. He fought hard to win the war. But every step of the way, he strove to create peace." Ernie Pyle, who covered the European Theater in 1943–44, suggested another possibility in the conclusion to *Brave Men*, a collection of his columns: "Submersion in war does not necessarily qualify a man to be the master of the peace."

Who's the Greatest?

Donald Trump's juvenile refrain about national greatness expressed most clearly in his two presidential campaign slogans, "Make America Great Again" and "Keep America Great"—seems like a fun-house echo of a national preoccupation with exceptionalism dating back centuries. The first slogan is a retread: Ronald Reagan had used the phrase "Let's Make America Great Again" in his 1980 campaign. In the republic's early days, the prevailing conceit was one of greatness in prospect. In 1839 the journalist John L. O'Sullivan, a proponent of westward expansion and the popularizer of the term Manifest Destiny, celebrated America as "the great nation of futurity." Racialist and other alarming assumptions are bound up in Manifest Destiny, inextricable from its conceptual force, but perhaps the idea's most enduring and potentially radical significance is its orientation toward the future. Ironically, by the late twentieth century, even as America became a seemingly unchallenged global power, greatness was becoming the subject of a backward rather than a forward glance: a precious, endangered commodity irrevocably linked to the past.

Brokaw's fascination with World War II began with a 1984 visit to Normandy undertaken as part of a documentary on the fortieth anniversary of the D-Day landings. By 1994, when he returned for the fiftieth anniversary, he had developed "a kind of missionary zeal for the men and women of World War II, spreading the word of their remarkable lives." The zeal manifested by Brokaw and others in the years since has been accompanied by an increasing sense of urgency. The media never tire of the morbid veteran deathwatch: stories tally the number of World War II veterans who die each day. Brokaw calls theirs a generation "birthmarked for greatness," possessing a distinct set of virtues, among them personal responsibility, a predisposition for Good Samaritanism, honesty, hard work, a capacity for sacrifice, and a sense of honor: "This is the greatest generation any society has produced," he insists. "I have the facts on my side." The thesis is impossible to prove, the narrative driven less by facts than by emotion.

Describing a country of unparalleled unity and commitment to the war effort, Brokaw comes to the overdetermined conclusion that by 1940 it was apparent "to all but a few delusional isolationists that war would define this generation's coming of age." To the extent that any one phenomenon can shape a generation, the Great Depression arguably did more than anything to define this one. Brokaw also dramatically undersells the fervor and reach of the nation's fascist sympathizers, who, as Bradley W. Hart documents in *Hitler's American Friends: The Third Reich's Supporters in the United States*, were more extensive and organized than has generally been assumed. While groups like the Silver Legion and the German American Bund collapsed after the country's entrance into the war, as the historian Stephen H. Norwood and others have demonstrated, the Christian Front pursued a violently anti-Semitic campaign that persisted throughout (and outlasted) the war. Another vocal group, the America First

Committee, was led by a national hero, the aviator Charles A. Lindbergh, who delivered a notoriously anti-Semitic speech on September 11, 1941, and was still championing isolationism at a rally at Madison Square Garden on October 30, 1941. The journalist Eric Sevareid recalled returning from Europe after the war began to a decidedly neutral United States, with which he felt himself at odds. The country, he reflected, "was just entering . . . the tortures of trying to make up her mind." When he, like others who had recently returned from abroad, vainly tried to inspire Americans to the cause of fighting fascism, he confronted "a fundamental suspicion in the American character . . . an outgrowth of the democratic habit, part of its bulwark in normal times, but now a downright menace as precious time rushed by. It was an American trait," Sevareid explains in *Not So Wild a Dream*, "not so much to avoid action, but to avoid the humiliation of being 'taken in.' America was terribly afraid of losing its fancied status as the 'wise guy,' of being a 'sucker.'"

There was no official government unity either: Senator Burton K. Wheeler headlined a "Keep America Out of War" rally in Chicago in July 1940. The North Dakota senator Gerald P. Nye found himself on the stage at an America First rally in Pittsburgh on December 7, 1941. When the reporter Robert Hagy brought him word of the attack on Pearl Harbor, Nye responded, "It sounds terribly fishy to me." Even after Hagy relayed that Japan had declared war on the United States, Nye proceeded to deliver his talk, telling his audience, "I can't somehow believe this." Given a third piece of news, that Roosevelt had convened a meeting of his cabinet and congressional leaders, Nye, albeit flustered, carried on with another speech that evening and told reporters, "We have been maneuvered into this by the President." Robinson Jeffers's poem "Pearl Harbor" opens with the same claim: the attack is portrayed as the work of those who sought to "embroil" the country in Europe's "wreck" through Lend-Lease and other policies. To Sevareid, by contrast, Roosevelt's course was evidence of a superior understanding: "He knew that he must act and that only in the test of action would the people rally and this democracy become more than a debating society in a world of violent action."

The Japanese attack on Pearl Harbor did not entirely silence the dissenting voices, but it did provoke a reaction: vengeance became the goad used to generate public enthusiasm. Contemporary observers nevertheless perceived a general American indifference to the fact that the world was on fire. Returning from a fallen France on a Norwegian freighter in December 1941, the *New Yorker* correspondent A. J. Liebling learned the news of Pearl Harbor from an officer, who shook his hand and declared, "We both allies now!" Liebling observes, "It felt more natural to be a belligerent on a belligerent ship than that anomalous creature, a neutral among belligerent friends." On docking in New Orleans, Liebling was surprised by the fact that even now America looked no different and bore no scars of war: "There were plenty of lights visible on the shore, more than I had seen at a comparable hour since leaving New York in the summer. Somehow I had expected our lights to go out when we entered the war. It seemed strange coming in our blacked-out ship to a country that was neither neutral *nor* dark."

More provocatively, on December 13, 1941, Noël Coward confided to his diary, published as *The Noël Coward Diaries* in 1982, "Cannot help being delighted about America being so dumbfounded at the Japanese attack. This feeling is not malice but a genuine relief that (a) they have at last been forced to realize that this war is theirs as well as ours, and," he continued, no doubt thinking of American triumphalism in the wake of World War I, "(b) that whatever the future brings they will never be able to say that they came in to pull our chestnuts out of the fire, as they were quite obviously caught with their trousers down." Yet Americans have liked to claim precisely that ever since. The Pacific war, begun in revenge and complicated by bitter racism, has long been eclipsed in national memory by a narrative of liberation focused largely on the European Theater. Ernie Pyle spent 1940, Brokaw's year of perfect harmony, writing his column in England, trying to impress upon his American readers that the world was in grave danger: "There is a lot of sudden dying in London every night." But Pyle did not lean heavily on ideology or throw around words like *liberty* and *democracy*: "I simply wanted England to win," he would write of his feelings once he returned to the States, "because it seemed to me safer and sounder for England to be running the world than for Germany to run it."

When Pyle returned to resume his prewar travels across America, he was still nonplussed about the state of affairs at home and about the United States' relationship to the rest of the world. In the foreword to *Ernie Pyle in England*, written in July 1941, he mused, "But maybe we're only fooling ourselves. Maybe we're just pretending that we've picked up the world where we left it last fall. For there is probably something to the theory that our lives, in common with all others, can never again be just as they were before 1940." This is an openly uncertain, searching voice. Pyle sounds very much like someone trying to convince his country (and himself) that the United States was not, and no longer could be, alone in the world. Pyle's columns offered Americans inspiring portraits of British resilience in the face of emergency. "It is true," he wrote in January 1941, "that all eyes in England look toward America." Among his several accounts of tours to underground shelters is an especially weird and haunting description of two dozen Londoners gathered in a basement around a piano, singing "Marching Through Georgia," the song written about Sherman's army—Sherman hated it—during the Civil War. Toward the end of the book, Pyle writes of the British response to the passage of the Lend-Lease Act: "Now that the lend-lease bill is law, the British talk more frankly to Americans. 'Why shouldn't you give us the stuff?' my barber asks. 'You don't ask a man to repay you a shilling when you're both running for your lives.'" Pyle reports that Americans are "rolling in" to London "to study this, and study that," but that even among those Americans there was no clear consensus about joining the war effort: "It is the belief of most Americans I know over here that America is headed rapidly toward war. Their feeling seems about fifty-fifty for and against the idea."

Liebling, in a later reflection on his encounter with the chairman and national director of the America First Committee in Chicago in the spring of 1941, also reveals a lack of national unity. He notes that the organization's mission to keep "the United States from aiding Great Britain in her war effort" was also the Communist Party line in the wake of the Nazi-Soviet pact, but, he quips, "there was no reason to suspect America First of Leninism." The leaders of the committee were the chairman of the board of Sears, Roebuck and a vice president of Quaker Oats, hardly the lunatic fringe Brokaw imagines but bastions of the Middle American establishment. Ironically, the Midwest is the epicenter of American values for Brokaw. General Robert E. Wood, the committee chairman, informed Liebling that "a German victory could not possibly endanger the United States, then as naked of armament as a garden worm." The foundation for Wood's belief—and for his desire to stay out of the war—was his service in World War I. What proved most unsettling to Liebling, who had just returned from Europe, was the confident insularity of the committee leadership:

All things, national and international, were manifest to the manufacturers of overalls and breakfast cereals, and the America First letterhead showed that the General and the oatlet had behind them the man who made Spam and a man who made steel and a man who had investments in salt, teletype machines, and wristwatches. As intellectual reference, they offered Robert Maynard Hutchins, the president of the University of Chicago . . .

I could not understand why what was so plain, in the spring of 1941, in New York and Washington and Lisbon and London should be so bitterly denied by so large a segment of the dominant group in this particular city and region.

Liebling attributes this dissidence to a regional chauvinism and disappointment: "As much as any unreconstructed Confederates, the mail-order giants and puffed-fluff kings have found themselves the leaders of a lost cause. Their personal fortunes may be great, but the world has not gone as they willed it. Chicago's bid for grandeur has failed." Liebling had entered what Sevareid referred to as the country's "isolationist heart." Others noted the region's worrisome lack of interest in the world beyond. As late as August 1942, in order "to wake up the Middle West to the grimness of our national situation," Thomas Hart Benton felt the need to paint a series of propaganda pieces, including the starkly titled and controversial *Embarkation—Prelude to Death*, which depicted soldiers at the Brooklyn Navy Yard boarding ships en route to North Africa.

The Chicago committee's opposition to the East Coast establishment is echoed in the current antagonism between the coasts and the so-called flyover states. In 1941, it took the form, as it has in recent years, of a preoccupation with the ethos of America First. It is no accident that Trump invoked that particular phrase to such success. Nor indeed was this sentiment limited to the middle of the country in the 1940s. Even in New York City, a sizable population voiced pro-German sentiment in movie houses and other public venues, as Thomas Doherty has documented in *Hollywood and Hitler, 1933–1939.* Far from admitting the inevitability of war, American industries, including Hollywood, had spent a decade tempering their politics and championing neutrality in order to retain the profitable German market.

In February 1939 a German American Bund rally at Madison Square Garden attracted as many as twenty thousand people. As Marshall Curry's 2017 documentary *A Night at the Garden* reveals, the Bund strutted in fascist uniforms in front of a huge banner of George Washington, their co-opted patron saint, and asserted a direct line between fascism and the founders. The Bund also gathered in the summers throughout the 1930s at Camp Siegfried, in Yaphank, Long Island, where they sang the "Horst Wessel Song," read propaganda directly supplied by Germany, and strolled along paths named for Hitler and Göring.

"The Japanese attack on Pearl Harbor brought war but not unity to the American people," the historian Richard W. Steele observed in an article that appeared in *The Journal of American History* in 1978. Opinion polls in 1942 revealed a "peace bloc" comprising fully twenty percent of the adult population; these post–Pearl Harbor "divisionists," Steele notes, "were strikingly similar in numbers and attitudes to the isolationists of 1941." By February 1942, the Roosevelt administration was concerned about "the shallowness of public commitment to the war . . . The consensus was that after the initial shock of Pearl Harbor had worn off, the public had lapsed into complacency." A large portion of the population was still confused about war aims and insufficiently committed to the war effort. Six months into the country's involvement, fifty-three percent of Americans polled "admitted they did not have a clear idea of what the war was about." Roosevelt believed that proponents of a negotiated peace included leaders of the Republican Party, some of whom had been contacted by German agents. Steele observes, "Apparently only a lack of organization significantly differentiated sentiment for a negotiated peace from the isolationism of 1941."

Calling attention to the deep cynicism with which many Americans responded to the war, Eric Sevareid remembered the spendthrifts, bootleggers, and profiteers he encountered in New York and Washington, where they danced in nightclubs to a "saccharine" tune Sevareid mockingly calls "Remember-r-r Pearl Harbor-r-r," complained about sugar rationing, or derided "the Four Freedoms, and the great vision of the century of the common man . . . as 'globaloney.'" Seeing the advertisements proclaiming "Lucky Strikes had gone to war" or advising the country "that its war production would be increased if everyone masticated a few extra sticks of Wrigley's per day," Sevareid confronted the general mood of a nation that "was encouraged to believe that it could produce its way to victory, or buy its victory by the simple measure of writing a check. Life was easy and getting more prosperous every week, and nobody believed in death," a fantasy further encouraged by the War Department's censorship of photographs depicting dead service members.

But for the myth to work its magic, unity must always prevail, as it does in the celebratory narratives of Ambrose and Brokaw. Public opinion must turn overnight after Pearl Harbor, while the various regional, racial, and political divisions that roiled the country must be immediately put aside as Americans rally toward a shared cause. The temporary nature of the gains made by certain segments of society— the short-lived burst of self-sufficiency enjoyed by women, for example, which gave way to the reactionary conservatism of the postwar world and the deep resentment of men at women's newfound independence—must be submerged in the explicitly messianic agenda of *The Greatest Generation*. The faith expressed by one war industry worker in the book encapsulates the whole: World War II, she concludes, was "the last time 'in the history of our country when a full-blown spirit of true patriotism was in every heart.'" My point is not that some Americans didn't feel that way—at least in retrospect—but that platitudes and generalizations ignore the welter of contradictions to be found in period writing.

Leave No Man Behind

Steven Spielberg's *Saving Private Ryan*, made in the wake of the war's fiftieth-anniversary celebrations, offers a provocative visual expression of the school of remembrance I have been outlining. The highest-grossing film of 1998 in the United States, *Ryan* also heads the domestic lifetime gross list of all World War II films, followed by *Pearl Harbor* (2001), *Dunkirk* (2017), *Captain America: The First Avenger* (2011), and *Inglourious Basterds* (2009). *Ryan* was Spielberg's second World War II epic in five years, the first being *Schindler's List* (1993). While the latter film, much celebrated in certain quarters, was criticized by Jason Epstein and others for its sentimental reading of the Holocaust as the triumph of one righteous man, *Saving Private Ryan* was largely forgiven analogous indulgences because of the graphic depiction of the D-Day landing on Omaha Beach, which overwhelmed the saccharine quality of the prologue and epilogue, in which the older Ryan and his family appear at the American Cemetery in Normandy. At the end of the film, before the grave of one of the men who died to save him, Ryan asks his wife to tell him that he is "a good man" who has "led a good life."

At the time of the film's release, the Associated Press reported that the Department of Veterans Affairs had "set up a national hotline for veterans or their family members traumatized by the combat scenes in the movie." A VA therapist in Portland, Oregon, explained, "I think it's going to hit a lot of people hard." She added, by way of context, "John Wayne made a lot of movies examining that World War II experience but not as graphically as I understand this one will be. It's a much different perspective on the pain, the suffering and the actual killings." For Paul Fussell, the film's value lay in its willingness to show a gruesome truth other films had not: "In war films you don't often see arterial blood pumping out." Other veterans agreed: the film "couldn't be more real," said one on PBS's *NewsHour with Jim Lehrer*; it was "a very real experience," offered another.

Spielberg declared his intention to give the film the greatest possible sensory realism and thus to "approximate" actual combat. He and his cinematographer, Janusz Kaminski, worked to achieve their goal by electing not to storyboard the scene and by using a handheld camera. The film stock itself was run through a desaturation process that would reproduce the bleached-out look of color footage of the actual invasion filmed by the director George Stevens Sr. In this way, the film ends up evoking less the actual experience than the way it would have looked at the movies. Claims about *Ryan*'s unprecedented realism, even when voiced by veterans themselves, might thus give us pause. A combination of a technological process and our impressionable eye makes *Saving Private Ryan* seem an authentic reproduction rather than what it is: an effective illusion that satisfies a viewer's (and a moviegoer's) nostalgia. Stevens, Frank Capra, John Huston, John Ford, William Wyler, and other Hollywood professionals filmed real or simulated battles for the armed services, an experience Mark Harris chronicles at length in *Five Came*

Back: A Story of Hollywood and the Second World War. Some of that footage was later incorporated into feature films such as Allan Dwan's *Sands of Iwo Jima* (1949), one of the John Wayne films to which the VA therapist alluded.

Apparent verisimilitude isn't the only sleight of hand in *Saving Private Ryan.* The plot itself, in which soldiers are sent by no less an authority than Army Chief of Staff George Marshall to rescue James Ryan, the last remaining son of a family of soldiers killed in action, is wholly unrepresentative of World War II–era attitudes toward individual soldiers. In 1942 the armed forces instituted a "sole-survivor policy," later called Directive 1315.15 Special Separation Policies for Survivorship, in response to the fact that several sets of brothers, the most celebrated of which were the five Sullivans, all assigned to the USS *Juneau,* were killed in action. They were the subject of Hollywood's *The Fighting Sullivans* (1944). *Saving Private Ryan*'s plot is based on the story of Frederick Niland, a soldier fighting in Normandy. On receiving word that his brothers had been killed, Niland informed a chaplain of the distressing news; the chaplain thereupon sent up a request that Niland be transferred out of harm's way. There was no search required, let alone one ordered by the army chief of staff.

As the title of another John Wayne vehicle, *They Were Expendable* (1945), suggests, many casualties were necessarily left behind in this war. There were simply too many lost or missing bodies to allow a preoccupation with the individual. By training a spotlight on the fate of a lone survivor, however, Spielberg's film effectively transforms the conflict from one characterized by mass mobilization and modern industrial warfare to something more old-fashioned, recalling the heroism of the ancient epics, in which battles between individuals come to seem more important than the big picture, and in which personal causes—avenging the death of a comrade, securing an adversary's magnificent armor or other spoils, maintaining or reclaiming one's honor—assume an outsize role. In *Saving Private Ryan*, the tension between the communal and the individual is palpable, but the latter eventually wins out. The film's reason for being is the fulfillment of an anachronistic obligation to leave no man behind that more properly belongs to earlier (and later) wars.

The creed of leaving no one behind did not become an American social and political obsession until the latter part of the twentieth century, when casualties, while still high, again become low enough to count. In the years following Vietnam, when the reasons for that war became murkier and less popular than ever, the black-and-white POW/MIA flag, with its message—YOU ARE NOT FORGOTTEN—directed to prisoners of war (POW) and soldiers missing in action (MIA), became the emblem of a national backward glance. Larry Greer, an official at the Defense Prisoner of War/Missing Personnel Office (DPMO), explained the origins of the commitment to Caroline Alexander in a 2004 *New Yorker* article: "Vietnam was significant because it saw the beginning of grassroots and particularly family pressure on our government . . . Frankly, what you're seeing today is a result of this."

The mission of the Defense POW/MIA Accounting Agency (DPAA), formerly the Joint POW/MIA Accounting Command (JPAC), which deploys recovery teams to Southeast Asia and elsewhere, is to "provide the fullest possible accounting for our missing personnel to their families and the nation." According to DPAA, there are approximately 72,000 American bodies missing in action from World War II and more than 8,000 from all conflicts since. Many—those lost at sea, for example—are deemed unrecoverable. In 2004, when the total of bodies that could theoretically be recovered stood at 43,000, Alexander calculated that it would have taken "the United States government four hundred and nine years to make good its pledge."

Such pledges have an ancient history. Thucydides's account of the annual Athenian military funeral rites during the Peloponnesian War suggests the long-standing political importance of identifying and repatriating all bodies even as it reveals the practical impossibility of full accounting: bones were sorted by tribe, warriors' remains solemnly interred in a public burying ground outside the city walls. Also part of the procession was an "empty bier . . . for the missing, whose bodies could not be recovered." Pericles's funeral speech, recorded by Thucydides and later reimagined by Abraham Lincoln at Gettysburg, reveals the political capital to be made of such funerary ceremonies and their role in unifying a community by reinforcing shared values. One can thus read the renewed focus on the repatriation of U.S. soldiers' remains as a direct consequence of the ambiguities and divisiveness of Vietnam.

A determination to go back for the wounded and the dead—to leave no one behind, no matter the immediate danger or the prospects for successful rescue or retrieval—has also become an increasingly visible aspect of military operations. In 1993, when Americans operated in Somalia with a knowledge of the enemy practice of mutilating bodies, the compulsion to leave no one behind at one point took precedence over even the care of the wounded and the mission itself. When Major General William F. Garrison ordered an entire rescue convoy, and with it the evacuation of the wounded, to halt for hours in the streets of Mogadishu while a downed Black Hawk was disassembled in order to extricate the remains of Chief Warrant Officer Cliff Wolcott, the mandate not to leave the fallen behind seemed to acquire a paralyzing grip. "Placing three hundred men at jeopardy in order to retrieve the body of one man," Mark Bowden observes in *Black Hawk Down: A Story of Modern War*, ventriloquizing Captain Mike Steele, who waited in the column, "was a noble gesture, but hardly a sensible one."

The film *Black Hawk Down* (2001), with its tagline, LEAVE NO MAN BEHIND, helped to popularize the gesture for a wider civilian audience. Instead of elevating a cause, the film removes combat action from its political context and fixates on the sacrifice of the living for the dead. In an era of unconventional, asymmetrical warfare—one in which missions are more difficult to explain and victories more difficult to recognize, battles are witnessed by commanders in real-time video, and risk aversion is paradoxically magnified by the fact that casualties are low enough to be individually reported—an ancient warrior ethos exalting a particular kind of sacrifice exerts an almost irresistible appeal.

In the absence of more tangible, near-term goals, the gesture of risking one's own life to rescue the wounded and recover the dead has emerged as a recognizably heroic ideal for American service members and for the nation they serve. Six servicemen were killed in Afghanistan in early March 2002 as they attempted first to rescue—and then to recover the body of—Petty Officer First Class Neil Roberts, a Navy SEAL who had fallen from a Chinook helicopter into enemy hands. Responding to the incident, U.S. Air Force Brigadier General John W. Rosa Jr., then deputy director for operations for the Joint Chiefs of Staff, told reporters simply, "We don't leave Americans behind." Offered as explanation, justification, or praise, such responses have become de rigueur for military commanders. For a long time the mandate of small, unconventional forces such as the U.S. Army Rangers, the U.S. Marine Corps, and the French Foreign Legion, leaving no man behind became part of the U.S. Army's Soldier's Creed in 2003. Embraced by the media and popularized by films like *Black Hawk Down* and *Saving Private Ryan*, the creed uses a vocabulary historically associated with elite bands of warriors in distinctive, closed cultures.

This could not be further from the prevailing ethos of World War II, but one would not know that from watching *Saving Private Ryan*, in which Captain Miller (Tom Hanks) is ordered to find Mrs. Ryan's last surviving son. As a company commander, Miller has routinely been forced to make the choice of mission over men. It is only when his mission suddenly becomes a man, as Sergeant Horvath (Tom Sizemore) reminds him, that he begins to reflect on his moral calculus. Resting for the night in a church, Miller and Horvath reminisce about soldiers who have died. There have been so many that Miller momentarily forgets one of their names. This lapse prompts him to explain his decision-making process:

CAPTAIN MILLER: You see, when . . . when you end up killing one of your men, you see, you tell yourself it happened so you could save the lives of two, or three, or ten others, maybe a hundred others. Do you know how many men I've lost under my command?
SERGEANT HORVATH: How many?
MILLER: Ninety-four. But that means I've saved the lives of ten times that many, doesn't it? Maybe even twenty, right? Twenty times as many. And that's how simple it is. That's how you—that's how you rationalize making the choice between the mission and the men.
HORVATH: Except this time the mission is a man.
MILLER: This Ryan better be worth it. He'd better go home, cure some disease or invent a longer-lasting light bulb or something, 'cause the truth is I wouldn't trade ten Ryans for one Vecchio or one Caparzo.

Private Ryan (Matt Damon) is still very much alive when Miller finally finds him, but he initially refuses to be rescued. Ryan's own calculations suggest to him that he counts for the same thing as his fellow soldiers and must therefore face the same risks. The accident of his brothers' deaths does not in any way change his status as a combatant, only as a son. And how could Private Ryan be worth it—worth, that is, the lives of several other privates—unless one were to apply some undemocratic measure? This is the argument one of Miller's men makes while on the march. Private Ryan's identity as Mrs. Ryan's last surviving son has increased his relative value for only the high command. First Miller suggests that Ryan might redeem himself by making a great contribution (curing a disease), but this resolution is immediately undercut by the cynical reference to the longer-lasting light bulb, as the captain realizes the injustice of using potential to measure the value of any given soldier. In the end he further devalues the man he must save by claiming that he would not trade one of his men for ten Private Ryans.

The ambiguities probed in this scene, and the rich complexities of the film's middle part, are abruptly erased by its high-octane conclusion. We are never given a rational answer to the question Miller's own soldiers ask repeatedly: Why does Mrs. Ryan deserve more consideration than their own mothers? Instead, we are swept up by the sentimentality of the end of the film, which returns to the frame story of Private Ryan as an old man paying his respects to the captain who saved his life. The repeated shot of an American flag snapping in the breeze, a tearful Ryan, his affectionate wife, children, and grandchildren—all these images, accompanied by swelling music, are offered as visual argument that saving Private Ryan was worth the exorbitant cost. We are meant either to forget that Mrs. Miller and Mrs. Horvath also lost their sons, or to believe that they should have been consoled by the noble gesture of self-sacrifice.

That Captain Miller fulfills his mission at the cost of his own life and those of his men demonstrates his strong sense of duty. However, he is forced by the nature of the enterprise, imposed by no less a figure than General Marshall, to forsake the command principle by means of which he had heretofore accorded dignity to his men even as he led them into harm's way. Miller cannot imagine Ryan to be worth more than another man. Instead of sacrificing one to save many, Miller must now sacrifice many to save one. The movie's final battle scene culminates, to borrow Rachel Bespaloff's description of Hector's death in Homer's *Iliad*, in an "ecstasy of self-sacrifice," as Miller dies telling Ryan, "Earn this." It partakes of the rapturous self-destruction of the ancient warrior, which, according to Bespaloff, is produced by a "force . . . detestable insofar as it contains a fatality that transforms it into inertia, a blind drive that is always pushing it on to the very end of its course, on to its own abolition and the obliteration of the very values it engendered." The ending of *Saving Private Ryan* succeeds in obliterating the values it means to exalt: namely, the worth and dignity of the individual. The monomaniacal drive to save one man effectively negates the value of all those individuals sent to rescue him. Humanity is supplanted by a humanitarian fiction.

Whether one admires the esprit de corps that drives soldiers to return for comrades left behind, or one criticizes it for interfering with missions and contributing to the deaths of more soldiers, it must be acknowledged that the roots of this ethos are ancient and literary. Film may be the most powerful modern medium for the war story, but it is to Homeric epic that the idea can be traced. In the *Iliad*, the stated reason that the Greeks have come to Troy—the return of the kidnapped Helen to her husband, Menelaus—recedes before

a tight focus on individual contests between warriors trying
to win battlefield honor, the highest kind they know. A recognition of this genealogy is essential to a full understanding of
the concept's significance for today's military and the ways in
which it has been read back onto World War II, when the sheer
numbers of dead made such attention impossible. The late-
twentieth-century and early-twenty-first-century emphasis on
retrieving the fallen—not only the wounded but, more provocatively, the dead—reveals the enduring appeal of aristocratic
sentiment to a democratic force and the society it serves.

In Homer's time, as M. I. Finley notes in *The World of
Odysseus*, armor had come to serve the "honorific purpose"
satisfied in more primitive cultures by enemy heads. Failure
to obtain, or retain, such treasure brought a corresponding
shame. Many of the battle scenes in the poem are therefore
nothing other than contests over the armor-clad bodies of the
slain. Ancient codes of loyalty and honor manifest themselves
nowhere more clearly than in a steadfast determination to
protect a body from the enemy even at the loss of one's own
life. Indeed, the corpse acquires a value independent of its armor; it becomes a tactical objective on Homer's battlefield—
the vehicle through which one reclaims honor.

The imperative to retrieve a fallen comrade's body from
the field regardless of tactical cost also suggests the preeminence of the dead over the living. The death of the soldier is "a
spectacle," observes Simone Weil, "the Iliad never wearies of
showing us." Finley put it in slightly different terms: "The poet
and his audience lingered lovingly over every act of slaughter."
At a fundamental anthropological level, such scenes express
the fact that, as Phyllis Pagli and Henry Abramovitch write in
"Death: A Cross-Cultural Perspective," "Death awareness is
a natural sequel to the development of self-awareness—an intrinsic attribute of humankind." Yet these demonstrations also
reveal more culturally specific attitudes; the representation of

death in the epic signals the centrality of the physical body to Homeric conceptions of honor and integrity. This frenzy over bodies was, in truth, almost exclusively literary in classical Greece. As the classicist Pamela Vaughn explains, only rarely, when the "fighting was uncharacteristically indecisive," did victory depend on "the return of corpses." The decision by the Athenian general Nicias to forfeit a battlefield in 425 BCE in order to retrieve bodies was a notable instance. But in Homer, the compulsion to recover bodies reshapes battle plans and distracts participants from their original objectives. This is the rich poetic history behind the rescue of Mrs. Ryan's remaining son.

Saving Private Ryan effectively reduces World War II to a contest of individuals. Its anachronism can be illuminated through a comparison with an earlier film's treatment of a similar theme. In *Twelve O'Clock High* (1949), Gregory Peck plays Brigadier General Frank Savage, who takes over from a friend the command of a bomb group that has come to regard itself as a "hard-luck" outfit. Although he will learn to care as deeply about his men as his less stoical predecessor, Savage attempts to instill discipline by retraining personal loyalties into unit and institutional ones. In the briefing that follows the group's first mission under his command, the general asks a pilot why he broke formation. The aviator replies that he saw another pilot, who happened to be his roommate, in trouble and tried to help him home. The damaged plane is shot down anyway. A coldly furious Savage replies with a clinical analysis of his subordinate's decision:

> So for the sake of your roommate, you violated group integrity. Every gun on a B-17 is designed to give the group maximum defensive firepower. That's what I mean by group integrity. When you pull a B-17 out of formation, you reduce the defensive power of the

group by ten guns. A crippled airplane has to be expendable. The one thing which is never expendable is
your obligation to this group . . . That has to be your
loyalty—your only reason for being.

Like Captain Miller's war, Savage's consists of a series of unromantic calculations. "Consider yourselves already dead,"
he tells his men on first meeting them. This attitude is interpreted by the man he has replaced, Colonel Davenport, as
callousness. Soldiers, Davenport remonstrates, "can't be just
a set of numbers" to their commander.

Nevertheless, in contrast to *Saving Private Ryan*, this film
provides further endorsement of the general's methods. Only
once, on what turns out to be his last mission, does Savage
deviate from his principles. After the group has released
its bombs, he decides—against the advice of his now well-
trained executive officer, Major Cobb—to turn over a heavy
flak area in order to protect some stragglers from approaching German fighters. As a result of this decision, Cobb and
his entire crew are lost; their plane explodes before they can
bail out. This crisis, his effective killing of Cobb, precipitates
Savage's own breakdown. Seventy years ago, Hollywood
could portray Savage's philosophy as military virtue; it could
portray without criticism a sense of duty that seemed to have
no room for individual attachments at the expense of the collective, even as it registered the toll such an approach took on
decision-makers. Today, however, when on-screen soldiers
face similar dilemmas, they are more likely to eschew Savage's corporate sensibility in favor of the noble gesture and a
celebration of the individual.

For the ancient warrior, the political theorist Michael Wal-
zer proposes in *Just and Unjust Wars*, war was not yet "ugly,"
because not coerced, as it would be on such a large scale in
the democratic armies of the modern era. "For a man of the

people to die in war is terrible," an aristocratic French officer tells his similarly patrician German captor in Jean Renoir's World War I film *La Grande Illusion* (1937), "for you and me it is a good solution." Renoir's film marks the passing of the old order and the rise of a new one with delicacy and without nostalgia. All U.S. soldiers are "of the people," and it is therefore "terrible" for them to die in war. Returning for the dead satisfies many impulses—loyalty, fear, vengeance, honor— and it also simplifies the confusions of modern war and helps to disguise their ugliness. Wars kill civilization, concludes one of the characters of John Horne Burns's bitter World War II novel *The Gallery*: "The gentle die in battle. Your crude extrovert comes out of his ordeal more brutal and crass and cocky than when he went in. That's the way civilizations die, gradually. A premium is put on physical courage in wartime which kills off the gentle, because they're too noble to admit of cowardice . . . Death to them is terrible."

The War Before the Good War

"Now, fifty years later, there has been so much talk about 'The Good War,' the Justified War, the Necessary War, and the like," Paul Fussell wrote in 1989, "that the young and the innocent could get the impression that it was really not such a bad thing after all." Fussell's paramount goal, in *Wartime* and elsewhere in his work, was to disabuse anyone of the notion that war itself could ever be "good," regardless of the ends to which it had been the means. One of the most remarkable aspects of the triumph of the Good War mythology is how thoroughly it has obscured the altogether more open, ambivalent, reflective mode of remembrance that has persisted all along, in parallel to the mythmaking. In 1984, Studs Terkel produced another in his series of masterful oral histories, *"The Good War": An Oral History of World War Two*. Terkel conceived the project as an antidote not to *mis*-remembrance but to "disremembrance," a goal central to all of his oral history projects, which derive their strength from contradiction and ambiguity. The books recover as wide a collection of often-conflicting memories as possible. *"The Good War"* revels in its many voices, which range from the deeply nostalgic to the bitterly disaffected. Terkel talked to everyone: from admirals to merchant marines, GIs to government officials, defense workers to USO entertainers, nurses to the so-called premature anti-fascists who had fought in the Spanish Civil War. And he made no attempt to reduce the cacophony to a single refrain, to reconcile differences of opinion, or to shape contradictory accounts into a coherent narrative. As his prefatory note suggests, incongruity is a Terkel specialty: the book's title appears in quotation marks, he explains, "because the adjective 'good' mated to the noun 'war' is so incongruous." The strength of communal memory as Terkel assembles it lies in its multiplicity and disunity. The sentimental and the disillusioned, the jingoistic and the thoughtfully patriotic, the nostalgic and the dismissive—all these perspectives share the stage in *"The Good War."* And this fundamental disagreement over what to make of the war becomes by far the strongest evidence of authentic democracy. The polyvocal nature of the text fights against the reductive force of myth.

Perhaps the most important work Terkel does is to knit the war into a larger pattern of national history rather than considering it as a self-contained event: "1939 was the end and the beginning," he writes in his introduction. "Hard Times, as though by some twentieth-century alchemy, were transmuted into Good Times. War was our Paracelsus." Terkel's reference to Paracelsus, the sixteenth-century alchemist, is instructive, for it captures the illusory, almost accidental nature of the transformation that has been read as national destiny. Terkel revealed the extent to which many Americans understood the war not as sacrifice or even vengeance, but, more simply and practically, as deliverance from the misery of the Depression: "We were ready for a war," opined the conscientious objector John H. Abbott. "We'd had a long depression . . . Get off those bread lines. Build another bomber for peace . . . That was the most popular war we ever have had. People sang, danced, drank—whoopee, the war." Other interviewees by no means as cynical as Abbott likewise emphasized the difficulty of disentangling patriotic and economic motives. Lee Oremont, a supermarket comptroller, noted that the war could seem very far away to those without relatives in harm's way. Oremont enjoyed unaccustomed prosperity: "We really didn't suffer." John Kenneth Galbraith, the deputy head of the Office of Price Administration and later one of the members of the Strategic Bombing Survey, reflected, "Never in the history of human conflict has there been so much talk of sacrifice and so little sacrifice."

Women, who contributed so much materially to the war effort, also brought to it a range of responses, hard-edged realism notable among them. Peggy Terry, a Kentucky native who worked in defense plants during the war, described herself as ignorant of the larger picture. Her perspective was rooted in the poverty and desperation of the Depression rather than in the consequences of her work: war work was a job like any other for Terry, and she traveled wherever she had to in order to find it. Other defense workers, such as Sarah Killingsworth, who moved to Los Angeles from Tennessee to find employment, shared Terry's unconcern with such labor as anything but a source of pay. Killingsworth, who got a job as a washroom attendant in a defense plant, described for Terkel the attitudes of her coworkers: "They weren't interested in the war. Most of them were only interested in the money. Most of us was young and we really didn't know."

Among those Americans initially seized by war fever was a retired music teacher named Dellie Hahne. At first everyone thought the war "the greatest thing since the Crusades," she recalled, but soon "enthusiasm waned and we became cynical and very tired and sick of the bloodshed and killing." Hahne remembered all those who "didn't want to fight" as well as those who did, including her brother, who was killed in a training exercise. She offered Terkel a portrait of wartime America as complex and contradictory as its peacetime version. The very phrase *good war* infuriated her:

> World War Two being called a good war is a horrible thing . . . If they had said to me, Look . . . we'll all get our arms and legs blown off but it has to be done, I'd understand. If they didn't hand me all this shit with the uniforms and the girls in their pompadours dancing at the USO and all those songs—"There'll Be Bluebirds over the White Cliffs of Dover"—bullshit! . . .
>
> Maybe you have to get people to fight a war, maybe you have to lie to them.

Hahne's complaint alerts us to the danger of imagining any war as simply good. This was the source of Fussell's rage as well. There could be nothing inherently "good" about an enterprise motivated by vengeance and won with "insensate savagery." Fussell divides the war into two phases in *Wartime*. The first was infused by the delusion that "civilized restraint and New World decency could overcome brutality and evil," which early reversals in Africa and the Pacific would dispel. The second was driven by "the cynicism, efficiency, brutality, and bloody-mindedness . . . required to win."

One of the most powerful accounts in Terkel's collection of the gulf between the home front and the theater of war comes from Betty Basye Hutchinson, a nurse in Pasadena who recalled the shock of the city's finest citizens at the presence in their midst of wounded soldiers billeted in a downtown hotel after the closure of a nearby hospital. She would walk through town with the convalescents, one of whom had a grievous wound to the face: "Half his face completely gone, right? . . . Nicely dressed women, absolutely staring, just standing there staring . . . It's like the war hadn't come to Pasadena until we came there." Residents wrote letters to the editor of the local newspaper demanding that the patients be kept on the grounds of the hotel and out of sight of the population: "It's only the glamour of war that appeals to people," Hutchinson concluded. "They don't know real war."

The many veterans Terkel interviewed likewise revealed a diverse range of opinions and emotions: love (of country and comrades), fear, anger, regret, and numbness—sometimes all at once. He found men who wanted to be in combat but ended up as orderlies; teenagers who cared less for country than for proving their manhood and soldiers whose patriotism reached incalculable depths; men who performed extraordinary acts of courage as well as indiscriminate killing that had "the flavor of murder." For many, it was the most momentous passage in their lives, but its significance had little to do with why they were there and owed almost everything to their proximity to danger. Robert Rasmus, an infantryman who later became a Chicago business executive, told Terkel that the war provided "the most tremendous experiences of all of life: of fear, of jubilance, of misery, of hope, of comradeship, and of the endless excitement, the theatrics of it."

Eddie Costello, a journalist and navy veteran who began the war as a naïve teenage patriot, shared far less romantic memories. He summed up the experience as "four years of nervous diarrhea." Nevertheless, Costello revealed that reminiscing gave him the opportunity to improve upon his war: "Enlarge it, embroider it, and come out . . . smelling a little better than I do." Fish stories, tall tales, exaggerations—war has always had an uneasy relationship with the truth. Another of Terkel's interviewees, Roger Tuttrup, sixteen at the time of Pearl Harbor, worried that he would miss out. Once he joined the marines, the training simultaneously humiliated and validated him: "You're part of something. When you're there and you need somebody, you got somebody. It was the high point of my life." Tuttrup, late to the action, worked as a stevedore in the Pacific, but like Costello, he tended to embroider his record: "Everybody embellishes the truth a little bit. I don't lie, but I don't always tell it a hundred percent. So I says I was in on the invasion of Okinawa. That's true. The outfit I was in made a diversionary trip to the southern end of Okinawa. Then we went back to Saipan."

Lies are one of the compensations of war for those who fight it, but there's also a relationship between lying and war at the level of decision-making. That relationship has intensified for many Americans since Vietnam. The Pentagon Papers find an echo in the Afghanistan document trove. It is no accident that the Vietnam veteran Tim O'Brien's meditation on lies, "How to Tell a True War Story," is so often invoked in discussions of recent American wars: "If at the end of a war story you feel uplifted," O'Brien writes, "or you feel that some small bit of rectitude has been salvaged from the larger waste, then you have been made the victim of a very old and terrible lie." But even legitimate causes are often served by illegitimate propaganda. Motivating people to risk death involves a certain degree of deception. What the World War I poet Wilfred Owen called the "old Lie" always hovers around wars—even just and necessary ones that end tyrannies and liberate peoples—at home and in the combat theater itself, where dreams of martial glory give way before the stark truth of destruction.

Perhaps few understood this dynamic better than Robert Lekachman, an economics professor interviewed by Terkel. Lekachman was drafted after Pearl Harbor, and the army gave him regular employment for the first time. So inept during training that he wasn't sent to OCS, Lekachman was grateful that he didn't become one of those second lieutenants who were "slaughtered in heaps." Instead, he was sent to headquarters staff, an assignment that increased the odds of his survival considerably and taught him many life skills. There, as a self-described ghostwriter, he crafted the letters of condolence that company commanders are supposed to write to next of kin. He called this work "creative fiction." He also wrote citations for medals, a task he described as "really creative fiction. There was an awful lot of hustling for awards. Each one was worth five points. People were shipped back home in the order of points accumulated. But there were so many genuine acts of bravery, too."

Lekachman's remembrance of World War II, like that of so many of Terkel's interviewees, was shaped in no small measure by the war in Vietnam, in contrast to which his war seemed "idealistic . . . the last time that most Americans thought they were innocent and good." Joseph L. Rauh Jr., a public-interest lawyer in Washington, D.C., put it more pithily: "There may be no such thing as a good war," but, in contrast to Vietnam, "at least World War Two had a purpose." Terkel's engagement with World War II's Cold War legacy proves just as revealing as his attention to its prehistory in the Depression. The veteran Johnny DeGrazio reflected in his interview, "World War Two is naturally different . . . Vietnam was treacherous fightin' . . . World War Two, everybody was behind it. Five hundred percent." The divisions of Vietnam surely made the World War II–era United States seem unified by comparison. As John Bodnar suggests, "the more troubling legacy of Vietnam" primed Americans to "entertain highly laudable stories of national honor and bravery." But if the two wars seemed radically different to many Americans, a few perceived a profound resemblance. For Gene La Rocque, a retired rear admiral, the first war made the second possible by distorting our perspective: "We see things in terms of that war, which in a sense was a good war. But the twisted memory of it encourages the men of my generation to be willing, almost eager, to use military force anywhere in the world." The journalist Neil Sheehan referred to this mindset as "the disease of victory" in his revelatory 1988 book *A Bright Shining Lie: John Paul Vann and America in Vietnam.* "By the second decade after World War II," Sheehan writes,

> the dominant characteristics of the senior leadership of the American armed forces had become professional arrogance, lack of imagination, and moral and intellectual insensitivity . . . The attributes were the symptoms of an institutional illness that . . . arose out of the victorious response to the challenge of Nazi Germany and imperial Japan. The condition . . . had also touched the civilian bureaucracies . . . that joined the armed services in managing American overseas interests for the president. The attitudes had spread as well to the greater part of the political, academic, and business leadership of the United States. World War II had been such a triumph of American resources, technology, and industrial and military genius, and the prosperity that the war and the postwar dominance abroad had brought had been so satisfying after the long hunger of the Depression, that American society had become a victim of its own achievement.

If "the disease of victory" in World War II contributed to the colossal failure of Vietnam, it would be left to yet another war, superintended by World War II veteran George H. W. Bush, to cure what Bush himself liked to call "the Vietnam syndrome."

Epic Shock and Awe

The golden-anniversary celebrations of World War II worked to seal off the past as the lost, inviolable age of great men. In literary terms, they turned the event into the stuff of epic. In his essay "Epic and Novel," first delivered as a lecture in 1941, the Russian literary scholar Mikhail Bakhtin articulated what would become an influential theory about these two literary genres. The epic was the genre of the past, the novel that of the future. "The epic world is an utterly finished thing," argued Bakhtin, "not only as an authentic event of the distant past but also on its own terms and by its own standards; it is impossible to change, to re-think, to reevaluate anything in it . . . One can only accept the epic world with reverence; it is impossible to really touch it, for it is beyond the realm of human activity, the realm in which everything humans touch is altered and re-thought." Epic brooks no argument. The novel, by contrast, is, like the modern world itself, fluid, many voiced, and open-ended. It is a work in progress rather than a finished thing.

The lost world conjured by the epic has particular features, chief among them the assumption that glory and honor ᵃⁿᵉ the highest goods, and the battlefield the best place to ᵐ. War becomes not a means, but an end in and of ᵈᵘring the Spanish-American War, Thorstein ᵈ this as the ethos of the "primitive barbarian," which survived in contemporary culture as a preference for "heraldic devices" that employed "the more rapacious beasts and birds of prey." These were the vestiges of a world in which honor equated to "superior force . . . Under this common-sense barbarian appreciation of worth or honour," Veblen argued, "the taking of life . . . is honourable in the highest degree. And this high office of slaughter, as an expression of the slayer's prepotence, casts a glamour of worth over every act of slaughter and over all the tools and accessories of the act. Arms are honourable, and the use of them . . . becomes a honorific employment."

Forty years later, in World War II, this was not necessarily a widespread attitude toward the American exercise of force. Ernie Pyle ends *Brave Men*, his chronicle of the Allied advance through Italy and France in 1943–44, with a decidedly disquieting acknowledgment: "The strength we have spread around the world is appalling even to those who make up the individual cells of that strength. I am sure that in the past two years I have heard soldiers say a thousand times, 'If only we could have created all this energy for something good.' But we rise above our normal powers only in times of destruction." The primary lesson for the reporter in the thick of the fight is not America's aptitude for peace, but its capacity for destruction. Pyle repeatedly asserts that there is little romance in war, even if there is undeniable physiological exhilaration. In *Here Is Your War: Story of G.I. Joe*, the 1943 book of reportage about operations in North Africa that made him famous for telling the ordinary soldier's story with respect and affection, he explains that there is an air of "intoxication about battle, and ordinary men can sometimes soar clear out of themselves on the wine of danger-emotion. And yet it is false." The inherent falseness of danger's seductive thrill resounds through Pyle's wartime dispatches.

In his war journalism Pyle remains largely uninterested in what he calls in *Here Is Your War* the "big picture," and he elects to focus instead on the "worm's-eye view." Although Pyle is frequently remembered as the correspondent who turned the ordinary "Joe" into a hero, he repeatedly resists depicting GIs—whom he clearly loves—as champions of anything other than their own survival. Their political investment is limited to a desire to have things repaired in such a way as to prevent another war. Pyle acknowledges that by hunting around, he could unearth "plenty" of politically engaged or "internationally minded men" of various ranks in the army, yet he insists that most of the soldiers he encounters in Africa evince little interest "in foreign affairs . . . outside of battle affairs."

By September 1944, when it seemed that the war in Europe had been won, Pyle was cautioning against a reading of victory as the fulfillment of some exceptional predestination: "We have won this war because our men are brave, and because of many other things . . . Russia, and England, and the passage of time, and the gift of nature's materials," he writes in *Brave Men*. "We did not win it because destiny created us better than all other peoples." Pyle's worm's-eye view taught him that war "coarsens" soldiers rather than ennobling them. This is especially the case for frontline combat troops, who differ from the rest in their proximity to death. With the war in Europe won but the struggle for the Pacific still in progress, Pyle predicts a period characterized by "the new spiritual freedom of half peace and the old grinding blur of half war. It will be a confusing period for us." Owing in no small measure to the overwhelming force of which the United States has been capable ever since, as well as to the military-industrial complex's obsession with violent technologies throughout the Cold War and beyond, this confusion persists. The golden-anniversary propagandists, comfortable stipulating the nobility of the cause, spent the bulk of their energies glorifying not simply the act of liberation but also the American power that secured it. At the end of the Cold War, another war helped to cement the myth. The Persian Gulf War worked to restore the confidence so badly shaken by Vietnam.

Operation Desert Storm was my first television war. I watched this overwhelming demonstration of American military might in college, where I also happened to be reading *Richard II*, Shakespeare's play about the violent deposition of an inept king whose murder unleashes a prolonged civil war. The play depicts a battle between the language of power and the violent thing itself. Violence wins. A king armed only with the poetic symbols of authority is murdered while a usurper, backed by a flesh-and-blood army of thousands, is crowned. King Richard, who is fond of swearing by his scepter, is defeated by his cousin Bolingbroke, who knows how to swing a sword. The Gulf War presented, among other things, the spectacle of raw force: stunning, swift, (technologically) "smart"—all of it telecast live. The efficiency of this hundred-hour ground war ("the largest logistical move in history," according to the general who directed the effort) seemed to catch out even its protesters, who initially rallied under the slogan "No Blood for Oil," but dispersed rather quickly. Once the war was over, a sense of military invincibility eclipsed a reckoning with the inevitable, enduring costs of unleashing force: continued war in the air over a no-fly zone, ongoing internal violence in Iraq, crippling sanctions, and the lingering illnesses of many U.S. veterans. These details were obscured by the afterglow of American might and largely ignored in narratives of the war as a discrete, efficient success.

The American military power demonstrated by the Gulf War, a prelude to the shock and awe that would rain down on Iraq in 2003, also helped obscure in national memory the politically unavailing devastation of the Vietnam War. In 1975, the ignominious fall of Saigon left Americans with a graphic symbol of what happens when violence becomes unhinged from strategic outcomes. The event offered the United States a potent symbol of futility, a disillusioning end to what, until 2010, was the longest war in U.S. history. Perhaps it also made Americans nostalgic for a world in which sacrifice led to victory and in which victory looked sufficiently different from defeat. Although the process of rehabilitating our adventure in Vietnam began during the Reagan administration, the Gulf War, less than two decades after our failure in Southeast Asia, restored an apparent and a longed-for clarity. With a World War II combat veteran at the helm—ubiquitous allusions to President George H. W. Bush's military service as a navy pilot in World War II seemed meant to offer additional legitimacy and reassurance—the war had the imprimatur of being run by restrained professionals, even as it exploded on viewers' screens and launched the era of frenzied twenty-four-hour news coverage.

During our twenty-first-century wars, I have repeatedly returned to *Richard II*, often in the company of my students, cadets at West Point, where the preparation of future army officers carries on while the embers of recent wars slowly smolder out. That work continues regardless of national political drama—drama that for several years was characterized by a Trump administration at once isolationist and dictatorial in inclination. (How else could we read the simultaneous desires for military parades at home and a complete withdrawal of troops abroad?) Cadets not infrequently describe themselves as members of "the post-9/11 generation," a label that signals their solidarity in uniform even as it distinguishes them from their civilian peers and even as the nature of their future occupation grows increasingly uncertain, albeit no less vital, absent almost-inevitable deployments to Iraq or Afghanistan.

One day in class, a first-year cadet paused at a moment in *Richard II* when a conspirator who fears he has gone too far in open criticism of Richard—"most degenerate king!"— suddenly begins to speak in code, couching further observations about the kingdom's criminal mismanagement—and the prospect of armed insurrection—in the extended metaphor of a ship sailing into a "fearful tempest." A second conspirator, picking up the hint, likewise laments the impending shipwreck, until a third assures his cryptic friends that they can speak freely about the army massing across the English Channel under Bolingbroke's command. "What's he talking about?" my curious student asked on encountering the bit about the storm-tossed ship. It wasn't a passage I had planned to spend much time analyzing, but it turned out to be the perfect illustration of a point absolutely essential to the enterprise of understanding Shakespeare and, more generally, the significance of the ways we choose to talk about violence in real life. Shakespeare's images and metaphors, difficult and oblique though they might seem to a twenty-first-century audience, are inseparable from his meaning.

The language most often used today to talk about war is suffused with a sentimentality that seems to belong more properly to some lost romantic age. It certainly isn't Shakespearean metaphor, but it is a code of distortion, misdirection, and concealment. Even after the revolutions in modern consciousness supposedly occasioned by conflict in the twentieth century, a pernicious American sentimentality about nation and war has triumphed, typified by demonstrative expressions of, and appeals to, an emotion that short-circuits reason. In this respect, the conspirators' exchange in *Richard II* has broader resonance: whenever people describe violence with abstraction or indirection, in Shakespeare's time or our own, there's bound to be a reason. The conspirators' motives are particular, but their language offers a fine example of the stratagems people employ when they are trying to talk around ugly and dangerous things.

Now embarked on the third decade of the century, having seen the resurrection of the ugly rhetoric of the 1930s, we evaluate the exit from the costly, inconclusive wars in which the United States has been embroiled for so many years. Iraq and Afghanistan came to seem interminable and inconvenient, embarrassing to all save perhaps their most fervent original designers. Debates about force and the language through which it is described—issues of violent means and elusive ends—are as pressing now as they have ever been. Yet we seem unable to talk about these issues frankly or to recognize, as my perceptive student did, when and why people resort to linguistic subterfuge. This, too, is a legacy of World War II, specifically of a misapprehension about the meaning of American violence in the world. It leads us repeatedly to imagine that the use of force can accomplish miraculous political ends even when we have the examples of Vietnam, Iraq, and Afghanistan to tell us otherwise.

A language of the heart helps to insulate us from the decisions we have made and paradoxically distances us from those whose military service we seek to recognize. We see it in the empty profusion of yellow ribbons and lapel-pin flags. We hear it in the organized celebrations of American heroes and patriotic values: celebrity public-service announcements, beer commercials about military homecomings, the more jingoistic variants of country music, and the National Football League's "Salute to Service" campaign. All these observances noisily claim to honor and celebrate, in the words of the NFL, "the service and sacrifice of our nation's troops." We have become exhibitionists of sentiment: the more public and histrionic our displays, the better we seem to feel.

Yet sentimentality does more than shape the way we commemorate wars. It informs all those cultural and sociological attitudes in the shadow of which wartime and postwar policies are crafted, and it prevents a more productive and enduring sympathy that, in cooperation with reason, might guide our actions and help us become more careful readers of war's many ambiguities and false seductions. Our predicament calls to mind the eighteenth-century debate over the danger of confusing the exercise of pity with sympathetic action. The philosopher Jean-Jacques Rousseau, for example, differentiated true compassion from the emotion we might feel at the theater: "a sterile pity which feeds on a few tears" and never produces "the slightest act of humanity." The British writer and philanthropist Hannah More warned against "mistaking sentiment," which she defined as "the virtue of ideas," for principle, which she called "the virtue of action." The Scottish novelist Henry Mackenzie, meanwhile, observed that "refined sentimentalists . . . are contented with talking of virtues which they never practice" and "pay in words what they owe in actions."

American sentimentality about war suffuses political rhetoric, irrespective of party; Republicans and Democrats are equally adept at its tunings. World War II's transcendence is signaled by the fact that it is equally useful to presidents as different as Donald Trump and Barack Obama. The latter's 2014 State of the Union address contains a representative example. The address concluded with an appeal to American ideals "and the burdens we bear to advance them." "No one," the president insisted, "knows this better than those who serve in uniform." And then Obama called attention to Sergeant First Class Cory Remsburg, a U.S.

Army Ranger grievously wounded in Kandahar, Afghanistan, who was seated in the gallery next to the First Lady. The speech included the crucial detail that the president first met Remsburg on Omaha Beach during the sixty-fifth-anniversary celebration of D-Day. This allusion set the stage for the speech's emotional peroration, in which Remsburg became a symbol of something almost entirely disconnected from his own costly service and in which one war seemed to melt into another:

> My fellow Americans, men and women like Cory remind us that America has never come easy. Our freedom, our democracy, has never been easy. Sometimes we stumble; we make mistakes; we get frustrated or discouraged. But for more than 200 years, we have put those things aside and placed our collective shoulder to the wheel of progress—to create and build and expand the possibilities of individual achievement; to free other nations from tyranny and fear; to promote justice, and fairness, and equality under the law, so that the words set to paper by our founders are made real for every citizen.

Everyone rose in unison. Some members of Congress wept as Obama extolled the sergeant's sacrifice. In this, antagonistic leaders could evince a solidarity they had not shown since they united in sending Remsburg to war in the first place. Submerged in the celebration of a "new generation of heroes" were all those nagging questions about the use of force that ought to have provoked debate in the first place. Lawmakers seemed to be seeking absolution for their earlier uncritical enthusiasm by joining together in a tearful expression of feeling. That's the slipperiness of sentimentality, which is the natural ally of jingoism. So long as we indulge it, we remain incapable of debating the merits of war without being charged with diminishing those who fought it. Celebration of the humanity of the individual—calling attention to what is true about Remsburg's suffering, endurance, and commitment—is a vital national act. But once soldiers become symbols, abstractions available for political ends, we deny them the very humanity we claim to celebrate.

Just a few weeks prior to Obama's address, the fall of Fallujah had prompted comparisons to Vietnam. The battle for the Iraqi city in 2004 held great significance for the U.S. Marines who won it, and the raising of a black insurgent flag—like the hoisting of a pirate's skull and crossbones on a ship, or of enemy colors above a desert fort in a 1930s Hollywood movie—seemed another emblem of futility. Some of the marines who watched it unfurl began to wonder whether the lives of their comrades, as one veteran put it in *The New York Times*, "were sacrificed for nothing." "It was irresponsible," another said, "to send us over there with no plan, and now to just give it all away."

This is not what Americans expect to find at the end of their war stories. Indeed, if sentimentality tends to elicit the emotions without binding the will, an equally dangerous consequence of an overreliance on the heart is the compulsion to transform even the most ambiguous tragedies into inspirational "good-news" stories. Without a strong head to resist the temptations of sentimentality, a writer might find herself facing the predicament of Ivy Spang, the hapless protagonist of Edith Wharton's 1919 "Writing a War Story." When war breaks out, Spang forgets her ambitions to be a poet and goes to Paris to work in an Anglo-American hospital. There she is asked "to contribute a rattling war story" to a morale-boosting monthly being prepared for circulation among the wounded. "A good rousing story, Miss Spang," exhorts her editor. "A dash of sentiment, of course, but nothing to depress or discourage . . . A tragedy with a happy ending—that's about the idea." The editor is here paraphrasing William Dean Howells's explanation for the failure of the Broadway adaptation (by Clyde Fitch) of Wharton's novel *The House of Mirth*, which the *New York Times* drama critic proclaimed "doleful" and almost entirely lacking in "comedy lines." After several false starts, Spang serendipitously discovers a true war story, originally transcribed from a soldier's unvarnished account by her former governess, who had also worked for a time in a military hospital. The published story's first impartial reader, a soldier and novelist who happens to be among the war-wounded patients at the Paris hospital where Spang works, admonishes its author: "You've got hold of an awfully good subject . . . but you've rather mauled it, haven't you?" In adding "a dash of sentiment," Spang has ruined the material. She acquiesced to an editor's demand to shape the story of war into a sentimental absurdity by giving it a happy ending.

There was a time when we manifested at least some self-awareness about our irresistible desire for happy endings. MGM's *Cry 'Havoc'* (1943), based on a play of the same name, with a screenplay by Paul Osborn and Jane Murfin, tells the story of two army nurses stationed in the Philippines in 1942, on the eve of Japan's victory in the Battle of Bataan and subsequent takeover of the country. The nurses, Captain Alice Marsh (Fay Bainter) and Lieutenant Mary Smith (Margaret Sullavan), train a group of volunteer civilians, women from a variety of backgrounds and without experience or training, to do first aid and other hospital work. As General MacArthur departs for Australia, leaving General Jonathan Wainwright in command, and the prospect of being captured becomes a certainty, Marsh orders Smith to offer the civilians a last chance to be evacuated. The volunteers refuse, as Smith subsequently reports:

CAPTAIN ALICE MARSH: Well?
LIEUTENANT MARY SMITH: They're staying.
MARSH: All of them?
SMITH: Uh-huh.
MARSH: What did they say?
SMITH: I don't know, but they're staying.
MARSH: You told them, didn't you?
SMITH: Yeah, I told them. They didn't hear it. Or maybe they just didn't believe it. They're Americans, Cap, they believe in the happy ending.
MARSH: I'm an American, Smitty, I don't.
SMITH: Yeah, but it's different for us. We're part of the Army. This is our business.

The film ends with the off-screen voice of a Japanese soldier ordering all the women to surrender. There is little doubt about their fate, and at the time of the film's release, in February 1944, the happy ending had not yet been secured. Those prisoners of war who survived would not be liberated for more than year. Wainwright himself was freed by the Russians in August 1945.

Yet the kind of war story we crave today is the one that Ivy Spang would write. We search for a redemptive ending to every tragedy. After two decades of engagement, grasping wherever and however we can at a cleansing goodness that might close the book on two wars that launched so many more questions than they answered, we find no solace in the inconclusive, and we remain uneasy when asked to contemplate our own capacity for a violence that has not served a noble end. Witness the media coverage surrounding the 2013 opening of the film *Lone Survivor*, based on the book by former Navy SEAL Marcus Luttrell. In a January interview, CNN's Jake Tapper suggested that there was an air of "hopelessness" about the film—that the deaths of Luttrell's comrades in Afghanistan during an operation gone wrong "seemed senseless." Luttrell responded angrily, wondering what film Tapper had seen: "We spend our whole lives training to defend this country, and then we were sent over there by this country, so you're telling me that because we were over there doing what we were told by our country that it was senseless and my guys, what, they died for nothing?" The internet exploded with vitriol against Tapper for his failure to appreciate a true American hero. Only a few columnists subsequently weighed in about the need for a debate over whether Americans have in fact died for some enduring change in Iraq and Afghanistan.

Calling a death heroic gives shape to a life, salvaging it from the oblivion of destruction and shifting focus away from the merits of a cause. Calling a death on a mission gone wrong "senseless," as Tapper proposed, condemns that life to the relentless circularity of betrayal and doubt. Suggesting that a death in battle was in vain—"Lives were wasted" in Fallujah, a former marine told the *Times*, "and now everyone back home sees that"—also starkly exposes Wilfred Owen's "old Lie" about the unadulterated sweetness of dying for one's country. The imposition of happy endings on war's tragedies may momentarily assuage the heart. Who could fail to understand the intensity of Luttrell's desire to seek a balm for grief, guilt, and the constellation of emotions besieging the lone survivor of a battle? Yet the perpetuation of the "old Lie" also insults the head.

In a climate in which the pressures to sentimentalize are so strong and victory and defeat are so difficult to measure, it seems a moral imperative to discover another way to read and write about a war. Futility might be found at tactical, operational, or strategic levels. During wars, especially long ones, replete with confusion and fluidity, with losses and fleeting but costly gains, archetypal moments such as the raising of a flag—over Iwo Jima or Fallujah—offer discrete tableaux amid an otherwise indecipherable jumble. It isn't easy to determine whether a war is futile. Perhaps it never has been. Are all lost wars a waste? Are all victories worth their price? How many are Pyrrhic? Wait long enough, of course, and many of history's victories will be reversed.

It is much easier to tell a sentimental war story with a happy ending, in which valor eclipses causes and reconciliation triumphs over everything—a comedy, in other words—than it is to tell another, unsentimental kind of story. It is much harder to speak of war in a pellucid, forthright mode. Even our own wised-up age retains a misguided faith in the cleansing, redemptive power of violence. It is the faith expressed in President George W. Bush's remarks on the deck of the USS *Abraham Lincoln* in 2003, when he described the Iraq War as embodying "the highest calling of history" and the assembled sailors as bearing the message of the prophet Isaiah "wherever" they went: "To the captives, 'come out'— and to those in darkness, 'be free.'"

"I'm confused," one of the plebes in my class confessed when we reached the third act of Shakespeare's *Richard II* and he discovered his sympathies shifting from the apparently victimized Bolingbroke to the irresponsible, duplicitous, and initially self-deceiving King Richard. It is Richard who knows before everyone, including Bolingbroke himself, that his cousin cannot stop—the momentum of war will not let him—until he has secured the crown for himself. "Up, cousin, up," King Richard tells Bolingbroke, who has knelt before him: "your heart is up, I know, / Thus high at least [pointing to his crown], although your knee be low." To my student's surprise, it is Richard, the king of dreamy poetry, who now displays by far the keenest, most unsentimental understanding of the actual dynamics of force. As Simone Weil noted, force blinds those, like Bolingbroke, who imagine they can control it. In the collision between symbolic and practical might, the latter wins, and King Richard intuits that all will suffer for it. England's civil wars gave Shakespeare fodder for eight plays. When next he shows us Bolingbroke—now the title character of *1 Henry IV*—the energetic usurper is changed utterly: exhausted, he rules a kingdom full of trenches, a land soaked with the blood of "civil butchery." King Henry is cut by the double "edge of war" that he first unleashed.

When Fallujah fell in January 2014, some heard echoes of Khe Sanh in Vietnam, won at great human cost and then evacuated in 1968. Five years later, in 1973, Frederick Weyand, commanding general of Military Assistance Command, Vietnam, announced the deactivation of MACV: "Our mission has been accomplished. I depart with a strong feeling of pride in what we have achieved and in what our achievement represents." Weyand's rearguard rhetorical action, reported in American newspapers, sounds cynical given what we now know to be the outcome of the Vietnam War—until, that is, you have had the opportunity to listen to enough officers, whose earnestness you do not doubt, who have come home from Iraq or Afghanistan. They are heavy with the deaths of fellow soldiers and at the same time fighting a sense of futility with an insistence about the meaningful progress they saw. How many courageous and honorable friends, either on their way to war or relieved at their good fortune in coming home, have told me with a gallows-humor grin that no one wants to be the last American to die there?

We live in a historical moment during which it is necessary to reflect on our recent wars in the light of wars past. The way we think and talk about force will influence not only the use of American military might abroad but also our response to the violence that has increasingly been used as a tool of insurrection at home. To the degree that we allow the undeniable suffering and sacrifice of war somehow to redeem all causes— that we allow our guilt to obscure the realities of devastating, indecisive wars—we increase the likelihood of finding ourselves in a similar predicament once again. In focusing on a moment of linguistic indirection in *Richard II*, my student found the key to unlocking an entire play. Reading closely in this way isn't a skill we tend to take very seriously—until we find that we cannot live without it.

2
DEAD-SHOT AMERICAN COWBOYS

> "Did you ever hear of Karl May?" asked Marlene Dietrich, suddenly . . .
>
> "He died long ago, a year or so before the other World War of 1914," said Marlene.
>
> "It was just as well," nodded Pasternak. "He didn't live to see his German boys picked off in the war by the dead-shot American cowboys and Indians they had read about in his books."
>
> —"Reite Ihn, Cowboy!" *The New York Times,* December 3, 1939

Box-Office Poison

In the spring of 1938, the Independent Theater Owners Association (ITOA) took out a full-page advertisement in the Hollywood trade publications declaring Marlene Dietrich, along with eleven other movie stars, box-office "poison." Faced with shrinking attendance numbers and forced by the major studios' block-booking system to exhibit—along with surefire crowd-pleasers—many films with little appeal for their patrons, the theater owners helped to redefine, and in some cases to derail, the careers of a group of stars whose personas were thoroughly identified with the 1930s. Tempered or outlawed outright would be the European exoticism of Dietrich and Greta Garbo, the homegrown bawdiness of

Mae West, the cosmopolitan sophistication of Fred Astaire, and the eccentric androgyny of Katharine Hepburn. (Dolores Del Río, Luise Rainer, Norma Shearer, Edward Arnold, John Barrymore, Kay Francis, and Joan Crawford rounded out the list of newly toxic icons.) From gangster gore to art deco chic, the eclectic fantasies served up to movie audiences in the early and mid-1930s—the worst years of the Depression—would be largely replaced by less politically radical and more provincial wholesome fare, especially during the war years.

The prewar period was also marked, as Thomas Doherty has argued in *Hollywood and Hitler*, by a general reluctance among the major studios to address the dangers of fascism and the coming crisis in Europe. Instead, with the conspicuous exception of Warner Bros.—which Groucho Marx reportedly toasted as "the only studio with any guts"—the majors tried not to antagonize Germany, for years their most lucrative overseas market. When the German émigré director Fritz Lang was asked in an interview at the American Film Institute in 1973 why the budget of his 1941 film *Man Hunt* had been so small, he replied, "Darryl [20th Century Fox studio head Darryl F. Zanuck] said, 'Don't show too many swastikas. We don't like that.' For me, it was the first time that I could really show what the swastika meant, you know, and I showed it as often as I could. Zanuck never said anything, but maybe, because of this, he didn't want to spend."

When confronted by what Doherty calls "incendiary" political material, Joseph Breen, the head of the Production Code Administration, would invoke the following clause in the Code: "The history, institutions, prominent people, and citizenry of all nations shall be represented fairly." The first film to deal earnestly and openly with fascism came in 1939, with Warner's *Confessions of a Nazi Spy*, a hard-hitting, documentary-style drama deemed so sensitive that its production was robed in secrecy. Breen approved the script, which was based on an FBI agent's account of the 1938 infiltration of a Nazi spy ring in New York. The federal trial of several of the conspirators had revealed that the dangers of Nazism were both quite real and uncomfortably close to home.

In addition to this groundbreaking film, the year 1939, often cited as Hollywood's *annus mirabilis*, saw the production of a group of memorable films that arrived at a transformative moment in world history: *The Women, Mr. Smith Goes to Washington, Young Mr. Lincoln, Stagecoach, The Adventures of Huckleberry Finn, Wuthering Heights, Love Affair, Dodge City, Gunga Din, Ninotchka, Destry Rides Again, The Hunchback of Notre Dame, Beau Geste, Only Angels Have Wings, Drums Along the Mohawk, The Roaring Twenties, Gone with the Wind, The Wizard of Oz, Union Pacific, Jesse James, Idiot's Delight, Of Mice and Men*, and the indefatigable Bette Davis's four pictures: *Dark Victory, Juarez, The Old Maid*, and *The Private Lives of Elizabeth and Essex*. This is a remarkable set of films, noteworthy for their initial impact as well as for their staying power. A number of them, including *Mr. Smith Goes to Washington, Young Mr. Lincoln*, and *Gone with the Wind*, have (for good and ill) come to occupy a place in our national mythology. Several turn inward to explore grand American themes—the Civil War or the western frontier—at a moment when the commitment to isolationism that followed World War I and dominated much of the 1930s was at long last being challenged by European realities. Films ostensibly unconnected with the present-day situation nevertheless inserted significant messages about liberty (*Juarez, Drums Along the Mohawk*) or slavery (*The Adventures of Huckleberry Finn*). And one of the films of 1939, a tragicomic Western called *Destry Rides Again*, brought Marlene Dietrich back to Hollywood in what amounted to a new configuration of Old and New Worlds. The film might also be read as a fable of America's relationship to global events in the late 1930s.

The first chapter in Dietrich's Hollywood career had begun, on the heels of her international success in the German production *Der blaue Engel* (1930), with the shimmering artifice and pre-Code decadence painstakingly cultivated by the director Josef von Sternberg in a series of films for Paramount. In these films Dietrich played nightclub singers, women of adventure, a spy, and a Russian empress. After her collaboration with Sternberg dissolved, less successful partnerships with other directors helped earn her ITOA's "box-office poison" label. One of them, *Angel* (1937), directed by another German émigré, Ernst Lubitsch, suggests at least one of the reasons for her newfound notoriety. Unimpressed by its plot of marital infidelity and reconciliation, *The Hollywood Reporter* deemed it "an extremely well bred continental comedy of manners." Continental comedies of manners, especially those involving lax sexual mores, were a staple of the 1930s, but they had become suspect. As Dietrich's biographer Steven Bach notes, the world's highest-paid woman had now become "virtually unemployable." Fired by Paramount, her projects at other studios canceled, Dietrich decamped to Europe, briefly returning to the United States only to finalize her American citizenship, thereby cutting ties with her native Germany, whose politics she deplored. The doomed summer of 1939 found her in the South of France, where fellow European expatriate Joe Pasternak offered her the role of "Frenchy," a singer from New Orleans—all foreign accents were interchangeable in Hollywood—performing in a saloon in the lawless western town of Bottleneck in *Destry Rides Again*. Although she initially thought the proposition ridiculous, Dietrich needed the money, as Bach has documented, and knew that Europe was on the precipice, so she accepted and sailed for New York in August.

Typical of so many of the films of Hollywood's Golden Age, *Destry* was a thoroughly international confection, its cast and crew an amalgamation of American-born personalities and immigrants from a variety of countries. The Russian-born Mischa Auer plays a Russian who wants nothing more in life than to be a cowboy; the film's producer, Joe Pasternak, had emigrated from Hungary; the music was by one of the leading composers of the Weimar cabaret scene, Friedrich Hollaender, who had escaped Nazi Germany in the early 1930s. Frank S. Nugent of *The New York Times* alluded to the film's international dynamic in his review: "With a sweep of his Hungarian fist," Pasternak "has taken Marlene Dietrich off her high horse and placed her in a horse opera and has converted James Stewart, last seen as Washington's timid Mr. Smith, into the hard-hitting son of an old sagebrush sheriff." Hollywood alchemy worked in such a way that a Hungarian could transform the most highfalutin European into a woman equipped for the frontier, and turn an American boy into a real man. The New World had triumphed over the Old, the virile over the effete, the masculine over the feminine. Such priorities had long been essential to the genre, but *Destry* is not an entirely conventional Western. Stewart's portentously named Thomas Jefferson Destry Jr., the newly appointed sheriff's deputy of Bottleneck, is an initially reluctant gunfighter. He must be provoked into violence; the resonances with the United States in 1939 are clear. Young Tom, who saw his father, a celebrated lawman, shot in the back, refuses to carry a gun, much to the consternation of the townsfolk and to the amusement of Bottleneck's actual boss, a crooked gambler named Kent (Brian Donlevy). It is only when Kent's henchmen murder the good-natured old sheriff (Charles Winninger), who hired Destry to clean up the town, that the outraged deputy straps on his gun belt and fulfills the expectations of the genre by gunning down his man. After this explosion of violence, in which Frenchy is shot saving Tom's life and then dies with a kiss in his arms, the final scene returns us to an unarmed Destry presiding over a now-tranquil town.

There is an elemental playfulness to *Destry*: Mischa Auer's character is continually losing his pants, Winninger is an amiable drunkard, Dietrich sings several memorable numbers and gets in a raucous saloon fight in all her feathered finery, and Stewart's Destry is constantly telling folksy stories that make him sound Lincolnesque. In addition to not taking itself too seriously, the film also refuses to turn the final showdown between Destry and Kent into the archetypal duel on a dusty street. Instead, the shoot-out takes place inside the saloon, which is crowded with a mob of brawling men and women; the latter have organized in order to stop the violence, but they end up taking part in a nonlethal variety by knocking men unconscious with bottles and stowing them behind the bar.

In *The Invention of the Western Film*, a history of the genre's first fifty years, Scott Simmon proposes that prewar Westerns attempt "to test whether the idea of law and order is possible without violence." Simmon argues that similar tests and debates over "political questions of disarmament and isolationism," which were often found before the war, had largely disappeared from Westerns by the 1950s, when "sheriff-cleans-up-town" stories seemed to encode "cold-war arguments interpreted by everyone from President Eisenhower on down." *Destry* has a deeply ambivalent attitude toward violence as an inherently tragic remedy to the very real problems of lawlessness. It also has a far more sanguine perspective on the relationship between the lawman and the community he protects. The townsfolk are with Destry, not, as they will be in *High Noon* (1952) and many other postwar Westerns, indifferent or fearful, willing to leave their fate to a coterie of weary professionals.

On December 3, 1939, *The New York Times* published

a story called "Reite Ihn, Cowboy!" about a reporter's visit to the set of *Destry* during which Dietrich and Pasternak reminisce about growing up on the Westerns of Karl May. The Americans, Stewart and Winninger, have never heard of May. Stewart assumes they are talking about a baseball player, while Winninger simply asks what the joke is. May is still largely unknown in America, but as Rivka Galchen suggests in "Wild West Germany," a 2012 article in *The New Yorker*, his "stories of the American West are to this day better known to Germans than the works of Thomas Mann . . . Though May never visited the American West, he told everyone that he had, and he wore a necklace of bear teeth, as if in proof." Most of his stories involve an Apache named Winnetou and his "blood brother," a German immigrant called Old Shatterhand, often thought of as May's alter ego. To this day there is an annual Karl May Festival in the German town of Bad Segeberg, northeast of Hamburg.

The European fascination with the American West was not limited to Germany. It also animates the French director Jean Renoir's 1936 film *The Crime of Monsieur Lange*, in which the title character, a lowly employee of a French pulp publishing house, becomes a sensation among the young boys of France with his tales of "Arizona Jim." Lange is a dreamer: he gazes longingly at a map of the United States affixed to the wall above his bed and stays up all night concocting adventures that delight his French readers, who find Arizona as exotic as Americans have tended to find Paris. Made during the time of Léon Blum's Popular Front government, the film also expresses a working-class solidarity that can be found in some depictions of Western townsfolk.

On the set of *Destry*, Dietrich fishes from her knitting bag a copy of May's *The Revenge of the Farmer*, which she had purchased for her daughter, Maria, on her last visit to Salzburg. Pasternak, who grew up in Austria-Hungary, begins to translate a passage from the pulp novelist, to whom he and generations of German-speaking children had been devoted, and declares: "I was worse than the kids now with 'Hi-yo, Silver.'" When the film's director, George Marshall, asks how May likes it in Germany now, Pasternak reveals that he died before World War I. "It was just as well," the producer adds. "He didn't live to see his German boys picked off in the war by the dead-shot American cowboys and Indians they had read about in his books." As the cowboys of German pulp melt into the doughboys of the American Expeditionary Force, the reporter veers away from melancholy back to the weirdness of the cinematic West, which is compared favorably with the ersatz West imagined by May, who had never been to the United States and whose idea of the frontier was inadequate. The admiring Old World, in the form of Pasternak, Dietrich, and Auer, must go as far West as it can—to Hollywood—to become thoroughly schooled in the ways of the New.

This vignette, published a few days into the film's run at New York's Rivoli, is suggestive of the global instability—and permeability—of 1939. The United States' eventual entry into the war in 1941 confirmed a realignment of Old and New Worlds by unsettling the myth of geographic exceptionalism that had held sway, in one form or another, in the United States essentially since its founding, but that had further crystallized in the historian Frederick Jackson Turner's Frontier Thesis, which held that American democracy was a unique phenomenon linked to westward movement across the continent. Greg Grandin, who demonstrates the suppleness of the frontier myth throughout American history in *The End of the Myth: From the Frontier to the Border Wall in the Mind of America*, argues that the more progressive members of the Franklin D. Roosevelt administration recast Turner's Frontier Thesis during this period: "New Dealers . . . read the frontier less as mythology and more as pathology, a social disorder manifested in an insistence on national uniqueness. Such a reading made space for a new kind of tolerance and openness." But the "one world" idea championed by Roosevelt, Wendell Willkie, and other globally minded politicians gave way soon after the war's end. And, as American "confidence" returned after the doldrums of the Depression, Grandin notes, the frontier resumed its psychic power as the quintessential expression of an exceptionalist myth.

As one of the most spectacular representations of the frontier, the Western film offers an ideal testing ground for mythological reworkings, which continued throughout the Cold War. As Jane Tompkins proposes in her book *West of Everything*, the imaginary West was empty and blank:

> The desert offers itself as the white sheet on which to trace a figure. It is a tabula rasa on which man can write, as if for the first time, the story he wants to live. That is why the first moment of Western movies is so full of promise. It is the New World, represented here, not for the first time, as a void, the *vacuum domicilium* the Puritans had imagined, waiting to be peopled. The apparent emptiness makes the land desirable not only as a space to be filled but also as a stage on which to perform and as a territory to master.

As Tompkins notes, the initial sense of promise contained in that emptiness was confounded by the aura of apocalypse. Beginning in the 1940s, it would become the landscape of Los Alamos, Area 51, and atomic bomb tests, of missile silos and Strategic Air Command. The West was also the home of the loner at odds with community.

The distinctively American figure of the rugged individualist—celebrated in literature, film, and culture more generally—militated against the ideals of unity and community that we project back onto the period. As Thomas Doherty notes in *Projections of War: Hollywood, American Culture, and World War II*, "the necessity of personal sacrifice and the value of communitarian purpose were not exactly main currents in American thought." Doherty continues: "The native self-made man made an unlikely candidate for selfless devotion. The cheeky newspaperman, the lonesome cowboy, the private detective, the single-minded inventor, even the will to power of the urban gangster strike chords unsounded by the rewards of group solidarity and communal work." But if the empty land nurtured solitary heroes, it was also the perfect setting for the reinvention—and Americanization—of Europeans.

Dietrich's career was resurrected by *Destry*, but the war also put it on hold. Now an American—officially as well as cinematically—she committed herself to the war effort. At first this meant working long nights in the kitchen of the Hollywood Canteen and volunteering to be sawn in half by Orson Welles in the magic show he staged in a tent for the benefit of GIs. Eventually, however, it meant donning a (bespoke) GI uniform and deploying to North Africa and Europe, where she tirelessly entertained troops. Many Hollywood personalities did similar work, but only Bob Hope came to be so completely identified as Dietrich with World War II. At the end of 1943, as Bach records, Dietrich auctioned most of her belongings and left for the front to do, as she would later insist, "the only important thing I've ever done."

One of Dietrich's complaints, often echoed by journalists like A. J. Liebling and Ernie Pyle when they returned from abroad, was that in America "one was hardly aware of the war." After returning from North Africa and Italy, Dietrich gave an interview to Leo Lerman for the August 15, 1944, issue of *Vogue*. War, like the Western before it, seems somehow to have liberated Dietrich from Hollywood's obscuring fantasy: "Dietrich is funny," Lerman revealed, "with that baggy pants comedian funniness, that belly-laugh vigour which her friends adore, but which Hollywood hid behind six-inch eyelashes and a million-dollar languor." Throughout the interview Dietrich expresses her frustration with home-front attitudes. She is outraged, for example, that blood donations require "propaganda . . . that you've had to beg for it . . . that's amazing." Having seen the demand for various resources at the front, she expresses similar frustrations at complaints regarding gas rationing and other domestic restrictions. Dietrich's experience also gave her an appreciation for a cooperative spirit and for an "extraordinary confidence in everybody who's around" that seemed unique to military life. Her sympathies are entirely with the GI. She even tells the story of being introduced to something called the "4-F Brushoff Club": soldiers pinned up pictures—inscribed with phrases like "Forever yours" or "I'll be waiting for you always"—of "girls who promised to wait and forgot about their promises." Unlike these women, Dietrich signed up for the duration: "I won't sign any contracts here that would tie me down. I will not sit here working my little job and let the war pass me by. Over there, no one says, 'Let the other fellow do it.' They do it themselves."

Right before "Welcome, Marlene" in the same issue of *Vogue*, a feature called "Woman's Work" appears. As late as the summer of 1944, the magazine was exhorting its female readers to do something for the war effort: "There are in this country," it begins, "nearly five million women, between twenty and forty-nine, with no responsibilities, and not doing a lick of real war work." The article goes on to enumerate several of the objections offered up by these women, including: "BUT ISN'T THE WAR NEARLY OVER?" "COLLEGE TRAINED, I AM AN INDIVIDUALIST, AND I HATE REGIMENTATION." "MY PAR-

ENTS WON'T LET ME." In cataloguing and responding to these objections, the magazine portrays a readership apparently characterized by selfishness over an inclination for sacrifice, individualism over community spirit, personal ambition over patriotism. The answers themselves tellingly appeal as much to self-interest as to public-spiritedness. To readers who fear losing their appeal to men, *Vogue* helpfully replies:

> Listen, baby, a girl who attracts men attracts men.
> Want some more answers to this vital question? There is hardly a marriageable man left in the U.S.A. outside of an Army camp. So, joining the Army, you go to the source of desirable material. He—the guy you're waiting for . . . [will come back] older, wiser, battle-worn, and look beyond the mascara deep into your eyes, and find a vacuum. His mind will wander to the girl in uniform who worked beside him, who KNOWS what he's been through. There's a bond between them you can't overcome.

Here the author explores sexual and social anxieties; elsewhere he or she predicts the harsh economic realities of the postwar world. To the concern expressed by some respondents about employment in a world full of returning servicemen, *Vogue* tells its female readers to face the fact that they will have no chance for "a foothold" in the job market against "twelve million men returning from the dust and agony of battle . . . no matter what little foothold you have, they are going to see that they get theirs first." The significant reduction of women in the postwar workforce bore out this warning.

The period also marked a change for Dietrich's work. Although she continued to make films, she would reinvent herself yet again as a cabaret performer. She toured the world tirelessly in sequined gowns and tuxedos as she once had toured it in her army uniform. Her contributions to the war effort were recognized the world over: she received both the Presidential Medal of Freedom in the United States and the French Ordre National de la Légion d'honneur for her work in the European Theater. At least one fan dated her contributions all the way back to *Destry Rides Again*. Reporting from England in January 1941, Ernie Pyle devoted a column to Lord Beaverbrook, the Canadian newspaper magnate turned efficient British minister of aircraft production. Pyle attributes Beaverbrook's effectiveness and his ability to speed up production to a certain "American sense for ignoring tradition," and he numbers him among the "little knot of half a dozen or perhaps a dozen men" who "will emerge at the end of this war as the great leaders who pulled England through." Nicknamed "the Beaver," and sharing that animal's reputation for industriousness, Lord Beaverbrook apparently found his only relaxation in the movies. "He's crazy," Pyle reports, "about Marlene Dietrich. As one of his fellow workers said, Lord Beaverbrook probably thinks the greatest contribution America could make to Great Britain would be to send over more Dietrich films. They say he has seen 'Destry Rides Again' nine times." The films would have to do for England until the United States could send Dietrich herself, together with the Eighth Air Force.

Premature Anti-Fascists

When Marlene Dietrich returned to the United States in the summer of 1939 to begin filming *Destry*, it was only natural that she should sail aboard the SS *Normandie*, a magnificent but star-crossed French liner built for speed that could

make the transatlantic crossing from Le Havre to New York
(by way of Southampton) in just under four days. Movie
stars, potentates, and titans of industry all sailed on this, the
world's largest and fastest ship. On its maiden voyage in the
spring of 1935, the three-deck liner was greeted at Pier 88
on Manhattan's West Side by one hundred thousand people
who, F. Raymond Daniell reported in *The New York Times*,
had "gathered to marvel at the great ship's size and grace of
line." The *Normandie* happened to be docked in New York at
the outbreak of war in 1939. It was detained and, after Pearl
Harbor, seized by the United States government as the property of Vichy France, an enemy nation. The navy began to
refit it as a troop carrier renamed the USS *Lafayette*. These
plans were interrupted when a fire broke out on board during
retrofitting operations in February 1942, and the ship cap-
sized at the pier as a result of the volume of water pumped
into the hull. The salvage operation cost millions, and when
the badly damaged ship was finally righted months later, it
was judged too expensive to repair and ultimately scrapped in
1946, a relic of the prewar world.

Before this inglorious end, however, the *Normandie* set
new standards for luxury as well as speed. Its first-class accommodations were sumptuous. There is a photo of Dietrich on her November 1939 voyage in one of four Grand
Luxe suites, the Rouen, in front of its piano. Pieces of the
ship survive in private collections, occasionally showing up
at auctions. New York's Metropolitan Museum of Art and
Pittsburgh's Carnegie Museum own several of the murals
that adorned the dining rooms and other public spaces. The
whistle now resides at the Pratt Institute but used to blow
the shift changes at Bethlehem Steel; the wheel is on display
at the South Street Seaport Museum; and the magnificent
doors of the grand dining room now adorn Our Lady of Leb-
anon Cathedral in Brooklyn, New York.

The *Normandie* catered to the elite, but it also carried tourists and other unknown (if no less extraordinary) travelers in second- and third-class accommodations. One of them was Esther Silverstein, a nurse who left her job at the Marine Hospital in San Francisco to aid the Republican side in the Spanish Civil War. Silverstein sailed on the *Normandie* in May 1937, served with the 35th International Division Sanitary Corps for more than a year, and subsequently joined the Army Nurse Corps during World War II. She joined almost three thousand American volunteers in the Spanish Republic's fight against Franco, whose military coup was from the outset supported by men and matériel from Italy and Germany. As the historian Peter N. Carroll has documented, the first contingent of eighty-six volunteers sailed on the *Normandie* in 1936. The indifference with which Europe's democracies met the upheaval in Spain, and Italy's takeover of Ethiopia before it, was not lost on the Europeans and Americans who joined the International Brigades to fight fascist aggression. Two journalists who covered the war, Virginia Cowles and Vincent Sheean, spoke for many observers when they traced the origins of World War II directly to the Spanish Civil War. Watching the Battle of Britain in the summer of 1940 from a cliff in Dover, the two reporters had the following exchange, which Cowles later recorded in *Looking for Trouble*:

> Vincent turned to me and said, "It's funny to think all this business started down there." He nodded toward the mists.
> "Down there?"
> "In Spain."
> Undoubtedly future historians will puzzle over the lessons that were never learned from the first world war; they will shake their heads that the three great

democracies refused to join hands and accept their responsibilities as the guardians of world peace. They will trace the causes of the present conflagration to the breakdown of the League of Nations, pointing to Manchuria in 1931 and Abyssinia in 1935. But they will have to turn to Spain in 1936 for the first rumble of gunfire to break the stillness of the European continent . . .

I saw the villages of Spain burning and followed the flames across the map of Europe.

Franklin Roosevelt's October 5, 1937, speech at a bridge dedication in Chicago, known as the "quarantine" speech, gave hope to the interventionists with its characterization of the world's "political situation" as "a reign of terror and international lawlessness" and its warning that the United States could not "have complete protection in a world of disorder." But the United States continued to adhere to the series of Neutrality Acts passed earlier in the decade while the great democratic powers of Europe refused to respond to the overt fascist interventions in Ethiopia and Spain. Italy, and to an even greater extent Germany, used the latter conflict as a dress rehearsal for battles to come, especially for the Luftwaffe. The only power to intervene on the Republican side was the Soviet Union, which joined with avowed communists, socialists, anarchists, republicans, and others in their fight on behalf of the Republic.

Hollywood offered somewhat belated representations of those who were early to the fight against fascism. In *Casablanca*, which had its New York City premiere on November 26, 1942, we learn that Humphrey Bogart's Rick Blaine, who claims to stick his neck out for no one, "ran guns to Ethiopia" in 1935 and "fought in Spain on the Loyalist side" in 1936. As M. Todd Bennett notes in *One World, Big Screen: Holly-*

wood, the Allies, and World War II, the script was supervised by the Office of War Information, which saw its utility as propaganda to galvanize audiences still uncertain about U.S. involvement in the war. In *The Fallen Sparrow* (1943), based on the eponymous Dorothy B. Hughes novel published in 1942, John Garfield's John McKittrick fights in the Spanish Civil War, survives imprisonment by the Nazis, and returns to New York to solve a murder committed by German agents. This cinematic return to Spain also signified that the USSR, the old enemy (albeit briefly the friend) of our new enemy, had become our new friend.

It is estimated that about seventy percent of the Americans who fought in Spain with the Abraham Lincoln Brigade were communists; others were fellow travelers or simply understood the fight as anti-fascist. During the confusing interval between their experience in Spain and the attack on Pearl Harbor—and after the 1939 German-Soviet Nonaggression Pact—some communists broke with the Party. Others, disgusted by the abandonment of Spain by the democratic powers, found themselves temporarily aligned with American isolationists. As the classicist Bernard Knox, who fought with a British contingent in Spain and with the U.S. Army in World War II, noted, "The American volunteers of the Abraham Lincoln Brigade were known to the FBI as 'premature anti-Fascists'; it was an accusation but it is a designation that all those who fought for the Republic can accept with pride. We were ahead of everybody else in something that had to be done." Even in the light of later revelations about the extent of Soviet "interference and manipulation," Knox refused to repudiate the Republican cause: "War is an ugly business at best; as Thucydides said long ago, it is a teacher of violence and reduces most men's tempers to the level of their circumstances." Under the auspices of the U.S. Army's Morale Services Division, the psychologist John Dollard conducted a study of behavior in combat based on interviews with veterans of the Lincoln Brigade. His findings, published as *Fear and Courage under Battle Conditions*, revealed that at least for these volunteers, ideology was a crucial motivator in the face of fear.

Whether or not they had been Communist Party members, the veterans of the Lincoln Brigade were put under government surveillance ostensibly because of their earlier violation of the U.S. Neutrality Acts. When they volunteered to fight fascism once again after Pearl Harbor, they learned that they had been blacklisted as "premature anti-fascists." Despite the fact that they were among the few Americans with recent combat experience—including valuable experience against modern German weaponry such as the Stuka and the 88-mm artillery gun—they were initially prevented from obtaining commissions and often shunted off to camps for troublemakers and politically suspect conscripts. The poet John Ciardi, for example, was denied a commission in the Air Corps after successfully completing navigation training. Ciardi did not even fight in Spain; as a graduate student, impressed with those who had volunteered, he had signed various petitions. After Milton Wolff's commanding officer learned that he had served in Spain as a member of the Lincoln Brigade, Wolff found himself assigned to a unit of misfits and malcontents, the majority of whom were Nazis and fascist sympathizers. Most of the rest were foreign nationals, while a few were, like Wolff, premature anti-fascists who had joined the battle against Mussolini and Hitler too soon. The irony of being lumped in with fascists was not lost on veterans of the Lincoln Brigade, who were generally more politically engaged than many of their fellow soldiers and who had in any case been thinking about the global struggle in one way or another since the mid-1930s. Until the press picked up the cause, many were restricted to support jobs and kept out of combat. The hounding of the veterans of the Lincoln Brigade, even those who went on to serve honorably in World War II, resumed in 1947, when the Red Scare began in earnest.

Several premature anti-fascists ended up in the Office of Strategic Services (OSS), headed by William "Wild Bill" Donovan, who cared less about men's politics than about their willingness to fight. One of these men was Bernard Knox, a naturalized U.S. citizen who had fought in the International Brigades in Spain while still a British subject. Knox would later become a celebrated classicist for whom the relationship between ancient and modern wars was deeply intertwined. As a World War II commando who did dangerous work behind the lines with the French Maquis and later with Italian partisans, Knox, who had taken an undergraduate classics degree at Cambridge, made a promise to himself: "If I ever get out of this, I'm going back to the Classics and study them seriously." Only after he had survived the war and applied for graduate school did Knox learn of his official designation as a premature anti-fascist. In 1946 his Yale interviewer, the chair of the classics department, nonchalantly used the term on discovering that he had served in the Spanish Civil War. Knox was completely nonplussed: "How, I wondered, could anyone be a premature anti-Fascist? Could there be anything such as a premature antidote to a poison? . . . If you were not premature, what sort of anti-Fascist were you supposed to be? A punctual anti-Fascist? A timely one?" If you were not early, Knox added, you were like those Frenchmen who joined the Resistance in 1944, and whom the real French maquisards with whom Knox worked derided as *Résistants de la dernière heure*" [last-minute anti-fascists]. "It is a perfect description," Knox adds, "of Neville Chamberlain and Lord Halifax. But in 1939, last-minute was too late."

As early as 1938, Roosevelt had authorized the Department of Justice to investigate Nazis, fascists, and communists. Long before the end of the war, communists became the government's chief preoccupation, a phenomenon that manifested itself in all sorts of unexpected ways. According to the historian Peter Carroll, the FBI opened files on more than two hundred veterans of the Abraham Lincoln Brigade. The term *premature anti-fascist*, abbreviated PAF, became a code word for *communist*. Congressman Martin Dies's committee to investigate un-American activities ferreted out PAFs in Hollywood, too, among the members of the Anti-Nazi League and other organizations, some of them communist fronts, that showed sympathy with the Spanish Republic or early on expressed alarm about the regimes of Italy and Germany. Various commentators have noted that World War II was marked by a lack of the kind of ideological rhetoric that had accompanied our participation in the First World War, but the crusade against communists had a decidedly hysterical fervor, and the supposed communist enemy within would become as terrifying as the communists abroad. Ignoring what Knox calls the "surreal" complexity of the time, the United States adopted the Manichaean worldview that sustains us to this day: "Islamofascists" have replaced the fascists of World War II, the axis of evil the Axis Powers, global extremists the communists of the Cold War. It was easier to think of all those veterans of Spain as premature anti-fascists than it was to accept that one had been too late. Their precocity proved something of an embarrassment, and it would serve as sufficient proof in the 1950s of a dalliance with communism that would outweigh any subsequent displays of loyalty.

Knox's own commitment to ancient literature, like that of fellow veteran Robert Fitzgerald, was galvanized by his wartime experience. And in the complex, nuanced attitude toward war in the work of these two classicists can be

found another antidote to the sentimentality that suffuses
so much war remembrance. Knox's reading often provided
him an analogue to his experience of modern war. Grievously
wounded—his comrades "sure that I was dying," he would
recall—in Spain, he did not respond with tranquility or satisfaction. This would be no nineteenth-century "good death,"
but an occasion for "furious, violent rage." When he returned
to ancient epic, he discovered that his "reaction was not ab-
normal." He explains: "In Homer's *Iliad*, still the greatest of
all war books, this is how young men die . . . And Virgil's
Turnus [in the *Aeneid*] goes the same road." Knox fought in
two wars for the same anti-fascist cause, but he was too astute
a reader to confuse the necessity of violence with glory. In an
introduction to Robert Fagles's translation of Virgil's *Aeneid*,
Knox recalled a venerable practice called the Virgilian lottery, in which people consulted the poem to learn the future:
"You took a passage at random and it foretold your future.
Often it was consulted in temples, as it was regarded as an
oracle; Hadrian and other men who became Roman emper-
ors first learned of their future eminence from this source,"
Knox explains. During the English Civil War, King Charles I
consulted the lottery "and put his finger by chance on Dido's
curse on Aeneas," in which the forsaken Carthaginian queen
expresses the desire that her former lover be plagued by war,
meet an untimely death, and be left unburied on a lonely
beach.

Knox played the lottery himself in a wrecked villa in
Modena, Italy, while fighting the Germans alongside a group
of Italian partisans. His war, carried out on foot, largely
without the benefits of mechanized transport and modern
technology, put him in mind of "the legions of Octavian and
Mark Antony," which had marched across the same region.
Occupying the villa in the middle of a skirmish against a German machine-gun crew, Knox found a copy of Virgil printed

"By Order of Benito Mussolini." Closing his eyes, he played the lottery and opened by chance to a page from Virgil's first *Georgic*, which offered a vision of Italy as appropriate for 1945 as it was for any other historical moment:

> . . . a world in ruins . . .
> For right and wrong change places; everywhere
> So many wars, so many shapes of crime
> Confront us; no due honor attends the plow.
> The fields, bereft of tillers, are all unkempt . . .
> . . . throughout the world
> Impious War is raging.

Knox's affinity for Virgil and Homer had to do largely with their refusal "to gloss over the harsh realities of the work of killing." These poets made "no attempt, either, to sentimentalize the pain and degradation of violent death." Knox catalogues, in an essay on the *Iliad*, the many ways in which men die in that poem: "In agony; they drop, screaming, to their knees, reaching out to beloved companions, gasping their life out, clawing the ground with their hands; they die roaring . . . raging . . . bellowing . . . moaning." Death, moreover, "is the end." There is no consolation and no afterlife; even the heroic code the poem seems to celebrate is something "war imposes on its votaries." There is a recognition of the brutal exhilaration, the "intoxicating excitements," and the "deadly fascination" it exerts. It is a poison, never a tonic. Responding to the insights of Simone Weil, Knox concludes, "Three thousand years have not changed the human condition in this respect; we are still lovers and victims of the will to violence, and so long as we are, Homer will be read as its truest interpreter." And in subscribing to that code, the warrior commits himself to "a solitary line," a tragic rejection of "community" in the embrace of violent death. The warrior's solitude becomes the chief subject of the *Odyssey*, which traces the circuitous homeward path of Odysseus cast adrift in a postwar world of isolation, occasional imprisonment, and periodic returns to violent action, culminating in the mass slaughter of trespassing guests in his own home.

Knox wasn't the only one thinking about ancient wars as he fought a modern one. Robert Fitzgerald, a naval officer stationed on Guam in the Western Pacific, spent three seasons of 1945 making his way through the *Aeneid*, of which he would later render a magisterial translation. It was the first time Fitzgerald had read the entirety of Virgil's epic in the original Latin, and the project became an antidote to the boredom endemic to off-duty life as a staff officer on a well-manicured island just far enough away from the fighting to preserve its aura of tranquility: "The scene," he writes, "could not have been more imperial or more civilized." Meanwhile, a vicious war—and the vicious war talk that accompanied it—persisted all around him:

> I read Virgil by the light of a good lamp. I heard young submarine skippers, the finest Annapolis products, give their lighthearted accounts of shelling poor junks to smithereens in the China Sea. Meanwhile, offshore of the big Japanese island to the north, picket ships were having their prows or upperworks and the men who manned them smashed into flaming junk by Japanese fighters aflame; ashore, men with flamethrowers were doing what I had heard a briefing officer in San Francisco, with an insane giggle, refer to as "popping Japs"; and a good many young and brave of both sides were tasting the agony and abomination that the whole show came down to, in fact existed for. The next landings

would be on Honshu, and I would be there. More
than literary interest, I think, kept me reading Virgil's
descriptions of desperate battle, funeral pyres, failed
hopes of truce or peace.

Fitzgerald highlights the ease with which violence as a means
turns into violence as an end in and of itself. He intimates the
particular brutality of the war in the Pacific Theater, where
the violence was admixed with and intensified by racial ani-
mosity, which expressed itself in mutilation and the taking of
trophies and reached its apogee in the firebombing of scores
of Japanese cities and the dropping of atomic bombs on Hiroshima and Nagasaki. The Japanese surrender obviated the
need for the prospective landings on Kyushu and Honshu,
which were a part of the invasion plan "Downfall."

Like Knox, Fitzgerald discovered in ancient literature
numerous examples of war's coarsening effect. The context
of the *Aeneid*'s composition was, he reminds us, a Rome in
which civil war was still a green memory. War, that "Roman
specialty," had "gone fratricidal and got out of hand." For
Aeneas, the poem's hero, as for the emperor Augustus, under
whose rule Virgil wrote—as for the world in 1945, Fitzgerald
implies—the most difficult task "was waging war to end war,
to work out settlements so magnanimous as to challenge no
more strife but to promote *concordia* and the arts of peace."
Not for nothing did the postwar period come to be called the
Pax Americana, even if, like the Pax Romana, during which
the gates of war were open more than they were closed, it
amounted to a fantasy of peace, under cover of which wars
cold and hot simmered continuously.

In the *Aeneid* one discerns, as scholars have noted, a shift
in sensibility from the individually heroic to the unroman-
tically corporate. In this sense, it resonates to a far greater
degree than does the *Iliad* with the historical dynamic of

World War II service. In the *Aeneid*, for example, the dead are routinely left behind. "Uniform and anonymous, undifferentiated in essentials," Fussell writes of the effects of mass mobilization in wartime, "boys turned by training into quasi-mechanical interchangeable parts." They were, as the name "GI" communicates, "faceless young automatons." In his 1942 poem "To a Military Rifle," Yvor Winters suggests that in war individuals do not count "at all." During World War II, Virgil's poem illuminated a world at war for soldiers and civilians alike. In 1945 William Hardy Alexander and George E. Duckworth published articles about the poem as a "military manual" in *The Classical Journal*. They began what scholars subsequently called the "pessimistic" reading of the poem, in which the explosive violence with which it ends constitutes a commentary on the cost of founding nations. It has been argued that this reading responded to the fascists' use of Roman symbols; it gathered momentum during the Cold War, especially during Vietnam. The "pessimistic" reading of Virgil's epic refused to find something redemptive and meaningful in violence.

"Among My Souvenirs"

William Wyler's *The Best Years of Our Lives* (1946) chronicles the uneasy return of three servicemen to Boone City, a fictitious midwestern stand-in for Cincinnati. Restless and confused on his first night home, one of them, a banker turned infantry sergeant named Al Stephenson (Fredric March), insists on a night on the town with his wife, Milly (Myrna Loy), and daughter, Peggy (Teresa Wright). After doing the rounds of the city's nightspots, they end up at homely Butch's Bar, where the proprietor himself (Hoagy Carmichael) provides the entertainment on an old upright piano unworthy of his talents. The drunken Al requests "Among My Souvenirs," an old tune from the late 1920s, and asks Milly to dance. Twirling rather dizzily around the floor, Al is thrown back, in his confused intoxication, into another evening sometime during the war, when he danced with another woman. "You remind me of my wife," he informs an amused Millly, who patiently plays along.

Written by Edgar Leslie and Horatio Nicholls, "Among My Souvenirs" is a prewar tune—Paul Whiteman's version for Victor Records became a chart topper in 1928—and it sounds decidedly quaint on Carmichael's piano. Although it would be recorded well into the 1950s, notably by Connie Francis in 1959, "Among My Souvenirs" is meant to evoke a bygone era in a film that is postwar in mood. Milly's reaction reveals that it is the couple's song. However, as Sarah Kozloff notes in her companion to the film, it is not a love song, but a melancholy remembrance of things past and impossible to retrieve. The song begins with the revelation that nothing is left, and its ensuing itemization of souvenirs concludes with the revelation of "a broken heart." In a sense it is ideal for describing Al's confusion and anxiety as well as the new awkwardness between him and Milly. Even though they find each other again, it is clear that things will never be quite the same as they were before the war.

The song serves to emphasize that Al, like his fellow veterans, is out of sorts. His trousers don't fit; he drinks too much; he is uncomfortable, even a little irritable, around his children; and he clashes with the bank president over whether ex-GIs are good credit risks and should get the loans sponsored by the GI Bill. But the song is fitting for another reason. Al has brought home souvenirs for his high-school-age son, Rob (Michael Hall): a cap, a samurai sword, and a flag he "found" on "a dead Jap soldier." Rob seems far less interested in these spoils of war than in the aftereffects of radiation on

the inhabitants of Hiroshima, a phenomenon about which Al
knows nothing:

> ROB: You were at Hiroshima, weren't you?
> AL: Mm-hm.
> ROB: Did you notice any of the effects of radioactivity
> on the people who survived?
> AL: No, I didn't. Should I have?
> ROB: We've been having lectures in atomic energy at
> school . . . Oh, you're just kidding me, Dad. You've
> been to all these places and you've seen everything.
> AL: I've seen nothing. I should have stayed home and
> found out what was really going on.

The bond between father and son is tenuous at best—Rob
disappears entirely from the film after one more fleeting
appearance—and the awkward presentation of the souvenirs
amounts to a failed ritual of reacquaintance. Rob has to be
prompted by Milly to thank his father for these gifts, which
he does in perfunctory fashion, and it is quite clear that they
are more likely to end up in the back of the closet than to be
displayed on the wall of his room.

A version of this scene presumably played out in households throughout the country. Contemporary accounts suggest that souvenir hunting was something of a mania among
GIs, as it reportedly had been in World War I. J. Glenn
Gray hypothesizes in *The Warriors* that the "passion for
souvenirs . . . may have stemmed not so much from a primitive desire to loot" or to prove that a soldier had "been there,"
as from a need for "some assurance of his future beyond the
destructive environment of the present." In the midst of his
dramatic account of navy lieutenant John F. Kennedy and the
sinking of PT109, published in *The New Yorker* in 1944, John
Hersey took care to point out that when the young officer

was eventually rescued from a canoe by another PT boat, he brought along some spoils of war: "In the American tradition, Kennedy held under his arm a couple of souvenirs: one of the improvised paddles and a Japanese gas mask." Writing from the Mediterranean Theater in the fall of 1943, John Steinbeck devoted an entire dispatch to the subject: "It is said, and with some truth, that while the Germans fight for world domination and the English for the defense of England, the Americans fight for souvenirs." Steinbeck reckoned that the ancient temples of Salerno "have suffered more from chipping by American soldiers in two weeks than they did during the preceding three thousand years." He reports seeing entire pup tents crammed with worthless "mementos" and notes that a post office in Africa prevented a soldier from mailing a jar filled with brandy-soaked fingers. Steinbeck watched the Italians cashing in on the American craze for souvenir hunting by manufacturing all sorts of fake relics for the invaders. In one column, he tells the picaresque tale of a PFC called "Bugs," who discovers a six-by-four-foot, seventy-five-pound mirror that had miraculously survived the battle for Gela, Sicily, and decides to cart it on his back more than a hundred miles across the island all the way to Palermo, where he finally hangs it on the wall of the house in which he is billeted. The nail shortly comes loose, and the mirror shatters into countless shards. The stoical Bugs simply shrugs and declares that it probably wouldn't have looked very good in his house anyway.

The acquisitive American GIs are the strange descendants of the Gilded Age robber barons who scoured Europe for more valuable artistic treasures. The souvenir hunter was a frequent subject of journalists, including Pyle, who reported from Tunisia in 1943 that Americans started collecting souvenirs on the very day of the German surrender on the Bizerte-Tunis front. He hastens to reassure his readers that these items were, for the most part, willingly handed over, not looted from supply depots: "The Germans gave away helmets, goggles and map cases, which they will not be needing any more. The spoils of war which the average doughboy took were legitimate, and little enough recompense for his fighting." Pyle writes that almost every truck has a helmet affixed to the radiator. Motorcycles were fitted for "a carnival, with French flags and the colorful little black-and-yellow death's-head pennants the Germans use for marking their own mine fields." Pyle himself had a Volkswagen, "a topless two-seater with a rear motor, camouflaged a dirty brown," presented to him by the First Armored Division in thanks for his "sweating it out with" them during the winter. Innumerable Lugers appeared in GI holsters. Death's-heads would become the signatures of veteran motorcycle gangs such as the Hells Angels after the war, while souvenir pistols often turn up as murder weapons on the silver screen, where they place veterans under suspicion. A common device of film noir—the German Luger in *Somewhere in the Night* (1946), for instance, or the Japanese Nambu pistol in *Undertow* (1949)—the souvenir also appears in more lighthearted fare such as the 1947 comedy-mystery *Song of the Thin Man*, in which a Nambu is used in a homicide to throw suspicion onto a veteran. The fear of veterans with firearms was not exclusive to the movies. According to *The New York Times*, in May 1946 the Kings County district attorney convened the leaders of thirteen veterans organizations in his office to ask for their help in getting their members to surrender all "souvenir weapons . . . as a crime prevention measure."

In the Pacific, in April 1945, not long before Pyle was killed by a Japanese machine gunner, he once again noted the alacrity with which marines collected souvenirs at Okinawa, where the caves concealed a trove: "They were a rich field for souvenir hunters, and all marines are souvenir hunters.

So immediately two of our boys, instead of resting, started up through the brush, looking for caves." When the marines Pyle is accompanying stumble on some Japanese soldiers and capture them, a corporal named Jack Ossege seizes a special prize:

> That rifle was the envy of everybody; later, when we were sitting around, discussing the capture, the other boys tried to buy or trade him out of it. Pop Taylor offered him $100 for it, and the answer was no. Then Taylor offered four quarts of whiskey. The answer still was no. Then he offered eight quarts. Ossege weakened a little. He said, "Where would you get eight quarts of whiskey?" Pop said he had no idea. So Ossege kept the rifle.

The promise of trophies of one sort or another have always been one of the attractions of war. Today, U.S. and international laws make distinctions between "spoils of war," which the U.S. Code defines as "enemy movable property lawfully captured, seized, confiscated, or found which has become United States property in accordance with the laws of war," and illegal pillage or plunder. Rule 49 of the Red Cross's International Humanitarian Law concerns something called "war booty," which includes equipment and personal property found on the battlefield. It cites as precedent the Lieber Code, the U.S. Civil War document that was the first modern codification of the laws of war. According to the Lieber Code, such booty belongs to the "party," or state, as opposed to the "individual" who seizes it. The U.S. Law of Land Warfare directs that items "found on the dead," including an "identity disc, last wills or other documents of importance to the next of kin, money and in general all articles of an intrinsic or sentimental value," be returned to the enemy government.

In addition to prohibiting "looting or pillaging," Article 108a of the 2019 Uniform Code of Military Justice holds in violation anyone who "buys, sells, trades, or in any way deals in or disposes of captured or abandoned property, whereby he receives or expects any profit, benefit, or advantage to himself or another directly or indirectly connected with himself." In 2003, after several incidents in Afghanistan and Iraq, General John Abizaid, the CENTCOM commander, saw fit to reinforce the message. A DOD news article headlined "No War Trophies Allowed from Iraq, Afghanistan" explained that the acquisition of weapons, antiquities, drugs, as well as "plants, animals or other organic material" were all prohibited. Several soldiers were court-martialed for attempting to bring home weapons, and customs agents seized sheep skulls, which marines had attached to their guidons. In language that reflexively echoes World War II rhetoric, a CENTCOM spokesperson proclaimed, "We didn't go into Iraq or Afghanistan to conquer them, but to liberate them. Taking articles from those countries sends the wrong message." Legally obtained "souvenirs" are, however, authorized. I have a few of these myself: rugs and scarves purchased from Afghan vendors by soldiers of my acquaintance, as well as commemorative shot glasses painted with desert scenes and other paraphernalia, obtained from in-theater post exchanges that cater to the enduring American mania for mementos.

The wartime expression of American acquisitiveness, admixed with a certain entrepreneurial spirit, has spawned a rogues' gallery of literary figures. From the enthusiastic souvenir hunter to the expert "scrounger" typified by James Garner's character in the film *The Great Escape* (1963), countless GIs parade through popular culture "liberating" property from its owners. The resourceful scrounger is a figure of romance, but at the worst, he turns into a black-market opera-tive or war profiteer. In his satirical novel *Catch-22*, published in 1961, Joseph Heller offers an extreme example of greed in the figure of Milo Minderbinder, a supply officer who runs a syndicate from which he profits enormously. Minderbinder maintains a veil of secrecy, but everyone knows about his schemes, including the commanders, who allow them to continue because they receive a share of the take. The protagonist, Yossarian, learns that Milo has been made the mayor of Palermo and several other towns "because he had brought Scotch to Sicily."

> Yossarian was amazed. "The people here like to drink Scotch that much?"
>
> "They don't drink any of the Scotch," Milo explained. "Scotch is very expensive, and these people here are very poor."
>
> "Then why do you import it to Sicily if nobody drinks any?"
>
> "To build up a price. I move the Scotch here from Malta to make more room for profit when I sell it back to me for somebody else. I created a whole new industry here. Today Sicily is the third-largest exporter of Scotch in the world, and *that's* why they elected me mayor."

Minderbinder is, in short, a criminal, but the point is that his efforts are sustained by the impulses of his comrades—from the opportunism of the colonels to the collusion, greed, and sheer boredom of his peers—and by an ambient rapaciousness that seems to flourish during war.

Heller's profiteer is outlandish and extreme, but the avarice he highlights is also the central subject of a grim novel published soon after the war in 1947, John Horne Burns's *The Gallery*, which became a bestseller before being forgotten in the ensuing decades. By contrast, readers would be slow to warm up to Heller's novel in 1961, but it has since become a cult classic. The literature scholar George Hutchinson reminds us of the initial critical as well as popular enthusiasm for *The Gallery* in his book *Facing the Abyss: American Literature and Culture in the 1940s*, where he emphasizes the degree to which the novel's portrayal of soldiers differed from those found in journalism and on the movie screen. Set for the most part in Casablanca and Naples, the action of *The Gallery* largely transpires, as its name suggests, in the Galleria Umberto, an arcade where soldiers and Neapolitans congregate to engage in all manner of illicit transactions—the incessant trading, buying, and selling of goods and human beings. The tone is set early in the novel, when the narrator embarks on a Liberty ship making the crossing from Camp Patrick Henry, Virginia, to Casablanca. Burns's narrator is a participant-observer. Most of the book's characters have a kind of outsider status, reinforced in several cases by the fact that they are gay. The novel was pioneering in its sympathetic treatment of homosexuality.

The pacifism of earlier decades hadn't yet killed the narrator's adventurousness, but what he sees belowdecks, where GIs live "off one another like lice," so disgusts him that he feels he has "died as an American." Parasitic relationships continue to dominate the novel: Americans exploit Neapolitans; starving Neapolitans take any advantage they can of the Allies, as they once tried to do with the Germans. It is a world of desperate survivalists and con artists in which even the combat soldiers who populate the Galleria seem to be working some kind of angle, all the while attempting to look like the scruffy infantrymen Willie and Joe in Bill Mauldin's cartoons. The film critic Pauline Kael observed that servicemen at home also imitated the wise guys and hustlers they saw at the movies. In an interview with Studs Terkel, she recalled that a GI would try to pick a woman up and if she "weren't interested, he would say, That's what we're fighting for, that's what we're giving our lives for. They tried to make you feel guilty for not wanting to go to bed with them." Kael notes that popular culture nevertheless depicted these GIs as "boys . . . twelve-year-olds at heart."

Burns reveals that the mercenary impulse dominates the home front as well. Hal, a lieutenant headquartered in Washington, D.C., finds that America has "grown sharp and young" after the Depression. "For the first time in a decade they were united, proud, and rather gay. Washington was a garden party." Hal later grows demoralized while deployed to a base section in Oran, in charge of American Military Police who look to him like Nazis in formation and who spend their time engaged in chickenshit arrests of soldiers for having loose buttons. Overhearing the tenor of conversations in the bars of Oran, he concludes that everyone is unwittingly part of a "vast and deadly scheme." A sense of corruption pervades the novel. The Allies are living it up, but Hal thinks of the American support soldiers "rolling in the materialism" behind the lines as "bloodsuckers" surviving on frontline troops.

What the unnamed central narrator of Burns's novel witnesses in Naples breaks his heart and transforms his vision of the United States. Indicting its commercial, material culture, he concludes that the U.S. "had most of the riches of the modern world, but very little of its soul. We . . . couldn't resist the temptation to turn a dollar or two . . . We didn't take the trouble to think out the fact that the war was supposed to be against fascism—not against every man, woman, and child in Italy." The novel catalogues systemic and individual crimes perpetrated against the beleaguered Italians, much of it motivated by American greed. In addition to the big-time criminals who steal goods from the ships in the harbor, there are petty profiteers selling PX rations or GI clothing. Even the comparatively harmless quest for souvenirs turns compulsive and ultimately damaging as heedless servicemen buy all the junk they can for the thrill of it, thereby causing inflation and making the local currency worthless. One character concludes, "An honest American in August, 1944, was almost as hard to find as a Neapolitan who owned up to having been a Fascist."

Ernie Pyle describes a similar sensibility at the end of *Here Is Your War*. Recollections of Pyle tend to omit his most critical and provocative passages. "Our men," he warns civilians on the home front, "have less regard for property than you raised them to have." Money, he suggests, doesn't mean much to them—and that is saying something for men raised during the Depression—and their elemental generosity prompts them to "give or throw away their own money." Pyle did as much as anyone to circulate the popular image of the generous American; his portrait of soldiers giving away all their rations in North Africa provides a fine example in *Here Is Your War*. He also situates this portrait within a larger system in which the disdain for property becomes less an indication of generous impulses than a by-product of the overarching wastefulness of war. The practice of giving and throwing things away is sustained by an almost pathological amassing of supplies in a combat theater, "where things are scarce and red tape still rears its delaying head, a man learns to get what he needs simply by 'requisitioning.' It isn't stealing," Pyle reassures his home-front readers, but "the only way to acquire certain things. The stress of war puts old virtues in a changed light . . . But what's wrong with a small case of 'requisitioning' when murder is the classic goal?"

Whereas Pyle attributes such behavior to the war, Burns concludes that war simply exacerbates inherent American

moral deficiencies, chiefly a vicious materialism that victimized the Italians: "We could prate of the evils of fascism, yet
be just as ruthless as Fascists." The novel concludes with
the story of a lieutenant named Moe, wounded in battle and
waiting out the end of the war in Naples. Moe complains in
a letter to a friend that he has grown weary of authorizing
packages full of the souvenirs the American "Liberators"
have seized—"anything they can lay their hands on"—from
the Italians. He explains that Americans refer to their looting
as "liberating material." At the end of his novel, Burns thus
leaves his reader with a debased image of Americans as liberators not of the oppressed, but of "loot."

An even more damning portrait of the American souvenir hunter can be found in E. B. Sledge's *With the Old Breed*,
which documents the general fragility of humanity under
fire and reveals how close the author came to losing his own.
Sledge recounts a scene in which a mortarman on Peleliu is
"casually" throwing coral pebbles into a Japanese soldier's
skull, the crown of which had been blown off in the fighting: "The war had so brutalized us that it was beyond belief." Sledge is similarly uncompromising in the revelation
of his own complicity in commonplace acts of barbarity. In
another episode he describes "one facet of stripping enemy
dead that I hadn't practiced so far," the extraction—Sledge
calls it "harvesting"—of gold teeth from enemy corpses
with a Ka-Bar, the Marine Corps fighting knife. As he begins an extraction, a medic, Doc Caswell, with an expression "of sadness and reproach," puts a hand on his shoulder
to restrain him. After failing to convince Sledge to leave the
tooth alone on the grounds of propriety, Caswell tells him
he might get an infection, a possibility that stops Sledge,
who settles instead for removing the soldier's collar insignia
as a keepsake. Only in hindsight did Sledge understand the
medic's real motives: "I realized that Doc Caswell didn't re-

ally have germs in mind. He was a good friend and a fine, genuine person whose sensitivity hadn't been crushed out by the war. He was merely trying to help me retain some of mine."

Sledge did retain his sensitivity. After he had retired from a career as a professor of biology at Alabama College, he finally published his memoir in 1981. It is suffused with sensitivity and understanding yet unclouded by sentimentality and romantic views of war. Sledge's refusal to shape his story into a palatable narrative, let alone one with a happy ending, is apparent throughout the book. Its final section cements this commitment: "If this were a novel about war . . ." it begins, "I would find a romantic way to end this account while looking at that fine sunset off the cliffs at the southern end of Okinawa." Instead, he goes on, relentlessly, to chronicle Company K's one last "nasty job." Years of doing nasty jobs left indelible marks. In the epilogue to a second memoir about his postwar military assignment in China, he recalled that science and the works of Mozart were the antidotes that helped him "conquer the curse of combat nightmares." Sledge was a naturalist, but it took him a long time before he could see the outdoors from anything other than "an analytical perspective of its features as military terrain . . . possible avenues of enemy attack or ambush." His first postwar hunting trip ended with Sledge in tears contemplating a dead bird, in his "mind's eye still clearly seeing those beautiful brown eyes bordered by those fleshy pale blue eyelids." Sledge understood that he was part of the savagery of the "giant killing machine." And he never fully let go of that wartime self: "To 'mellow' is to forget," he explained, and he remained "proud" of the enemy he killed while regretting those he missed.

From the collector of ersatz souvenirs manufactured by cagey Neapolitans to the harvester of gold teeth, the American GI might become skilled in the ways of the operator, trafficker, thief, and profiteer. The GI was transformed by a wartime world of extremes: shortage and abundance, riotous generosity and stunning rapacity. As chapter 3 will show, it turned out to be similar in crucial ways to the world to which he would return. The postwar United States, rescued at last from the deprivations of the Depression, seemed as crazed by materialism as the GIs the country exported.

A Pocket Guide to Hamlet's Ghost

The ubiquitous characterization of the American souvenir hunter reveals many things, among them the GI's peculiar status as a tourist. In at least certain respects, that's the way the government thought of him, too, as evidenced by the series of pocket guides and instructional pamphlets the War Department produced for postings throughout the world. These booklets were regularly updated during the Cold War; the latest revisions date from the 1980s. In recent years, this kind of informational material has been produced more or less on demand for Iraq, Afghanistan, and other relevant theaters of war. Present-day publications are largely businesslike in tone and utilitarian in scope, but the early guides were wildly idiosyncratic, often witty, and—owing to the volatile nature of the landscape they described—sometimes unintentionally bizarre. As Rick Atkinson explains in his introduction to a recent reissue of *A Pocket Guide to France*, originally published by the Army Information Branch of the U.S. Army Service Forces in 1944, booklets for various European countries were prepared by civilian experts and members of the Office of Strategic Services. They were given "secret" classification until issued so as not to compromise invasion plans. Guides for Australia and Britain had been distributed as early as 1942; John Steinbeck alludes to the latter in *Once There Was a War*, where he describes GIs getting a laugh out of the book's attempt to explain linguistic differences. He overheard soldiers "talking a curious gibberish which they imagine is a British accent." Pyle took delight in highlighting the several inaccuracies of the North Africa guide. Indeed, the only volume for which Pyle had any use was the navy's *Guide to the Western Pacific*, which he calls "wonderfully informative."

It is easy to understand why the books came in for ridicule. "Back in the good old days, as we like to refer to peacetime, most Americans visited CHERBOURG through the water entrance, often coming in on the *Normandie* from New York," proclaims the *Pocket Guide to Paris and Cities of Northern France* (1944) in a typically breezy tone. "You, of course, will more than likely pay your visit via one of the highways or railroads that converge on the town from the base of the peninsula." The authors went on to acknowledge that jeeps and tank landing ships (as opposed to, one presumes, Daimlers, Delahayes, or Isotta Fraschinis) would be the troops' likeliest modes of transport. Nevertheless, after reading a large sampling of guides, one begins to discern an animating philosophy. The authors took seriously the question of what it might mean for an American who had quite possibly never been away from home to find himself among strangers about whose language, history, allegiances, values, and principles he knew next to nothing. Although there were women in uniform, the guides are unambiguously designed for male service personnel.

The early Cold War guides, geared for a potentially long-term occupation, are aimed at the "ugly American"— loud, impatient, largely ignorant of the various customs and hardships of the host country—but the wartime guides, obviously inspired by the authors' deep affection for their destinations, try to convey all the thrill of discovering new places even in the midst of war's destruction. Although there is certainly a recognition that the consumers of these guides might not know precisely how to behave when confronted with the alien charms of the Old World, the authors evince optimism about both the survival of Europe and the average American's potential for appreciating the Continent's rich history and culture. Consistent with the prevailing didactic spirit, there is even a space for taking notes at the end of some of the volumes. The guides vary in format and, to a lesser extent, style, but in their desire to disabuse visitors of common assumptions, they share a spirit with the WPA guidebooks produced for domestic travel in the 1930s. The several guides broken down by cities—e.g., *Cities of Denmark*, *Cities of Southern France*—could often be mistaken for civilian publications such as Baedeker. After the war, the large numbers of GIs abroad in turn inspired Arthur Frommer's first guidebook, published in 1955: *The G.I.'s Guide to Travelling in Europe*, on the cover of which the author is referred to by his rank as "Pfc. Arthur Frommer."

The city-by-city guides all begin with the following disclaimer, which establishes the confused state of affairs surrounding their production:

ATTENTION

About the only thing in this booklet that can be guaranteed is the terrain. The rest of it is up to the fortunes or misfortunes of war. Many of the towns and cities described here have been bombed and shelled by us as we approached, and shelled by the enemy as he retreated. And many of them will still show the marks of the destruction visited upon them when these lands were being conquered and occupied by the Germans.

The short historical notes and city plans concerning most of the towns are correct as of the outbreak of the war. But the changes of war were still happening in many places when this pocket guide went to press.

You may find that art treasures described and located in these pages have been looted or destroyed, and it may be years before those that can be restored are sights to see again. On the other hand, some of them, by a stroke of good fortune, may be left intact and you will be able to enjoy them.

The authors knew they might well be conducting readers through a world that no longer existed. Emphasizing the fragility of European civilization, several enumerate the long years of war's wreckage, as in the discussion of the serial invasions of Luxembourg in 1914, 1918, 1940, and 1944. In the face of this history of German destruction, the authors use a mocking tone to express a spirit of Allied resilience. "With the influx of Germans in 1940 Deauville's beach lost its glamour," declares the *Pocket Guide to Paris and the Cities of Northern France*, while the *Pocket Guide to the Cities of Denmark* (1944) announces, "Even the Germans could not obliterate the charm" of Copenhagen. Naples, the locus of so much corruption and confusion, and the target of so much destruction by Allies and Axis alike, also proves, according to the *Pocket Guide to Italian Cities* (1944), "beyond the power of the Germans to destroy." Rivaling Istanbul in picturesqueness, the book declares, Naples is the most naturally "beautiful" location in Europe, "and gutted and sacked though the city may be, the site retains its beauty and holds hope for the new Naples that will rise."

The authors' enthusiasm is somewhat muted by the recognition of a certain fragility and at times a melancholy resignation that in saving the soul of European civilization, it might be necessary to destroy some of its most iconic symbols. The tone is frequently elegiac, verb tenses shift back and forth between past and present, and the text is sometimes overwhelmed by nostalgia, as in the account of Monaco, which contains a wistful series of might-have-beens—a catalogue of sights the war has made impossible to experience. The guides are also frank about the damage done "by us" in contrast to that wrought by the Germans: for example, by Allied bombers "on the prowl after Germans" at Calais, where GIs are also enjoined to "prowl about" to see the attractions of the historic city while they can. In a landscape with such a long history, certain ruins become an occasion for humor. "You've seen a lot of ruins in Italy," explains that country's guide. "The Colosseum, however, wasn't wrecked by Long Toms [American 155-mm field guns]. It got that way through the passage of time." Similarly, a discussion of the Vichy regime situates the German occupation in a longer timeline, as if to say that this sordid and unpleasant episode will fade away like so many ephemeral conquests of the past: "Long before VICHY became the grim capital of occupied France in 1940 the old Romans were flocking there to bathe in and drink the water."

Written by people who knew and deeply loved prewar Europe, the guides are sometimes dubious about the typical GI's enthusiasm for the Old World. As a result, they have recourse to all sorts of practical as well as high-minded arguments in order to convince readers to expand their cultural horizons. Some of the city-by-city guides have a longer preface that concludes:

> And another thing: if some of these towns should be declared off limits, you'll bypass them, of course. Perhaps later, they may be open to you.
>
> Food and drink are discussed here so that as times

gradually return to normal, you may be guided in the tastes and customs of the country. But be sure that you are not encouraging a black market or bringing hardship to the native civilian population if you take advantage of what the town or region has to offer. You will receive direction from the proper authority in this matter.

Anyhow, so far as your military duties permit, see as much as you can. You've got a great chance to do now, major expenses paid, what would cost you a lot of your own money after the war. Take advantage of it.

After this exhortation, simultaneously practical and aspirational, the guides introduce service members to national histories (including comparisons to, or past relationships with, the United States whenever possible); art, architecture, and other cultural attractions; and local customs and traditions, including recreation. By turns chatty and earnestly instructive, the guides urge the novice travelers at whom they are directed to open themselves to new experiences.

Nostalgia, further complicated by a lack of up-to-date information, lends an air of unreality to the whole enterprise. For example, hungry GIs—Fussell notes that, despite the frequent reminders that they were the best-fed army in the world, GIs were perpetually hungry—could learn the following about Amsterdam from the *Pocket Guide to the Cities of the Netherlands*: "By 1940 it had sold something like four and a half million steaks, but there is probably a shortage now." The *Pocket Guide to the Cities of Southern France*, meanwhile, offered the following suggestion: "If you can arrange to drop in at Hyères in early summer, you'll be able to bite into some of the finest strawberries in the world."

Everything is normal, except that almost nothing is. The description of Rotterdam begins with the news that fully a third of the city was destroyed by the Luftwaffe in May 1940 but ends with a reference to the abundance of tennis courts. Arriving in Leiden in the right season would provide the spectacle of blooming tulips, among other attractions: "The tulip garden, or the picturesque windmill you may visit in the outlying suburbs of Leiden are places of as much interest as the university, according to your mood. Wherever you wander you will meet people of Leiden who will welcome your interest in their liberated city." At times the war recedes almost entirely from view: eat well in Belgium, go to the movies in Milan, see the fish at Trieste's aquarium, go for a swim on the Venetian Lido, play billiards or golf in Lyon, "*cherchez la femme*" in Paris, and "by all means" go to the theater before you depart. The exceptional wines and cheeses of specific regions are noted, as are the excellent service in Cherbourg and, in a moment of cruel irony, the picturesqueness of Normandy's hedgerows, which would help make the Allied advance so deadly in the period after D-Day.

While discussions of food and recreation are prominent, if incongruous, features of the guides—the frequent allusions to wine and beer accurately targeted their notoriously thirsty GI audience—in the main they aim higher. The authors rarely miss an opportunity to introduce readers to natural and architectural wonders as well as to the birthplaces of celebrated artists, musicians, and authors, including Montaigne, Charles Dickens, Adam Smith, and Hans Christian Andersen. Artistic merit is sometimes measured in a way calculated to appeal to an American pragmatism: Andersen's sales, they note, are surpassed only by those of the Bible. The guides assume a passing acquaintance with Shakespeare: the names of Padua and Verona should ring bells as the settings for *The Taming of the Shrew* and *The Two Gentlemen of Verona*, respectively. The guide to Denmark contains the most extended discussion of Shakespeare. The city of Helsingør, noteworthy because of its significance in the history of the Baltic trade, is also home to the castle on the terrace of which "Hamlet is supposed to have seen his father's ghost." The many Hamlet-related tourist attractions—Ophelia's brook, a bronze statue of the prince, a column said to mark his grave—are all recommended even if, as the guide informs the more literal-minded GI, "the Hamlet legend" isn't altogether true.

Giving service personnel an appreciation for European culture is critical to the guides' overarching tendency to try to shape American behavior. In particular, the authors seek to impress on GIs the courage and integrity of the people who suffered under German tyranny. In the tough maritime city of Skagen, the *Pocket Guide to the Cities of Denmark* reminds readers, "You can be sure that people such as these did not take kindly to their German 'protectors' and did all they could to make life miserable and unpleasant for them. You will be hailed as liberators and, as such, will be welcome wherever you go. Don't abuse the privilege. Boasting and bad manners will not go over very big with people, for whom the risking of one's life is merely part of a daily routine."

Frequent comparisons to American features, traits, or regions work to assert a fundamental kinship and understanding among allies. Of all the Allied nations, England and Australia make the easiest cases. The instructional pamphlets to these countries stress shared language, government, and values. The similarities between Australians and Americans are emphasized, while the differences are treated with humor: the Australians have a pioneer spirit akin to that of Lewis and Clark; like Americans (and, by implication, unlike Europeans), they live in the present and future and "have little use for the past." They are, in other words, a young people who like new things.

The same arguments can't be made about the English, of course, but the *Instructions for American Servicemen in Britain*

(1942) celebrates the long tradition of English liberty to which the United States owes its own form of government. It instructs GIs not to worry about "old wars" and redcoats. The authors also suggest how important it is to make a good impression because the English have gotten their ideas about Americans from the movies: "You have a great chance to overcome the picture many of them have . . . of an America made up of wild Indians and gangsters." The volume's illumination of key social and cultural differences in this and other guides betrays an underlying fear that servicemen will be hampered across the globe by their provincialism, chauvinism, and racism. This particular manual zeroes in on GI assumptions about masculinity and gender: British men aren't "panty-waists," the authors insist. Implicitly acknowledging that the American women serving in the WACS and WAVES are a subject of sport to their countrymen, the manual explains that the many heroic British women in uniform are taken quite seriously by their compatriots and should receive a corresponding respect from GIs. Other guides anticipate the reactions of white GIs to other races. Warnings to military personnel to leave their color prejudice behind feature in those guides designed not only for service in Africa or the Middle East but also for stations closer to home, in Hawaii. These admonitions contribute to what was evidently an overarching agenda. One of the running themes of the series is humility: "Crossing the ocean doesn't automatically make you a hero." It is never a good idea, the authors remind their readers, to tell the English that you won World War I.

But it is the French who proved the most challenging ally to explain. GIs tended to regard the French with greater suspicion than they did the Germans. Various observers noted the natural affinity many GIs had for the Germans and a corresponding distaste for the French. The guides therefore emphasize France's contribution to American independence

and assert the kinship between the American and French revolutions: "French ideas" and "French guns" "helped us to
become a nation." By 1945, the initial euphoria of liberation
had already dissipated to such an extent that the Information
& Education Division of the U.S. Occupation Forces, Paris,
issued a new book called *112 Gripes about the French*. It was
meant to defuse the tension caused by French resentment of
their new occupiers' misbehavior, which has been amply documented in books such as *What Soldiers Do: Sex and the American GI in World War II France*, by Mary Louise Roberts.

Gripes alludes to the feeling prevalent among GIs that their
hosts were particularly ungrateful toward their liberators. It
also calls attention to something that would be forgotten rather
quickly in American remembrances of the war. The United
States did not "come to Europe to save the French, either
in 1917 or in 1944. We didn't come to Europe to do anyone
any favors. We came to Europe because we in America were
threatened by a hostile, aggressive and very dangerous power."
In short, the guide concludes, "it was better to fight our enemy in Europe than in America." This view of things would
soon become eclipsed by a loftier one, but in 1945 it expressed
a clear-eyed understanding of not only American war aims
but also the challenges presented by disgruntled GIs stuck in
Europe at the end of the war. In addition to refuting various
stereotypes about the French, *Gripes*, like its forerunner, the
1944 *Pocket Guide to France*, insists on understanding what
military occupation does to a people's pride and self-esteem.
The 1944 booklet reminds skeptical GIs, "You are a member
of the best dressed, best fed, best equipped liberating Army
now on earth. You are going in among the people of a former
Ally of your country. They are still your kind of people who
happen to speak democracy in a different language." Even
French communists are described as really just New Dealers.

Admonitions about the Germans are as energetic as are

defenses of the French. The 1944 edition of the guide to Germany warns vehemently against fraternization and insists that the surface friendliness of the average German, who may look a lot like an American, conceals a ruthless and duplicitous enemy brainwashed in the "master race" theory. But there is also some attempt to lay the groundwork for a future relationship. Like the English, the Germans are said to have formed their impressions of Americans from the movies (and possibly from Karl May, although the guide doesn't mention him): "Many Germans grew up with the idea that America was mostly full of cowboys and Indians and rich uncles." The authors explain that during the interwar period, before the Nazis, the Germans had come to develop an appreciation, perhaps an envy, for the United States as "a country of skyscrapers and millions of automobiles, of mass-production and unlimited resources."

The 1945 guide, expressly designed for postwar occupation forces, adds some prefatory material. It begins with Eisenhower's Proclamation No. 1, addressed to the people of Germany, which announces, "We come as conquerors, but not as oppressors." This is followed by Truman's May 8, 1945, speech, in which he refers to "Our Armies of Liberation" and denounces the "evil from which half the world has been freed" and of which the other half had still to be "cleansed." Truman's emphasis on evil is consistent with the book's strenuous attempt to persuade service members of the depravity of Nazi ideology. Clearly, it could not be taken for granted that all GIs would instinctively recoil from that ideology. Taken together, these two proclamations also began to build the official memory of the war. The subtleties of timing and motive, frankly alluded to in *112 Gripes about the French*, have disappeared, while the more nuanced discussions about occupation and the damage done to countries and peoples by tyranny and war are replaced with platitudes about American decency: "The point is, we don't like to kick people when they are down." Or "This warning against fraternization doesn't mean that you are to act like a sourpuss or military automaton." Democracy is oversimplified as meritocracy and a sense of decency in contrast to the "tragic nonsense" of "the master race theory" and the Nazis' "gangster racket." The book repeatedly identifies the Nazi regime with gangsterism. The treachery of Nazis, who will attempt to melt back into the population, is accounted for by the fact that German boys do not have "the spirit of sportsmanship, decency, and fair play instilled" in American boys. Such rhetoric accompanied what turned out to be a fairly short-lived denazification policy, which lost momentum to the desire to reestablish law and order quickly.

As this guide reveals, by 1944 the story of the war was already being streamlined and simplified in some of the educational and instructional material provided to service members. One of the book's longer sections, "Why You Are Fighting Germany," differs markedly from the explanation of self-defense offered in *Gripes*. Instead of being late to the fight—having been wedded to isolationist fantasies and having ignored events in Ethiopia and Spain—the United States is here portrayed as having been invested in world events as early as 1931:

The fascist peoples of Italy, Germany and Japan first destroyed their own liberties; and then began to use force to destroy the liberty of their neighboring countries. We hoped it was just a series of neighborhood quarrels, that were none of our business. But suddenly we began to see that we were part of the world neighborhood: aviation and radio brought the nations of the world into close touch. Suddenly we saw things happen that were very rotten indeed. Japan attacked China in 1931. Fascist Italy attacked Ethiopia in 1935, and in 1936, interfered in Spain's Civil War . . .

Then began the bloody and crazy march of destruction: the remainder of Czechoslovakia in 1939, the invasion of Poland in the same year, the invasion of Denmark and Norway, followed by the conquest of France in 1940 and, in 1941, invasion of the Balkans and the attack on Russia. German aggression threatened the entire world.

No self-respecting man, or nation, could live in a neighborhood in which gangsters were having their way without trying to stop them. It was not only a matter of principle; it was a matter of actual personal and national safety.

The fascists all over the world made their alliance against the believers in freedom, and burst out of bounds whenever it looked favorable for a successful seizure of a peaceful country.

The free world couldn't go on taking that forever.

American engagement with the world's fight for freedom is effectively backdated while the crimes of the enemy remain rather vague. The guide alludes to concentration camps and "brutal acts of terror" but doesn't dwell on the identity of the victims. American hostility for Nazis—despite the death camps and the ample evidence of the regime's horrors—lacked the intensity of what Sledge calls a "burning hatred" for the Japanese because, as the instructional guide notes, Germans tended to look just like Americans. Hatred for the Japanese, by contrast, was sparked by vengeance, rooted in racism, and stoked by crude propaganda. Even Pyle, so circumspect in many ways, writes in *Last Chapter*: "Japanese were looked upon as something subhuman and repulsive; the way some people feel about cockroaches or mice. Shortly af-

ter I arrived I saw a group of Japanese prisoners in a wire-
fenced courtyard, and they were wrestling and laughing and
talking just like normal human beings. And yet they gave me
the creeps, and I wanted a mental bath after looking at them."

It was rather easy for Americans to regard the Japanese
as subhuman, but European fascists were more often described as gangsters. This vocabulary appeared in the artful
speeches of Churchill and Roosevelt as well as in the cables
of various diplomats. In a 1938 letter to Roosevelt, Ambassador Joseph Kennedy alluded to the "'gangster' technique" of
German annexation; in 1941 Myron C. Taylor, the American
representative to the Évian Conference, translated a French
diplomat's description of Italy and Germany as "two gangster regimes." That same year, in a speech on the Soviet-
German War, Churchill referred to "Nazi gangsters" and to
Hitler as "a bloodthirsty guttersnipe." Roosevelt began his
1944 State of the Union address by describing "a world that
has been gravely threatened with gangster rule." And to complete the picture, British command in Malaya characterized
the Japanese forces operating there "as a highly trained army
of gangsters equipped with a high proportion of tommy guns
and mortars and employing all kinds of ruses in an attempt
to lower the morale of our troops." Charles de Gaulle added a
new twist when, during an acrimonious meeting in London,
he declared Churchill himself a gangster; signally, he also
called the British prime minister "a great artist."

The Allies discovered in the grammar of 1930s Hollywood an ideal way to distill geopolitical complexities. Having
suggested that the English and Germans supposedly formed
their impressions of Americans from the movies, the authors
of the guides used a cinematic vocabulary to lay out the world
situation for GIs. *A Pocket Guide to France* takes this to an
extreme degree. After they liberate France from "the Nazi
mob," the GI will still have to beware of getting too friendly

"with a special sort of hard-boiled dame" (a prostitute), and he should remain on his guard against "tarts" in nightclubs. More important, he should stick by his "chum" so as not to end up a sucker at some Parisian "clip joint." Thus the pocket guide translates the war into a gangster film with an international cast. It is a universe in which the American hero triumphs because decency always wins in the end: "Mostly, the French think Americans always act square, always give the little fellow a helping hand and are good-natured, big-hearted and kind." Gangster films of the early 1930s atoned for their excesses and indulgences by offering a formal recantation and punishing the criminal in the final reel. Justice seemed somehow to reassert itself in the end. Post-war American cinema, like the literature on which much of it was based, told a different story. In the decade after the war, among the various messages communicated in film noir—that odd, rebellious child of the 1930s gangster picture—and the fiction on which much of it was based were that decency doesn't always win out and that heroes and villains can prove difficult to tell apart because their methods are very much the same.

3

THIEVES LIKE US

To England will I steal, and there I'll steal;
And patches will I get unto these cudgeled scars,
And swear I got them in the Gallia wars.

—Ancient Pistol after the Battle of Agincourt,
Shakespeare, *Henry V*

First Fascist

On February 20, 1939, the German American Bund held a rally in Madison Square Garden to celebrate the birthday of the man they hailed as "the first Fascist": George Washington. The Bund leader Fritz Kuhn expressed his patriotic "veneration . . . for the fathers of the republic," especially "the immortal Washington." The figure of Washington was essential to the Bund's meretricious selling of its message of Aryan supremacy as "pro-American." At an event the year before, *Life* reported, a New Jersey Bundsman celebrated Washington as a "realist" who "knew democracy could not work." Pictures of the first president were prominently displayed at Bund assemblies, just as they would continue to be at America First Committee events; a photograph of Charles Lindbergh addressing a large crowd in Fort Wayne, Indiana, in 1941 discloses a portrait of Washington on an easel behind him on the stage. At the Madison Square Garden rally, an enormous banner was unfurled behind the rostrum. Documentary footage shows a full-length Washington, dressed in military uniform and wearing a look of great severity, standing at a position of attention, his left hand resting on the hilt of his sword. American flags and swastikas flank him on either side.

The Bund was ostensibly arguing for American neutrality in European affairs, but Kuhn's oratory was unmistakably belligerent, while his venomous attacks on Jews, the press, and the Roosevelt administration were nothing short of incendiary. He called the New Deal the "Jew Deal" and Roosevelt, "Rosenfeld." The Bund's co-opting of George Washington perverted the legacy of a man in fact so committed to republicanism that during the attempted revolt of some monarchical military officers in 1782, an event known as the Newburgh Conspiracy, he refused a dictatorship when he might have had one. In *Two Frontiers of Freedom*, a 1940 reflection on American history in the light of contemporary crises, the journalist and critic John Corbin described the officers at Newburgh as "proposing a Fascist coup." Washington was likewise a staunch defender of religious pluralism. Finally, he was sufficiently perplexed by the circumstance of owning human beings that, unlike many of his contemporaries, he manumitted his slaves at his death.

Bundsmen, meanwhile, weren't the only ones looking to Washington for inspiration in the late 1930s; they were merely tapping into a broader national trend. The 1939 World's Fair commemorated the 150th anniversary of Washington's presidential inauguration by erecting a giant plaster likeness, dramatically backlit by the Perisphere. That same year, the Iowa painter Grant Wood turned to the subject of Washington in the wonderfully strange *Parson Weems' Fable*, which depicts the apocryphal incident of a young George Washington chopping down his father's cherry tree. As the art historian

Barbara Haskell notes, Wood was inspired by Howard Mumford Jones's 1938 *Atlantic Monthly* article, "Patriotism—But How?" Jones was prominent among a group of writers and artists watching with dismay as American fascists successfully ransacked national history for potent symbols. Fascists abroad, Jones warned, had put the glamour back into patriotism, while at home, it had been left to the extremists by "higher liberal circles," who regarded it as, to borrow Samuel Johnson's phrase, "the last refuge of a scoundrel." In view of what he called "the coming struggle," Jones insisted on the need to "revive patriotism without chauvinism, economic self-interest, or racial snobbery." Without a revival of "the history of liberty as a living faith," he challenged readers, how could the United States "combat an alien mythology of race, militarism, and an uncomfortable version of the heroic in history?"

With *Parson Weems' Fable*, Grant Wood answered Jones's call to, in Haskell's words, "mobilize nationalism while avoiding the chauvinism" linked with fascism and, ironically, with the school of American Regionalism with which Wood himself was identified. The political and aesthetic challenges presented by nationalistic or patriotic art in the 1930s were obvious, especially to those on the left who were taking note of international affairs. Once America entered the war, Haskell explains, nationalism would be effectively replaced by the ideal of internationalism. But in 1939 Wood elected to paint one of the most celebrated American myths. Critics would fault him for choosing a child's fairy tale rather than a more sophisticated story, but Wood was tapping into a deeply familiar fable. The episode he chose to paint was first popularized by Mason L. Weems, known as Parson Weems, whose *The Life of Washington* went through multiple editions after its initial publication in 1800. The cherry tree incident made its first appearance in a subsequent edition, where

Weems proclaims it "too valuable to be lost . . . too true to be doubted."

At the age of six, according to Weems, young George received a hatchet, of which he was "inordinately fond," and the boy proceeded to amuse himself by exploring his father's garden "chopping every thing that came in his way." This destructive spree eventually extends to the elder Washington's favorite cherry tree, and he demands to know the culprit's identity. George collects himself and eventually replies to Augustine: "I can't tell a lie, Pa; you know I can't tell a lie. I did cut it with my hatchet." To Weems, this illustrates George's virtue, but it also establishes a specific setting for its exercise. Augustine Washington's garden is Edenic: abundant, lush, innocent, "a wide wilderness of fruit" with a forbidden tree at its heart. Instead of spending his wrath on the boy and banishing him from the garden, however, the father forgives the transgression because of his son's manifest honesty and urges him always to be similarly forthright. George's moment of youthful excess proves to be an aberration in a career subsequently marked by discipline, rectitude, and restraint. His confession signals the promise of future virtue.

Wood's painting comments on the fable in several ways. First, the figure of the smiling Parson Weems himself occupies the foreground, where he is engaged in the act of pulling back a red curtain on the scene and pointing to the drama thereby revealed. Within this theatrical frame, Augustine, the stricken cherry tree grasped in his right hand, stretches out his left palm to George, demanding an explanation. George—not a child but a miniature adult Washington, complete with the head of Gilbert Stuart's well-known Athenaeum portrait—points guilelessly to his offending hatchet, which he holds away from his father with his left hand. The art historian Cécile Whiting proposes that this manual circuit (from Weems to Augustine to George and back outward again) involves the viewer in the drama. In the middle distance, before a solid brick house, an enslaved man and woman are in the midst of picking cherries from an unharmed tree, while the background is dominated by a manicured carpet of grass and meticulous rows of trees in the far distance. The scene is pristine and precise—almost sterile. Wood used his own Iowa farmhouse as a stand-in for the Washington manse in a gesture that, Whiting argues, collapses time and space: past and present, East and Midwest.

At first glance, the painting seems to create unity by evoking the plantation myth of idyllic Southern life: the enslaved persons, occupied with their agricultural pursuit and apparently oblivious to the great father-son drama unfolding nearby, melt into the landscape. Yet closer inspection reveals certain oddities. For instance, the male slave, dressed exactly like George in white shirt and blue breeches, doubling the national father, links master and slave and locates the latter at the center of the story. Moreover, well-lit though it may be, the entire scene is infused with an elemental starkness and coldness attributable chiefly to a dark and ominous sky. The trees themselves are shaped like globes, little worlds in danger of being jolted from their orbits by violence—by the violence of small hatchets, most immediately, but also by the adult violence of revolution, slavocracy, and civil war. Although brighter in tone, *Parson Weems' Fable* harbors the same sense of foreboding that dominates the artist's earlier meditation on American history in *The Midnight Ride of Paul Revere* (1931), as well as *Death on the Ridge Road* (1935), which depicts an impending traffic accident. *Parson Weems' Fable* also looks back to Wood's 1932 *Daughters of Revolution*, a portrait of three smug Daughters of the American Revolution in front of a painting of Washington crossing the Delaware. Stylistically, *Parson Weems' Fable* echoes Wood's earlier pastoral works, in which, as Haskell observes, "the combination of rigid geometries, shellac-like surfaces, and sharp, unnatural light produced landscapes that appear airless and still . . . a dollhouse world of estrangement and solitude."

The modernist painter Stuart Davis, the art historian H. W. Janson, and other influential critics dismissed as sentimental the various representations of the national past produced by Wood and his fellow midwestern regionalists. Davis attacked regional art as "antimodern, regressive, and even fascist in style and subject matter." Yet *Parson Weems Fable* is more complicated than this condemnation would admit, and it offers a window onto ways in which American artists and writers understood the relationship between history and their turbulent present in the 1930s and 1940s. The role of the artist within the state had been considerably altered at home by the New Deal initiative of the WPA—which supported a vast array of cultural projects, from art and architecture to music and dramatic performance—and abroad by the Nazis' sinister classification of certain artists as "degenerate." American artists wrestled with the question, posed in Howard Mumford Jones's article and elsewhere, of whether culture could productively serve anti-fascist ends without becoming a propagandist tool of the kind employed by the fascists themselves.

The answers were various, and the debate persisted after the war. The poet Robert Creeley described one of the conflict's effects on the artistic imagination: "Coming of age in the forties, in the chaos of the Second World War, one felt the kinds of coherence that might have been fact of other time and place were no longer possible. There seemed no logic . . . that could bring together all the violent disparities of that experience. The arts especially were shaken and the *picture of the world* that might previously have served them had to be reformed." The playwright Tennessee Williams acknowledged the role of technology in destroying the old logic when he described the late 1940s as "the beginning of an age of demented mechanics." The impassioned art criticism of the postwar period wrestled with these and related anxieties and, the critic Jed Perl suggests, instituted "a dramatic realignment in the relationship between the Old World and the New." Jackson Pollock's comparison of himself to Navajo sand painters, Barnett Newman's renewed poetic spirit—a response to the domination of man by science—and Mark Rothko's belief that "the familiar identity of things has to be pulverized" were all expressions of a postwar sensibility. The challenge was nothing less than to devise a new picture of the world.

Arts of War

Part of the difficulty in representing the New World amid the disintegration of the Old could be attributed to the type of war being fought. World War I, in particular the wholesale slaughter of trench warfare, had already presented significant challenges to twentieth-century artistic strategies of comprehension. That war's chroniclers, as Fussell and others have amply demonstrated, had to reckon with a new dispensation. Nevertheless, the scale and mode of mechanized warfare ushered in by the Second World War again demanded new modes of representation, of which Pablo Picasso's *Guernica*, depicting the effects of the German Luftwaffe's aerial bombardment of a Spanish town on April 26, 1937, was a harbinger. In his war reporting, John Steinbeck insisted on the impossibility of bearing witness to modern battles, in contrast to the comparatively organized affairs of the past:

> You can't see much of a battle. Those paintings reproduced in history books which show long lines of

advancing troops are either idealized or else times and
battles have changed. The account in the morning papers of the battle of yesterday was not seen by the correspondent, but was put together from reports. What the
correspondent really saw was dust and the nasty burst of
shells, low bushes and slit trenches. He lay on his stom-
ach, if he had any sense, and watched ants crawling.

Steinbeck's fellow war correspondent W. C. Heinz suggested
two emblematic subjects for any aspiring painter of the war:
"If you were a painter and could paint only one picture of
this war it would probably be of a battlefield with a dead GI.
But if you could paint two pictures, that second one would be
of the infantry moving up into the line." In fact there were a
number of visual artists working in the theaters of war, many
at the behest of the War Department itself. They included
prominent Hollywood film directors, deployed overseas as
part of photo units attached to the army or navy. As I noted
in chapter 1, the footage they shot during the war would later
make its way into feature films and documentaries alike,
mingling the fictional and real in new ways.

Various painters also found themselves at war. Jacob
Lawrence, who served in the U.S. Coast Guard, executed
a group of works called *War Series* (1946–47), completed
with the help of a Guggenheim Fellowship, an installment
in Lawrence's ongoing representation of American history
and the centrality of African Americans within it. Four
paintings, *Docking—Cigarette Joe?*, *On Leave*, *Untitled [Sail-
ors at a Bar]*, and *Naples—1944*, offer a visual realization
of John Horne Burns's account of the desperation of liberated Naples in *The Gallery*, the novel I discussed in chapter 2.
Lawrence's entire series—from *Shipping Out*, which reveals the indignities of the crowded hold of a transport ship,
to *Victory*, which depicts a GI with bowed head resting on

his rifle—offers a similarly somber and disillusioned view of wartime experience. As William I. Hitchcock notes in *The Bitter Road to Freedom*, the Allies arrived in Naples to find "the city . . . a total shambles and the people in a state of extreme filth and dejection." Moreover, they made matters even worse by initially shutting down the black market, which had been "a fairly regular source of food supplies in Italy's large cities." Another wartime artist, the GI cartoonist Bill Mauldin, popularized a similarly unromantic perspective on life in war. Pyle describes Mauldin's work as "funny" yet also "grim and real." His scruffy infantrymen Willie and Joe proved immensely popular with the GI readers of the military newspaper *Stars and Stripes*.

In *Brave Men*, Pyle introduces his readers to another artist, Lieutenant Rudolph Charles von Ripper, a man "so fabulous," Pyle explains, that he appeared to be a fraud at first glance. A wealthy Austrian by birth, von Ripper ran away from home at fifteen, traveled the world, and served in the French Foreign Legion for two years. At twenty-one he returned to Europe to study art, and Pyle thinks of him primarily as an artist. Von Ripper was also a committed anti-fascist who had been arrested by the Nazis and imprisoned for seven months in a concentration camp until the chancellor of Austria managed to free him. He then went to Spain, where he would further hone his art and serve as an aerial gunner on the Loyalist side of the Spanish Civil War. In 1938 he left Spain for the United States, became a citizen, and joined the U.S. Army. He served as a laboratory technician and as a member of something Pyle calls the Army Arts Corps before joining an infantry regiment, in which, after several engagements, he received a battlefield commission and was once again transferred, this time to the engineers. Eventually, Pyle reports, von Ripper began executing watercolors and sketches for the War Department in Naples. Pyle, clearly intrigued by von Ripper's strange amalgamation of qualities, describes him as fluctuating between "salon intellectualism" and a "hard, brutal reality" derived from long service. Pyle didn't normally "think of an artist as . . . tough or worldly," but he takes care to emphasize von Ripper's extensive combat service, even the number of times he has been shot. Although technically a kind of mercenary, von Ripper was motivated by political commitment in both his soldiering and his art.

Pyle has difficulty reconciling von Ripper's two careers, but he also surmises that his skills as a soldier might have made him a better artist. Ultimately, like almost everyone Pyle encounters in the war zone, von Ripper, committed anti-fascist though he was, "had finally become more interested in the personal, human side of war than in the abstract ideals for which wars are fought." As an artist, he avoided the all-too-familiar romance: "It's hard to be close enough to war to paint it," Pyle explains, "and still consider it heroic." Pyle describes the paintings as eventually verging on the "distorted" and "grotesque." Von Ripper gave Pyle one of his drawings, *Self-Portrait in Italy*, which shows the artist and a comrade, both wounded, along with starving children being led away by a laughing skeleton: "You get to seeing things like that when you've been a soldier for a long time," Pyle explains. Von Ripper followed a tradition of German and German-American soldier-artists such as the World War I veteran Otto Dix and the Civil War soldier Adolph Metzner, whose sketches share the element of the grotesque. After the war, von Ripper went on to practice his art. Like Jacob Lawrence, he won a Guggenheim, and he continued to paint until his death, in 1960.

The archetype of the soldier-artist has a strange odyssey in postwar culture. Sometimes sustained by the WPA before the war, but usually condemned to drifting through an inhospitable American landscape after it, artists join the many other war veterans popping up in pulp fiction, as well as in the highly stylized universe of film noir, the latter painted on the screen with chiaroscuro lights and shadows throughout the second half of the 1940s and into the 1950s. This world was in several senses the obverse of the official culture of postwar America, which was distinguished by conformity or an insistent normalcy and often represented visually in dreamlike, brightly colored advertising. Beneath this fantasy swirled another world altogether. Nelson Algren, whose 1949 novel *The Man with the Golden Arm* traced the postwar life of a veteran turned drug addict, called attention to an "enormous reservoir of sick, vindictive life that moves like an underground river beneath all our boulevards." This underground river runs through American culture, surfacing at particular moments: during the Depression, for example, and again after the war in the noir vision evoked by various novelists and filmmakers whose reflections on wartime experience expose a narrative of individual and collective disillusionment.

Numerous film historians have chronicled the rise and fall of film noir from the war through the middle of the 1950s and have analyzed its enduring stylistic, linguistic, and cultural influence. It was the French, starved of American film throughout the war, who later gave the style its name. In 1955, the critics Raymonde Borde and Étienne Chaumeton used *film noir* to describe a certain kind of American film that began to be shown in French cinemas in 1946. These films, some of which had been made during the war, include *The Maltese Falcon* (1941); *Laura* (1944); *Murder, My Sweet* (1944); *Double Indemnity* (1944); and *The Woman in the Window* (1944). Borde and Chaumeton proclaimed, "Film noir has renovated the theme of violence." Always an integral part of American film, violence, they argued, had previously been bounded by certain rules, as in the "fair fight" of the "adventure film." In place of the swashbuckling heroes of old, there now emerged "an unknown breed of men" who were ambiguous, various, and volatile: cool professional killers, unthinking brutes, or maniacal sadists, all of them equally at home in a world of chaotic violence. These films were often B pictures, the bottom halves of double bills that ran in typical movie theaters all over the country, as opposed to the grand movie palaces of New York, Los Angeles, and other major cities (although some noir ran in these grander surroundings, too). They exerted an influence on a generation of young moviegoers who might spend much of a day at the movies.

Most noirs, as James Naremore documents, had modest budgets. Studios found a "stable marketplace for low-budget thrillers," and the films were "reasonably popular and widely distributed" upon release. In subsequent decades they continued to make an impression on new generations of audiences at revival houses. To the critic Manny Farber, these were among the "underground films," best seen, as he wrote in 1957, in the "outcast theaters" of Times Square. Their "tight, melodramatic plots" were populated by a wild assortment of "stock musclemen," among whom Farber numbered the following: "A stool pigeon gurgling with scissors in his back; a fat, nasal-voiced gang leader; escaped convicts; power-mad ranch owners with vengeful siblings; a mean gun with an Oedipus complex and migraine headaches; a crooked gambler trading guns to the redskins; exhausted GI's." Unlike the crime films of the 1930s, which, as the film historian Foster Hirsch notes, "reflected their times in a direct way," 1940s noir was "less a matter of portraying specific social issues than of reflecting, generally and metaphorically, the mood of the country during and after the war." Arguably, as Hirsch contends, the most direct reflection was the portrayal of women, whose newfound independence during wartime came to seem a kind of threat once the war was over. As for the veteran, Hirsch concludes, "When he surfaces in noir, the returning soldier has the disconnectedness of the ex-con; he seems both amnesiac and somnambulist." Sometimes the veteran's problem is that he remembers all too well.

The pulps on which many of these films were based not infrequently center on the disaffected veteran. In part, of course, this owes to the simple fact that there were many millions of newly returned GIs. Charlotte Armstrong describes a hardened spirit among the young men who have returned from war in her 1950 novel *Mischief*, which tells the story of an attempted kidnapping at a Manhattan hotel. An elevator operator, Eddie Munro, notes that one of his passengers, Jed Towers, is an example of a new type of man:

> Out of the corners of their eyes, they typed each other, quickly. Eddie saw the easy grace of a tall body, the arrogant carriage of the high head, the crew cut that was somehow arrogant, too. The sharp cut of the good-looking face, the long nose with the faint flare at the nostrils, the cool gray eyes, long lashed, and almost beautiful in that hard-boned young face, but very cool and asking for nothing. A type. One of those young men who had come out of the late war with that drive, that cutting quality, as if they had shucked off human uncertainties and were aimed and hurtling toward something in the future about which they seemed very sure.

These are the men who populate "the boiling city," harboring little but mistrust for "a lousy world." Disillusioned by school, "the war, and the final bitter tutoring of the peace," Towers determines to use the doctrine of self-interest he has witnessed all around him to his own advantage—to achieve a kind of success wholly unconnected with any idealism. Resolutely cynical, he describes himself as "a young man out to 'make his fortune' as they used to say in the old stories when he was nine. Out to make his fortune without a dream in his eye." At the close of Armstrong's novel, another character offers a tentative, hardly reassuring philosophy for living in this chaotic, unfeeling world: "We oughta be scared, all right. Ignorant optimism won't do it," he insists. "But we've got *not* to be scared, just the same." Everything depends on "trust between strangers," he continues: "Everything else is a house of cards." This diluted version of FDR's counsel to fear nothing but fear itself fails to convince anyone in this bleak novel.

Few captured the new hardness Armstrong describes more effectively than Ross Macdonald (the pen name of Kenneth Millar), whose Lew Archer prowled California in eighteen novels from the 1940s to the 1970s. Macdonald published his first novel while he was still serving in the navy, and by the end of the run of Archer novels, he had earned widespread popularity and critical acclaim. Even in Archer's final appearance in *The Blue Hammer* (1976), the war continues to serve as a touchstone for the detective, as well as for the people with whom he interacts over the course of his investigations. Archer, whose military service is mentioned periodically throughout the novels, returns to find himself operating in a world altered by war. On occasion, however, he happens on "a preserve of prewar time": a neighborhood that "didn't know there had been a war" in *The Galton Case* (1959) or a woman with "a nice warm prewar . . . voice" in *The Way Some People Die* (1951).

Even the miserable relics (human and otherwise) of the Depression have for Archer a solidity and coherence absent from the postwar world, which he describes as dominated by "hardware in the sky, and dissension on earth." An attorney in *The Moving Target* (1949) delineates for Archer a "type" very much like the one Armstrong describes: "officers and gentlemen with high pay, an even higher opinion of themselves . . . War was their element, and when the war was finished, they were finished. They had to go back to boys' jobs and take orders from middle-aged civilians." Those who couldn't adjust, he concludes, tried to "snatch" success back: "They wanted to be free and happy and successful without laying any foundation for freedom or happiness or success. And there's the hangover." Almost all the Archer novels allude in one way or another to the war's cataclysm, and to the way it left Americans greedy and hard, their naked grasping after material wealth no longer softened by association with the democratic dream of a success unconnected with social class. In *The Barbarous Coast* (1956), Archer muses that "atomic fallout" has turned everyone mean. In *The Doomsters* (1958), he encounters rich men who made their money during the war by cheating interned Japanese farmers and buying up their land "at a few cents on the dollar." (Bill Mauldin illustrates this phenomenon in his second book, *Back Home*, which was published in 1947.) In *The Chill* (1963), Archer meets up with those who made out during the war but have never had it as good since.

Postwar film noir is dominated by a similar cynicism that Naremore attributes to the fact that "the war and its aftermath created a vision of ontological evil and a growing appetite for sadism." The film historian Sheri Chinen Biesen calls attention to the material, rather than simply thematic, connection between war and noir in *Blackout: World War II and the Origins of Film Noir*, in which she documents the degree to which wartime dimout and blackout restrictions, relaxed censorship, and the rationing of raw materials needed for filmmaking all contributed to the rise of noir. Yet the way these films addressed disaffection was also new, as Paul Schrader argues in the important essay "Notes on Film Noir" (1972), where he defines noir as a style rather than a genre. In a departure from American tradition, noir resolves "sociological problems" artistically rather than morally, Schrader writes. "Film noir attacked and interpreted its sociological conditions, and, by the close of the noir period, created a new artistic world which went beyond a simple sociological reflection, a nightmarish world of American mannerism which was by far more a creation than a reflection." Within a world dominated by aesthetics, the artist assumes a special significance. John Bodnar, Richard Lingeman, Mark Osteen, and others have all pointed to the special place of veterans within the film noir tradition, but the figure of the veteran-artist has a special role. As someone who makes a living by observing, reproducing, and reordering the world, the veteran-artist is an ideal tour guide through postwar noir.

The artists, writers, and actors who appear as characters in the novels and films of the period exhibit confusion, discontent, and disaffection. Take, for example, the veteran naval architect Peter Lapham (Henry Fonda), who struggles to resume his prewar life in *Daisy Kenyon* (1947); the psychopathic Lester Blaine (Jack Palance), an unsuccessful actor whose theatrical ambition was born while playing in a camp show during the war, who cons and ultimately attempts to murder his wealthy wife in *Sudden Fear* (1952); the confused and melancholy Corporal Arthur Mitchell (George Cooper), a WPA muralist before the war who ends up painting signs during the war and returns to the States only to become a suspect in a murder he didn't commit in *Crossfire* (1947); or Harry Jordan, the protagonist of Charles Willeford's 1955 novel *Pick-Up*, a failed painter and alcoholic skating on the edges of society—and sanity. Before the war, Jordan studied at the Art Institute of Chicago. Afterward, he used the GI Bill to resume his studies, but by the time we encounter him, he has given up: "I never could finish anything I started," he tells Helen, "the pick-up" of the book's title. When Helen's reaction implies that he should persist, he offers the following disillusioned meditation on American society: "The Great

American Tradition: *You can do anything you think you can
do!* All Americans believe in it. What a joke that is! Can a
jockey last ten rounds with Rocky Marciano? Can Marciano
ride in the Kentucky Derby? Can a poet make his living by
writing poetry? The entire premise was so false it was stu-
pid to contemplate." Harry's refusal to endorse the American
Dream is typical of the genre, which makes obsessive study
of the varieties of failure. The revelation on the book's final
page that Jordan is an African American further complicates
his relationship with the American Dream.

Harry and Helen drink their way through their pooled
resources and go through a series of schemes. Helen thinks
he can get in on the postwar boom because, as a veteran, he
can easily get a loan, but these schemes come to nothing, and
after a failed suicide pact, they commit themselves to drying
out in a psych ward. There Harry encounters another veteran
who has tried to kill his wife and confesses that he has "been
in and out of these places ever since the war." The hospital psychiatrist assumes that the war is the source of Harry's
self-destruction, but Harry insists that the army was not the
definitive experience in his life. The only great change his
service seems to facilitate is Harry's desertion of his family, to
whom he gives no further thought. "I don't think it affected
me at all. I was painting before I was drafted and that's all
I did after I got in." At Fort Benning, home of the infantry, Harry painted murals in mess halls and was happy. He
gave his superiors exactly what they wanted: "I painted army
scenes. Stuff like paratroopers dropping out of the sky, a
thick line of infantrymen in the field, guns, tank columns and
so on." He was dissatisfied artistically, but he also knew that
painting these dull murals was saving his life: "I was painting
while other soldiers were . . . getting shot at . . . As a special
duty man I was excused from everything except painting."
Harry resists what he judges the doctor's erratic methods and

contrasts them with his own "native intelligence" in putting together a jigsaw puzzle. "I wasn't a hero." He knows that he got "a damned good deal" while other soldiers with more talent "were never given the same breaks." And he will not blame the war for whatever prevents him from resuming his life afterward. In other words, he refuses to be pathologized by the doctor as a damaged veteran.

One of the earliest collisions of war and art in film noir occurs in the 1946 RKO film *Crack-Up*. It stars Pat O'Brien as George Steele, a former army captain who, in his capacity as a member of the Allied Reparations Commission, exposed forgeries the Nazis had substituted for stolen masterpieces and then unloaded on the global black market. Steele gives public lectures at a New York art museum; his desire to democratize art appreciation ruffles the feathers of the museum's patrician board members, one of whom calls his approach "revolutionary," while a disgusted Steele demands that the board decide whether they are running "a public institution or an exclusive tea party." Steele's politics may be radical, but his preference for traditional art and his ridicule of abstraction signal a cultural conservatism.

Steele is framed for murder when his plan to x-ray a painting in preparation for his next lecture threatens to expose a board member's complicity in an international forgery ring. As is typical of the way former service members are portrayed in these movies, Steele's war record is at once the foundation of his credibility, as acknowledged by his employer, as well as a liability, because it makes him somehow unpredictable and ultimately unknowable, even to his girlfriend Terry (Claire Trevor), who longs for some kind of postwar normalcy: "For the first time in three years I began to sense what life could be like again," she tells him after a romantic dinner that has been interrupted. Their recovered normalcy is now threatened by Steele's increasingly erratic, volatile behavior as he tries to clear himself. Steele himself feels that he has "time to make up"—as he tells a friend who urges him to relax—because the war has stolen three valuable years from him. In a subsequent discussion with Terry, he confesses his deep anxiety about cracking up: "I've seen a lot of good guys crack up in this war," he confides in her, "cool, composed cookies . . . snap like a tight violin string." Cracking up is the "one fear everybody had," he tells her: "I kept thinking it might happen to me." But Steele cannot rest; he almost destroys himself and Terry in his quest for the truth.

"Odd, isn't it, that truth should be a by-product of war?" muses *Crack-Up*'s villain, the doctor who has pretended all along to be helping Steele. Toward the end of the film, he prepares to inject Steele with truth serum, a process the doctor calls "narcosynthesis," which, he explains, was discovered during the war and which theoretically enables a man "to communicate with his true self." As is commonplace in noir, the most portentous statements about truth come from the mouths of criminals who appear to be the most respectable members of society. Steele's courageous postwar quest for truth dovetails with his wartime occupation of exposing forgeries. Perversely, by tracing the global black market to New York, he has discovered a connection between the American elite and the very enemy he had labored to defeat, as well as a corresponding divide between this elite and the people with whom he is trying to share his enthusiasm for art. The strongest kinship exists between the domestic villain (a respected physician, distinguished citizen, and board member of a civic institution) and the Nazis Steele has just returned from fighting.

Noir frequently asserts the uncanny resemblance between enemy governments abroad and home-front profiteers. While GIs have been away fighting, everyone at home seems to have gotten rich. *Nobody Lives Forever* (1946) opens with the con man Nick Blake (John Garfield) leaving a veterans hospital on Governors Island to reclaim the $50,000 he had entrusted to his duplicitous girlfriend. Al Doyle (George Tobias), the pal who meets him at the gates, happily reports that postwar business is booming, with Broadway full of "suckers" and demobilized "square Johns" ripe for the taking: "It's getting just like the old prohibition days. Loose dough. Everybody making it and throwing it away with both hands." Blake, meanwhile, as a result of his time away, seems to have lost his "nerve" for the con.

In *Ride the Pink Horse* (1947), the veteran Gagin (Robert Montgomery) gets off the bus in a small New Mexican town with his service revolver and a plan to take revenge on his friend's killer, a man named Hugo (Fred Clark). There he encounters a government agent named Retz (Art Smith), who warns him away: "You're like the rest of the boys—all cussed up because you fought a war for three years and got nothing but a dangle of ribbons." When Retz tells Gagin to let his "Uncle Samuel" take care of Hugo, Gagin responds, "Doesn't the government work for Hugo? It did all during the war."

Similarly, the protagonist of *The Phenix City Story* (1955)—a documentary-style noir based on the true story of a sensationally corrupt Alabama town just across the river from Fort Benning—returns from one war only to find another waiting for him at home. John Patterson (Richard Kiley) is an attorney who has just left the army and brought his family home from Germany to Phenix City. Soldiers from Benning provide an endless supply of suckers for the city's bars and gambling joints. Disgusted by the lawlessness and violence of his hometown, Patterson commits himself to fighting it, at no small risk to his family. When his wife, terrified by the murder of a child and a threat to her own children, tells him they should have stayed in Germany, where it was "safer," the analogy between the gangsters who terrorize Phenix City and those who tried to destroy Europe becomes clear.

Like Harry Jordan of Willeford's *Pick-Up*, Jim Vanning, the protagonist of David Goodis's 1947 novel *Nightfall*, is a visual artist and veteran. Having trained as an engineer before the war, Vanning first took up painting to relax. Upon discovering that he had talent, he determined to approach it as a vocation. At art school in Chicago he grows to realize that while he isn't good enough for "fine art," he can make a living as a commercial artist. During the war, as a damage control officer on a battleship, he saw action in the Pacific, but "luck stayed" with him, and he "wasn't even scratched." In contrast to many of the veterans in the pulps of the period, Vanning has a job waiting for him when he returns. Art is incidental to his story: it provides him with a career and stability, but it doesn't necessarily offer him particular insights or help him to make sense of all that happens to him. It is a means, like many other occupations, to achieving economic success—to making it. In a flashback, he remembers how it felt after he got his discharge papers and started for home, full of hope, in a convertible coupe he bought in Los Angeles:

> The top was down and the sky was very clear and . . . the war was over and that agency in Chicago was the kind that kept its promises . . . and . . . they had told him to come on back and go to work . . . He was thinking, before the war they had paid him five thousand a year. That was the kind of outfit it was. He felt good about going back. He felt good about everything. Chicago was an all-right place, and someday in the not too far distant future he ought to be meeting a nice girl and getting married and starting a home. It was a fine thing

to be thirty-two and alive and healthy. It was a marvelous thing to be starting fresh.

As this is a novel by David Goodis, not Horatio Alger, the
dream can't last. Soon Vanning finds himself the victim of
the "wrong man" plot so common to the genre. Stopping by
the side of the road to assist motorists at the scene of an accident,
an act that derails his life, Vanning ends up with a revolver in
his face. The accident victims turn out to be bank robbers, and
the Good Samaritan becomes a wanted man. When we first
meet him, he is on the run, keeping a low profile in Greenwich
Village and making his living as a commercial artist, but this
safety is impermanent. It is only the latest stop in a solitary
life on the run, to which Vanning long ago reconciled himself:
"This one tiny, moving, breathing thing called Vanning, and
what it meant to him was fear and fleeing. And hiding."

When a determined detective named Fraser enters the
scene, the novel addresses head-on the problem of returning veterans. Fraser develops sympathy for Vanning as he
surveils him and studies his habits. Having begun to question Vanning's guilt, the detective shares his doubts with his
wife. He can't figure out how this man without a criminal
record and with a stable employment history could end up a
bank robber and a murderer. His wife replies, "A lot of men
came back from the war and had the wrong outlook and got
themselves in trouble." Fraser admits that everyone else at
headquarters thinks the same thing. Scores of books and
films also express this anxiety—that men have come back
from the war changed for the worse. Yet Fraser remains unconvinced, and when he manages to find at least one other
detective who feels the same way, he gets the information he
needs to solve the case and clear Vanning. "Silver Star. Excellent record," Fraser's sympathetic colleague admits: "It's
an upside-down case."

Upside-Down Cases

Among the most disturbing "upside-down" cases of postwar noir is Dixon Steele, the serial-killer protagonist of Dorothy B. Hughes's novel *In a Lonely Place*, published in 1947 and adapted, with considerable alterations, into a 1950 movie starring Humphrey Bogart as a Hollywood screenwriter and Gloria Grahame as his lover, who can't quite rid herself of the suspicion that he's a murderer. In the film, Steele is wrongly suspected of killing a cloakroom attendant who works at the restaurant he frequents, but he is under suspicion because of his manifest propensity for violence. We discover that he was a good officer in the Air Corps, but his agent explains that he "hasn't had a hit since the war" because of an inability to concentrate on his work. When the police review his arrest record, they uncover a history of violence dating from 1946. The film thus implies that while Dix's volatility may have predated the war—his agent describes it as elemental to his personality— his service has somehow intensified it and prevented him from resuming the heights of his prewar career. (Critics have also argued that the film is an allegory of the Hollywood blacklist.)

In Hughes's novel, by contrast, Steele's guilt is unequivocal, and Hughes takes us deep into the mind of a serial killer whose first murder took place in England during the war. Unlike that of the celebrated, if troubled, screenwriter of the film, in the novel Steele's career as a writer is itself a fiction, which he invents to conceal his true vocation as a prolific serial killer: "Like ninety-three and one-half per cent of the ex-armed forces, I'm writing a book," he tells the wife of his war buddy, Brub, a detective who happens to be assigned to the case of the serial killer. Unlike the other aspiring veteran-writers, Steele announces that he is writing not a war memoir but a novel. Steele's life has been soured by resentment and laziness. He lives on the fringes of successful society, with a stingy rich uncle who allows him just enough money to go to Princeton. Once there, he sponges off his well-to-do classmates. After the war, with no interest in getting a job, he figures out a way to survive by killing a college friend and taking over his apartment, his clothes, his liquor, and his car. (There are parallels here to Patricia Highsmith's later and better-known Ripley novels.)

The war intensifies Steele's preexisting pathologies and unleashes his violence, but his rage originates—and has always been intimately bound up with—issues of wealth and social class. As the novel's title intimates, Dix Steele is a creature of the night, a solitary stalker in "a lonely place" who hates and preys on women in the dangerous urban landscape. Killing them gives him the only satisfaction he can get from postwar life. The novel opens with the restless Steele roaming the streets of Los Angeles, searching for the same thrill he once got from flying night missions: "He'd missed it after the war had crashed to a finish and dribbled to an end." There had been a "wildness" about dangerous missions that he is able to recapture only by killing women. The army brought Dix "the first happy years he'd ever known," not only because of the visceral excitement of flying but also because of the new socioeconomic status it conferred.

For the first time, Steele was well paid and didn't have to defer to the rich; he reveled in the particular prestige of pilots, his newly acquired "class," and the attentions of women. He rose to the rank of colonel and ended the war with a "cushy job" as adjutant to a general in England. So transformative was his status within military hierarchy that Dix was persuaded of its enduring reality even after the war ended. Only when he finds himself trapped in his uncle's house once again after his discharge does he realize that he has confused "interlude for life span." But the wholesale destruction of war—especially the air war of the pilot—teaches Steele how easy it is to kill and to get away with killing. He discovers that no one much cares about a single life amid so much death. The electric arousal of killing in war has no analogue in civilian life. Although he momentarily envies the normalcy and "happiness" he perceives in the homelife of Brub and his wife, Sylvia, he almost immediately rejects the mere "quicksilver" of such postwar contentment in favor of the "excitement and power and the hot stir of lust" he derives from stalking and murdering women.

At what amounts to a reunion dinner at the detective's house, the two men explore their motivations for joining up. Brub jokes that he fought the war to get home to Sylvia. When she in turn asks Steele why he fought, he decides to impress her with the following reply: "I've wondered about it frequently, Sylvia. Why did I or anyone else fight the war? Because we had to isn't good enough. I didn't have to when I enlisted. I think it was because it was the thing to do. And the Air Corps was the thing to do. All of us in college were nuts about flying. I was a sophomore at Princeton when things were starting. I didn't want to be left out of any excitement." Brub counters with some retrospective bombast of his own: "It was the thing to do or that was the rationalization. We're a casual generation, Dix, we don't want anyone to know we bleed if we're pricked. But self-defense is one of the few prime instincts left. Despite the cover-up, it was self-defense. And we knew it." Brub's explanation combines primal instincts and stoic masculinity, with perhaps a hint of duty or patriotism, but it is Steele's explanation that makes war seem less a cause than a fashion. The glamorous Air Corps becomes the social outsider's American Dream come true. The tragedy for Steele is not the war, but the fact that it had to end.

"I Steal"

Steele may be one of the most extreme incarnations of the alienated veteran in postwar fiction—his name itself an evocation of treachery and force—but his irascibility, emotional isolation, and inability to reacclimate to peacetime is consistent with the portraits of veterans found throughout the late 1940s and 1950s, not only in the cultural "underground," to borrow Manny Farber's term, but also in the mainstream. Scores of films throughout the period address—in ways direct or oblique, in the main or in passing—the challenges of veteran readjustment and examine the fate of veterans at the margins of American society. They include dramas that explore the physical and psychological wounds of war: *Pride of the Marines* (1945), *The Best Years of Our Lives* (1946), *Till the End of Time* (1946), *Homecoming* (1948), *The Man in the Gray Flannel Suit* (1956). They also include comedies that address readjustment in a different register: *Hail the Conquering Hero* (1944), *The Hucksters* (1947), *Good Sam* (1948). In the last of these, the title character's listless brother-in-law is one of the more than eight million veterans who took a year's "readjustment allowance" from the government. The allowance was made available to veterans who were unemployed or earned under a certain threshold. As the historian Joseph C. Goulden notes in *The Best Years: 1945–1950*, those who took it were regarded as loafers by civilians and fellow veterans alike. Finally, there were films that used the war and its veterans as an occasion to direct attention to various social injustices: *Bright Victory* (1951) and *Bad Day at Black Rock* (1955) dramatize racism against Black and Japanese American GIs respectively, while *Gentleman's Agreement* (1947) and *Crossfire* both treat the issue of anti-Semitism. The latter film substituted this issue for the anti-gay violence depicted in the original novel, Richard Brooks's *The Brick Foxhole* (1945).

Noir, in other words, offers only the most stylized, surreal reflection of the experience of war and its constantly recrudescing memories, memories that erupted across genres and registers, from highbrow to low: from Norman Mailer's *The Naked and the Dead* to the pulps, from the largely neglected tradition of American war poetry to the movies. In a review of *Poets of World War II*, an anthology edited by the veteran and poet Harvey Shapiro, the critic Helen Vendler describes this body of work as ranging from "lyric sweetness" to "self-exempting satire." If, as Vendler suggests, the tradition registers "a relative absence of guilt," it also evinces a lack of naïve enthusiasm or ideological commitment. This poetry tends to simmer with an anger more often directed at American institutions than at the enemy. Its speakers are often cast, Vendler notes, as the victims of the state that conscripted them rather than as the perpetrators of shocking violence.

It is the home-front crime story, however, that most urgently takes up the issue of an American violence come home to roost. Through the vehicle of the crime story—blackmail, heist, even murder—these works highlight the deep ambivalence, forgotten over time, that once characterized attitudes to the war itself and those who fought it. A rise in crime—fueled by veteran and nonveteran perpetrators, of course—followed the Civil War, World War I, and World War II. The rate of incarceration among Vietnam veterans is especially high. In 1978, at a time when nineteen percent of Americans had military service, twenty-four percent of inmates in state facilities were veterans. That percentage began to drop in 1998, and veterans are today no more likely than the nonveteran population to find themselves in jail or prison. A 2011–12 Department of Justice study revealed that of the country's incarcerated, eight percent, or 181,500, were veterans.

Historically, there has been a tendency to mistake a correlation between military service and incarceration for causation; crime among veterans is linked directly to military service while other aspects of a criminal's history are neglected. After World War II, a study of eleven prisons in the upper Mississippi Valley concluded that from 1947 to 1949 a little more than a third of those incarcerated were veterans of World War I or II. After extensive research, including interviews with prisoners and wardens, the study's author, Walter A. Lunden, who published his findings in the *Journal of Criminal Law and Criminology* in 1952, concluded, "It cannot be said with any degree of certainty that military experience causes service men to commit crimes after they return to civilian life." In perhaps ten percent of cases, he continued, "military experience may have had some connection with later civilian crimes."

Nevertheless, as Richard Lingeman notes in *The Noir Forties*, the "violent crime film" was also "the most commercially successful kind of veterans' stories." Audiences were primed to accept a connection between military service and crime. War service also tends to feature in the lives of the police and detectives as well as the criminals in these stories. In addition to Macdonald's Lew Archer, Chester Himes's Harlem police detectives "Grave Digger" Jones and "Coffin Ed" Johnson (and, a much later incarnation beginning in the 1990s, Walter Mosley's Easy Rawlins) have military experience that has shaped their worldviews and armed them with particular insights into violence and human nature. Whether private detectives who have been kicked off the police force or renegades working uneasily within departments for bosses who do not appreciate their idiosyncratic methods, the outlaw status of these detectives mirrors that of the criminals they pursue.

Bowing to government organs of censorship such as the Office of War Information and, after 1945, to other considerations such as the still-enforced Hollywood Production Code, many films offer a contrived resolution to the problems they explore: operations are successful, wounds are healed, veterans regain their equilibrium, prejudice magically falls before a demonstration of moral rectitude, criminals pay their due, platitudes abound. The film critic Pauline Kael told Studs Terkel that the "whole spirit of the country" during the war had a sanitized appearance: "Everybody was patriotic and shiny-faced. Wiped clean of any personality. Even after the war, when William Wyler made *The Best Years of Our Lives*, a sensitive movie, by no means cheerful—even that had the look of a *Life* magazine cover." The habitual optimism of Hollywood was expressed largely in the promise of economic success coated with the patina of moral restraint. For example, MGM's *The Hucksters*, a vehicle for Clark Gable, who had himself recently come home from wartime service as a pilot, tells the story of a veteran, Vic Norman, who has returned to the radio advertising business only to be disgusted by the hucksterism he had blithely participated in before the war. Everything "looks different" to him afterward, he declares to Kay Dorrance (Deborah Kerr), the very respectable war widow he wants to marry, yet the film ends not with his rejection of the advertising business, but with a new determination, articulated by Kay, to sell only things in which he "believes . . . with dignity and taste." Having signed on to this newly purified postwar capitalist dream, Vic gives away his last dollar, a symbolic gesture, before driving off into a future that looks bright, happy, and sufficiently remunerative.

It is chiefly in film noir that the relentless optimism of Hollywood recedes entirely before a far grimmer picture. In contrast to the establishment, the conformists, and the organization men, noir's sordid world of drifters, grifters, and con artists sounds a steady counterpoint to the mainstream Cold War narrative of American righteousness and self-satisfaction. A few movies, probing discontent before dismissing it, occupy a kind of middle ground. *Till the End of Time* is one of a trio of films—the others are *Pride of the Marines* (1945) and *The Best Years of Our Lives*—attempting to show the unvarnished truth about the struggles of the wounded. Like the others, it ends on a note of measured hope, but before it does so, its main character, Cliff Harper (Guy Madison), sounds what might be thought of as the keynote of veteran dissatisfaction. A marine who knows he is "normal" and "lucky" compared with one friend who has a steel plate in his head and another who has lost his legs, Harper nevertheless can't help feeling "edgy" and "out of things . . . because I've been scrounged. I'm robbed out of three and a half years. Somebody stole my time." When Pat (Dorothy McGuire), the war widow he wants to marry, warns him, "You can't twist up the rest of your life worrying about lost time," he remains unconvinced.

Having been estranged in one way or another—even from themselves—veterans come home in these films to operate at least for a time on the psychological and socioeconomic margins of civil society: most often in the harsh city, but sometimes in the seemingly idyllic small town (and, as I explore in chapter 5, on the lawless frontier of the resurgent Western). There is no clearer expression of the message of this category of film than the text superimposed over the nighttime urban street scene at the beginning of *Kiss the Blood Off My Hands* (1948), an American studio film about a Canadian veteran's misadventures in London:

> The aftermath of war is rubble—the rubble of cities and of men—They are the casualties of a pitiless destruction.
>
> The cities can be rebuilt, but the wounds of men, whether of the mind or of the body, heal slowly.

>This is the story of one such man; and of the girl
>whose path he crossed . . .

This title addresses not only the often-invisible wounds of veterans but also, in the allusion to "the girl whose path he crossed," the fact that the sometimes cruel chance that dominates war now seems to govern peace as well.

Like the credo of leaving no one behind, the motif of the veteran's voluntary or enforced marginality in the face of society's resentment and suspicion has ancient roots, most notably in circuitous tales of postwar wanderings, deferred homecomings, and intimate betrayals. One of the most celebrated of these stories is that of the Greek chieftain Agamemnon, who returns home to be murdered in his bath by his wife, Clytemnestra. Both have been adulterers, and this fable of mutual betrayal forms the subject of Aeschylus's *Agamemnon* and threads through Homer's *Odyssey*, where it serves as a repeated warning to Odysseus—gifted warrior, enforced nomad, ingenious criminal outlaw of the ancient world—about the dangers of homecoming and the need for the armor of disguise. In American film, the archetype of the returning veteran carries many of the attributes of the wandering Odysseus: an intimacy with violence, deep ambivalence about organized society, and an urge, or a practical need, to conceal certain aspects of the past in order to survive in an altered postwar landscape.

The *Odyssey* features a series of trials, one of the most devastating of which occurs on the island of Thrinacia, home of the magnificent cattle of the sun god Helios, when Odysseus loses his last remaining crew members. In the epic's opening lines we learn what will happen: Odysseus's courage will not be enough to save his crew from being destroyed by "their own recklessness" in slaughtering and eating a herd of cattle that belongs to Helios. Odysseus is admonished twice over the course of the poem—once in the Underworld by the seer Tiresias and again above ground by the sorceress Circe—not to touch the sun god's cattle, lest he be the lone survivor, adrift and alienated, his "house filled with trouble: insolent men / eating your livestock as they court your lady." When, halfway through the poem, the survivors finally reach the isle of Helios, the reader well knows the doom that awaits. Socked in by a contrary wind, running rapidly through their supplies, gazing daily on the cattle, sheep, and oxen that graze about the island, the Ithacans resist the temptation of cattle rustling until they begin to starve. Taking advantage of Odysseus's visit inland to pray to the gods for guidance, the desperate crew are spurred on to slaughter the cattle by the brazen Eurylochus, who declares, "Better / open your lungs to a big sea once for all / than waste to skin and bones on a lonely island!" Eurylochus gets his wish. Only Odysseus, who refuses to partake, manages to survive this ordeal; his entire crew dies soon after in a coastal shipwreck.

This single episode, foreshadowed no fewer than three times by Homer, its climactic significance underscored by appropriately horrific supernatural detail—"cowhides began to crawl, and beef, both raw / and roasted, lowed like kine upon the spits"—assembles essential elements of an enduring myth about a soldier's homecoming. Homer's veterans steal and thereby transgress established norms: the rightful owner of the property (Helios) demands redress, and the judge (Zeus, in this case) punishes the guilty veterans with death. The veterans, comrades in suffering, have been reduced to theft by desperation. They steal, yet they are simultaneously the victims of a less fungible swindle: war and the trials associated with homecoming have stolen years from their lives. Although Odysseus's restraint ensures his survival, he becomes an unwilling accomplice, helplessly enmeshed in the criminal acts of others. Finally, Odysseus himself comes home to find himself the victim of a monumental theft. As Tiresias promises, after twenty years away, he encounters "a house filled with trouble: insolent men" consuming his "livestock," just as his own men once did the cattle of the sun god, and aggressively courting his loyal wife, Penelope. He will ultimately avenge this theft with a terrifying explosion of violence.

In *Odysseus in America*, Jonathan Shay explores psychological aspects of the parallel between the warriors in Homer's *Odyssey* and American veterans coming home from Vietnam, but these correspondences reach further back in American culture. The specific story of veterans reduced to theft can be found in the early days of cinema, and it appears with increased frequency in the years following World War II. In 1944 the Columbia University sociologist Willard Waller had warned America of the dangers of the returning veteran in his study *The Veteran Comes Back*. Veterans, he wrote there, always had been, and would continue to be, "America's gravest social problem."

Forgotten Men

In addition to these long cultural roots, the character of the World War II veteran-as-thief also has a more immediate cinematic antecedent, found in the gangster and social realism films of the 1930s. In these films, the veteran is often an alien, the object of the same suspicions and resentments directed at immigrants and outsiders. The message repeatedly sounded in these films—that America must remember its veterans after the next war—seemingly would be forgotten. Throughout the interwar period, the World War I veteran served as a representative for millions of Depression-era dispossessed in films such as Mervyn LeRoy's *I Am a Fugitive from a Chain*

Gang (1932), in which James Allen (Paul Muni) is a veteran wrongfully convicted of a crime. The film historian David Thomson suggests that this film reveals the degree to which the United States is "a country where awkwardness is shut away and forgotten, or executed," a nation "still terrified of its own outcast energy." Based on the book *I Am a Fugitive from a Georgia Chain Gang!*, by Robert Elliott Burns, the film makes certain alterations to the original story, alterations that link the protagonist's fate to the war more directly. In real life, Burns was a drifter even before the war; in the film, it is the war that changes the course of his life. When his family insists that he return to his prewar job at a factory, he protests that he can no longer bear routine. "The Army changes a man," he tells his mother. He simply cannot "take up where [he] left off" but wants to get moving and accomplish something. Having had experience as an engineer during the war, he wants to do "a man's work" by building and creating things.

Wandering the country from job to job, Allen is unwittingly made an accomplice to a lunch counter stickup. Forced at gunpoint by another drifter to empty the cash register of its $5.81, he is sentenced to ten years on a southern chain gang. As the repeated indices of calendar pages dropping away emphasize, the state has effectively stolen his life. Finding this fate unendurable, Allen escapes to Chicago, where he works as a laborer on a bridge-building project by day and studies civil engineering by night until he rises to become a successful, well-respected engineer. He is eventually exposed and forced to return to serve what he is promised will be a ninety-day sentence, in exchange for a full pardon.

But the state reneges on the deal, and realizing that he will be imprisoned indefinitely, Allen escapes again from the prison farm and disappears. A headline asks "What has become of James Allen? Has he become one of the 'forgotten men'?" We see him one last time, when he returns to Chicago to visit the woman he loves. "How do you live?" she asks. "I steal," he replies in one of American cinema's most haunting final lines, as he slips into the darkness, presumably forgotten forever. The veteran who wanted only to be free and unfettered ends up being forced to "keep moving" perpetually. In its representation of the veteran's discontent and inability simply to resume his prewar life, *I Am a Fugitive from a Chain Gang* is representative: wrongly accused, sometimes partly complicit, the veteran steals and also has his life stolen from him in the films of the 1930s.

Released the following year, William Wellman's *Heroes for Sale* (1933) also entangles a veteran in a criminal plot. Its protagonist, Tom Holmes (Richard Barthelmess), is a wounded World War I veteran treated more humanely in a German prison hospital than he is at home. The protagonist's victimization begins in the war itself: a hometown friend, thinking Holmes dead, takes the credit for his battlefield heroism and the medals and accolades that are rightfully his. Back home, Holmes, working in a bank, contemplates stealing money to feed his morphine habit. In desperation, he goes to the town's doctor begging for help, but the doctor insists that he will have to report him to the state, despite the fact that the shame might kill Tom's mother. "It's not my fault," Tom cries. "It's not my fault if I steal. It's not my fault if I kill somebody. I'm going crazy."

Cured of his morphine addiction at the state narcotic farm, Holmes leaves town and ends up in Chicago, where his ingenuity allows him to rise from driving a laundry truck to middle management. Eventually, when an invention he helps to license ends up costing some of his fellow workers their jobs, Holmes becomes the target of their Luddite wrath as they decide to "smash the machines." Arrested for inciting a riot he was in fact attempting to put down, he also loses his wife, who is brutally clubbed in the chaos. Sent to jail, labeled a troublemaker by the police department's "Red Squad" when he returns, Tom signs over the royalties he has been earning all the while to his landlady, who runs a soup kitchen, leaves his young son in her devoted care, and joins the legion of "forgotten men" tramping from one town to the next. "Who you calling reds and hobos?" he asks a lawman herding a group of drifters onto a train headed out of town: "We're ex-servicemen." When Tom's young son asks the landlady about his father, she makes clear what the film has implied throughout: "He lives for everyone but himself. He's given everything and taken nothing."

In 1932, the year of *Fugitive*'s release, the government had violently quashed the "outcast energy" embodied by a "Bonus Expeditionary Force" of almost twenty thousand impoverished World War I veterans who marched on Washington demanding early payment of their promised pensions. Douglas MacArthur commanded the troops that advanced down Pennsylvania Avenue from the White House to disperse the veterans. Later that night, MacArthur ordered his troops to advance on the veterans' encampment on the Anacostia Flats and burn it. (The full story is told by Paul Dickson and Thomas B. Allen in *The Bonus Army: An American Epic*.) Seven years later, in 1939, Hollywood was still telling the story of the disenfranchised veteran reduced to a life of crime.

Acts of Violence

Raoul Walsh's *The Roaring Twenties* (1939) begins with a narrator's suggestion that the present unrest in Europe has eclipsed that earlier war, when so many Americans—like the film's unemployed protagonist Eddie Bartlett (James Cagney)—returned from the Western Front to join "a new kind of . . . criminal army" of bootleggers, America's new "adventuresome heroes." This film was a belated contribution to the Warner Bros. gangster cycle, a genre eloquently anatomized by Robert Warshow, an ingenious mid-twentieth-century critic of American popular culture, in a 1948 meditation on the significance of the gangster archetype. "The Gangster as Tragic Hero" begins with the premise that "America, as a social and political organization, is committed to a cheerful view of life." A "sense of tragedy," Warshow contends, "is a luxury of aristocratic societies" not committed to the social and political significance of an individual's fate, whereas the modern state—by which he means democratic as well as communist authoritarian societies—transforms happiness into a paramount political issue because the state exists for the sole purpose of augmenting "the quality and the possibilities of human life." Only in certain contexts can the tragic strain—the obverse of democracy's insistence on optimism—insinuate itself into art, and in the gangster film Warshow discovers "a consistent and astonishingly complete presentation of the modern sense of tragedy." The gangster, he asserts, in rejecting optimism, rejects "Americanism" itself. His urban dystopia, with its dangers and deceptions, stands as the antithesis to a bucolic idyll of America as old as Thomas Jefferson.

The gangster of the movies, in contrast to the mundane criminal of the real world, is the imaginary hero: "He is what we want to be and what we are afraid we may become." In a looking-glass inversion of the Horatio Alger story, the gangster—poor, lacking both social and institutional advantages—makes his way with a set of "ambiguous skills." Because it simultaneously involves both legitimate enterprise and sadistic violence, the gangster's career, Warshow argues, exposes the predatory nature at the root of all economic success: "In the deeper layers of the modern consciousness, *all* means are unlawful, every attempt to succeed is an act of aggression, leaving one alone and guilty and defenseless among enemies: one is *punished* for success. This is our intolerable dilemma: that failure is a kind of death and success is evil and dangerous, is—ultimately—impossible." According to War-show, the figure of the gangster, precisely because he is killed for his success, makes us feel safe: "For the moment, we can acquiesce in our failure, we can choose to fail."

A signal difference between the interwar gangster films and the later crime dramas often grouped under the category of film noir is that the latter rarely offer even the promise of success, legitimate or otherwise. The gangster film charts its protagonist's rise and fall; the noir begins, at best, at the central character's tenuous and usually modest height of happiness and success, and the only direction from there is down. More often, noir begins in the depths, flashing back to a wrong turn that can't be righted. Its plot is fueled by retri-bution for the errors of the past, its protagonist harried down lonely highways, through desolate diners, late-night bus ter-minals, and shabby hotel rooms decorated with the buckshot pattern of cigarette burns. Noir is a world ruled by bad de-cisions but also by bad timing. Chance, which plays such a pivotal role in war, bleeds into this world, too, to derail lives.

Those veterans who have achieved a modest version of the postwar American Dream are bored and frustrated by the routine. They don't want to be suckers, square Johns, or "or-ganization men," to use the phrase the sociologist William H. Whyte coined in 1956 to describe the legion of men who abandoned the American cult of the individual in favor of belonging to corporate America. Tom Rath, the protagonist of Sloan Wilson's *The Man in the Gray Flannel Suit* (1955), became one of American fiction's most celebrated organiza-tion men, his postwar disillusionment dissipating before the descent into tragedy typical of noir. The veteran Rath and his wife, Betsy, live in the Connecticut suburbs. Tom, donning his gray flannel suit for the daily commute to New York City, meets up with an old army acquaintance, who reveals that Tom's wartime affair in Italy resulted in a child. Established at the outset of the novel, the disrepair of the Raths' house is the unsubtle symbol of a general dissatisfaction. Betsy declares, "All I know is that I lived on the belief that everything would be marvelous after the war, and that we've both been half dead ever since you got home." Tom discovers that even the war itself, and his distinguished record in it, far from being the subject of congratulation or nostalgic reminiscence, has become unfashionable, eclipsed by another. When the topic of his service does come up during an interview, he feels the need to explain, "Not Korea. The one before that."

In fact, Tom has tried hard to forget about the war: "It is as necessary to forget it now as it was to learn it in the first place. They ought to begin wars with a course in basic training and end them with a course in basic forgetting. The trick is to learn to believe that it's a disconnected world, a lunatic world, where what is true now was not true then." One of the lessons of the novel is that the war is not disconnected at all: the illegitimate child, whose existence he reveals to Betsy, is proof of the fact that it is impossible to draw the "clear line" he wanted to insert between war and peace. The other lesson Tom learns is that he no longer believes in the prewar dream he shared with Betsy. It is an unselfconsciously white-supremacist Hollywood fantasy: "optimism, the implicit belief that before long they would move into a house something like Mount Vernon, with nice old darky servants nodding and singing all the time, a place where they would grow old gracefully, not getting fat, but becoming only a little gray around the temples, a mansion where they would of course be happy, real happy for the rest of their lives." He no longer credits "the dream," and he can't "even find it interesting or sad in its improbability. Like an old man, he had been preoccupied with the past, not the future. He had changed, and she had not." Wilson's novel ends with Betsy and Tom united in their desire to provide for Tom's child; Betsy's initial shock and flight precede acceptance, apology, and the prospect of some more mature version of domestic honesty and happiness.

Happy endings are much harder to come by in noir. *Pitfall* (1948) offers a sinister West Coast version of this story. John Forbes (Dick Powell) is an executive at the Olympic Mutual Insurance Company who lives a life of routine. The film opens with John confessing his discontent to his wife, Sue (Jane Wyatt). She was voted prettiest in the class, he most likely to succeed, he reminds her; they had once dreamed of building a boat and sailing it around the world. "What happened to those people?" he demands. When he complains of feeling "like a wheel within a wheel within a wheel," Sue replies, "You and fifty million others . . . You're John Forbes, average American, backbone of the country." The couple's familiar, largely good-natured banter makes it clear that this mood periodically descends on John. His malaise owes not to any war trauma. In fact, even his war experience was undramatic. Asked by his son, Tommy (Jimmy Hunt), what he did, he replies, "Anything I was told." When the boy—who tells him that his friend's father earned a Silver Star—asks where he was, he and Sue explain that he spent most of it in Denver, Colorado, and ended up with a Good Conduct ribbon. This time, however, John's malaise coincides with his meeting a woman named Mona Stevens (Lizabeth Scott), whom he happens to be investigating in connection with an embezzlement case for which the insurance company is liable. When he goes to her apartment to collect the goods her boyfriend has purchased for her with the stolen funds, she calls him "a little man with a briefcase. You go to work every morning, and you do as you're told." Forbes's frustration boils over at this point, and he embarks on a very brief affair that leads to a series of lies and a killing that is ruled a justifiable homicide.

Sue, increasingly concerned by her husband's erratic behavior, tries to get him to tell her what's the matter: "After all, nothing's too tough for us. We won the war together. You brought Tommy through pneumonia." But only after the killing does John confess the whole sordid story. The film ends not with a clear resolution, but with Sue's decision not to divorce him, after having asked herself how long a man who has been a good husband—except for one twenty-four-hour period—has to "pay" for his mistake. But the film refuses to end as most contemporaneous melodramas end, and the success of their reunion is by no means clear. Sue suggests that he ask for a transfer to a new town so as to avoid raising their son amid scandal. She makes no promises: "I'm not sure it will ever be the same. Not for a long time, anyway. But we've weathered other things. Maybe we can handle this." When John assures her that he wants to try, Sue replies, in the film's final line, "All right. That's what we'll do. We'll try."

Act of Violence (1948) tells an even more disturbing story of another apparently successful veteran, Frank Enley (Van Heflin), a former bomber pilot whose postwar respectability and prosperity is built on a lie. David Thomson describes the film's subject as "the slow stain of war." Enley lives in the small town of Santa Lisa, California, with his wife, Edith (Janet Leigh), and baby. His contracting business has prospered during the postwar housing boom. The fragility of this life is quickly exposed when a newspaper clipping touting Enley's wartime heroism and peacetime success reveals his location to Joe Parkson (Robert Ryan), his erstwhile bombardier and friend. The film opens on the rainy nighttime streets of New York City, the Chrysler Building looming in the sky. We hear Parkson's footsteps as he drags his wounded leg across the street and up the stairs of a dingy building so he can pack his service revolver in his army grip. He then boards a bus for Los Angeles on a vengeful quest to murder Enley, who betrayed the men under his command while they were POWs in Germany.

Parkson arrives in Santa Lisa on Memorial Day. The sun is so bright it seems to blind him, a figure only just emerged from nocturnal shadows, still wrapped in his trench coat. He suffers a further indignity when he is forced to wait for the parade to pass before limping across the street, while a radio announces, "A light breeze is whipping the flags of state and nation while a warm and bright sunshine streams down on the war veterans." Enley is the focal point of the town's celebration of the completion of a new housing development. The former captain is publicly lauded as a war hero and a pillar of the community whose determination and leadership kept everyone's morale up and helped them stick together throughout difficult moments during the construction process. Parkson's vendetta precipitates the unraveling of this life. Enley's hysterical response to his old friend's arrival prompts the innocent Edith—who has made it a policy never to ask her husband about his war experiences and occasionally inexplicable behavior—to confront Frank. She guesses that it was because of Parkson that Frank suddenly decided to move from New York to California without even bothering to collect his terminal pay from the army.

The sunny California of the film's beginning disappears into a stark nighttime world. In a chilling scene set in the vertiginous back stairwell of a Los Angeles hotel, site of a builders and contractors convention, Frank confesses. As the drunken conventioneers celebrate outside to the strains of "Happy Days Are Here Again," Frank tells Edith everything: how, as the senior officer, he was responsible for the men; how, nearly insane with hunger, Joe and the others dug an escape tunnel; how, knowing they had no chance, he informed the

SS colonel in charge where the tunnel was in order to get leniency for his men; how the colonel broke his promise. "They'd set a trap for them. They bayoneted them. They set dogs on them. And when it was over, they didn't even shoot them. They just left them there." Edith tries to reassure him that he simply did what he deemed best and that he should not be punished for the rest of his life for one dreadful mistake. But Frank refuses her consolation:

> I was an informer. It doesn't make any difference why I did it. I betrayed my men. They were dead. The Nazis even paid me a price. They gave me food and I ate it. I ate it. I hadn't done it just to save their lives. I'd talked myself into believing it, that he'd keep his word. But in my guts from the start, I think I knew he wouldn't. And maybe I didn't even care. They were dead, and I was eating. And maybe that's all I did it for. To save one man. Me. There were six widows. There were ten men dead, and I couldn't even stop eating.

Enley has tried to forget his past, to bury it in a new life in which he exerts the moral leadership within his community that he lacked in the POW camp.

Act of Violence dramatizes the contest between remembering and forgetting the war and one's deeds in it. Along the way, both men are drawn into criminal acts. Enley becomes almost accidently involved in a plot to kill Parkson: "You're the same man you were in Germany," one of his accomplices tells him, forcing him to own his past. "You did it once. You'll do it again. What do you care about one more man? You sent ten along already. Sure, you're sorry they're dead. That's the respectable way to feel. Get rid of this guy and be sorry later. It's up to you. He dies or you die. It's him or you." In the climactic scene that follows this exchange, Enley runs desperately through an empty tunnel in Los Angeles, trying to outpace all the voices in his head that reproduce that fateful night at the prisoner-of-war camp.

Parkson, meanwhile, by religiously preserving the past, kept "sane" during a long hospital stay while his leg healed: "I kept remembering. I kept thinking back to that prison camp." Determined to murder Enley, Parkson is prevented from committing the crime only by chance. Both men are deformed by their pasts; remembering proves as treacherous as forgetting. Ultimately, Frank expiates his crime by dying to save Joe's life, but visually the movie ends almost where it began, with Joe limping off into the damp night, this time on his way to tell Edith that she is a widow. In its exposure of the dank anxieties beneath the sunny exteriors of California, *Act of Violence* offers a vision of the state Joan Didion once described as a "place in which a boom mentality and a sense of Chekhovian loss meet in uneasy suspension; in which the mind is troubled by some buried but ineradicable suspicion that things had better work here, because here, beneath that immense bleached sky, is where we run out of continent." That edge-of-the-continent desperation also textures Ida Lupino's 1949 film *Not Wanted*. Set in a harsh, sunbaked Los Angeles, the film dramatizes the story of an unmarried mother and a wounded veteran, both rejected by society, who rescue each other from abandonment by finding what solidarity they can in their outcast status.

In contrast to John Forbes and Frank Enley, many of the veterans in noir are out of work, out of luck, or on relief. World War II veterans numbered in the millions, so the odds are that men of a certain age depicted in postwar films will have served, but these veterans often seem especially vulnerable to life's vicissitudes, and their service adds irony, and sometimes pathos, to their postwar predicaments. In *Desperate* (1947), Steve Randall (Steve Brodie) tries to make a go of a trucking company and is unwittingly drawn into a heist because the criminals know that he is struggling to feed his family and will eagerly take any job offered. In *Try and Get Me* (1950), the veteran Howard Tyler (Frank Lovejoy), having moved his family to California in an unsuccessful search for work, falls in with a stickup artist named Jerry Slocum (Lloyd Bridges), who spent his military service working the black market in Paris, where he heard "the rumor" that the war was tough. The pair botch a kidnapping and end up being lynched by a mob inflamed by the newspapers' sensationalized crime reporting. In *Side Street* (1950), the veteran Joe Norson (Farley Granger), a married letter carrier—still living with his parents and frustrated that his pregnant wife must seek treatment at a city clinic because he can't afford a private doctor—dreams of getting "something steady," until he happens upon some money that he impulsively steals. This one fateful act ensnares him in a ring of criminals.

The literary critic Jonathan Vincent has identified a figure in postwar culture he calls the "citizen-as-fugitive" in *The Health of the State: Modern US War Narrative and the American Political Imagination, 1890–1964*. This fugitive citizen has been permanently militarized, Vincent argues, by social alienation. Framed, trapped, driven to crime by desperation or uncontrollable rage, many of the veterans of noir become such fugitive citizens. The feeling that the veteran's youth, innocence, and prospects have been stolen from him by the war animates these films with currents of resentment and anxiety. The noir veteran is almost always on the move, sometimes simply restless but just as often committed to a desperate hunt for the truth: the amnesiac's search for his lost identity, the wrongly accused's quest to clear his name, the friend's attempt to track down a lost war buddy. His status as a wanderer, an Odysseus-like stranger turning up in a series of different towns, often asking uncomfortable questions about the past that the residents would rather forget, makes him inherently suspicious. War records—even good ones—provoke suspicion in film noir because the violence they document has become theoretically unacceptable in peacetime. Routinely investigated by law-enforcement officials and others, these records are invoked as evidence of good character, competence, or trustworthiness, even as they raise concerns that the erstwhile serviceman has developed a dependence on violence to solve problems. By proving a veteran's ability to kill, a service record makes him a likely suspect in violent crimes at home.

The *lack* of a service record also poses a recurring problem in fiction and films of the period. In David Goodis's novel *Dark Passage*, Vincent Parry is wrongly convicted for the murder of his wife. The prosecutor takes advantage of the fact that Parry isn't in the service: "That was about all," the narrator sums up the trial, "except the character stuff. A lot of people wanted to know why Parry wasn't in uniform. The prosecution played that up big. Parry was a 4-F" because of a sinus problem, a bad kidney, and, the implication is clear, a lack of moral fiber. This detail is eliminated from the 1947 Warner Bros. film starring Humphrey Bogart and Lauren Bacall because it would have been bad for the box office—and practically unpatriotic, after the heroics of *Casablanca* (1942) and *Sahara* (1943)—to impugn Bogart's masculinity. Men who were 4-F, dishonorable discharges, and those perceived somehow to have evaded the draft or secured themselves a "cushy" job in uniform become objects of derision and contempt and, in extreme cases such as *Crossfire*, of deadly violence.

But the more impressive the war record, the more decorations for valor, the greater the potential danger posed by the veteran. One of the central questions in *The Crooked Way* (1949), for example, is whether a commendable war record can erase an unsavory past. Noting the Silver Star on the lapel of a suspect he has just finished interviewing, a police captain muses, "You really do something to get one." "Yeah," replies his lieutenant, who is in the process of verifying Rice's service record, "buy it at a pawnshop for two bits." The lieutenant's cynicism illuminates the ease with which imposters can maneuver among civilians who admire and envy, even as they fear, veterans. War records provoke discomfort among civilians in these films not only because they might be fake but also because they show up the less heroic or imply that veterans are bringing war's violence back home.

Nefarious characters also manufacture tales of war service to deceive others or to gain sympathy. In *The Naked City* (1948), a person of interest in a murder investigation lies to a homicide detective when he recounts his combat service in the South Pacific as a captain in the 77th Infantry Division. It turns out, of course, that he had never even been in the army: "I tried to enlist," he explains once he's found out. "They wouldn't take me. I had a trick knee from college football. I just couldn't get in." A similar episode occurs in *Impact* (1949), a typical late-1940s noir: a low-budget, independent production nevertheless full of talent, including its cinematographer Ernest Laszlo, a master of the lights and shadows typical of the genre. A successful San Francisco businessman, Walter Williams (Brian Donlevy) is the intended victim of a murder plot by his wife and her lover, Jim Torrence (Tony Barrett). When Williams plans to drive east to inspect a new plant his company is thinking of buying, Torrence, posing as his wife's cousin, arranges to ride along. Williams grows suspicious on the way. The cousin's stories don't seem to add up. In one exchange, he claims that he was with Patton's Third Army and that his war was "rough except for the time in Italy. I kind of liked it there." Williams replies, "Patton's outfit never got to Italy." Unsettled, Torrence quickly thinks up an excuse for his lie: "Course, but most civilians never know or care, and I . . . I . . . figured you didn't either." In cynically manufacturing a war record—perhaps he served, but probably not with Patton—Torrence makes the presumably safe bet that most civilians wouldn't know the difference between a plausible and an implausible war story.

In *Boomerang!* (1947), a newspaper owner who wishes to help defend John Waldron (Arthur Kennedy), a veteran accused of murder, advises the defense attorney, "They'll never hang an ex-serviceman . . . Dig into that war record." Despite the claim that no one will execute a veteran, when things start going Waldron's way in court, the police have to defuse a would-be lynch mob. Based on a 1945 *Reader's Digest* story, *Boomerang!* takes place in a small Connecticut city, but the voice-over narration at the beginning takes pains to indicate that it might have happened anywhere in the country. A beloved minister is murdered brutally on the main street. Witnesses claim to have seen a man in a light fedora and dark coat. This flimsy evidence, along with some more damning details, is enough to pin the crime on Waldron. Nor does he help his own case. He acts suspiciously and lies. Deprived of sleep, mercilessly interrogated, and hounded by a psychiatrist who keeps telling him how bitter and resentful he must be at the success of the civilians around him and his own maladjustment, Waldron eventually signs a false confession. When the sympathetic state's attorney (Dana Andrews), who ultimately finds the exculpatory evidence, interviews him later, Waldron, who served five years in the army, endorses the psychiatrist's assumptions about his deep frustration even as he denies that it provided a motive for killing the minister: "That puts me five years behind the parade. I wanted to get moving. You can't wait. I'm not a kid anymore. I missed the boat. I had an idea once." The desire to make something of himself echoes James Allen's apologia in *I Am a Fugitive from a Chain Gang*. For Waldron, the idea has died. Only the tireless efforts of the state's attorney secure his eventual release. Yet the film's closing voice-over narration emphasizes the fact that some in the town remain convinced of his guilt.

In *The Strange Love of Martha Ivers* (1946), Sam Masterson (Van Heflin), on his way west, has a car accident near Iverstown, the hometown he ran away from almost twenty years earlier. There he finds that his childhood friends have married: Martha Ivers O'Neil (Barbara Stanwyck) runs a large factory inherited from her grandmother, and Walter O'Neil (Kirk Douglas) is now the district attorney. Fearing that Sam has returned to blackmail them over an old murder, which they mistakenly believe he witnessed, O'Neil asks a detective to do a background check on his old friend in the hopes of getting him out of town quickly: "He's a big shot gambler," the detective reports. "Broke many times, but always turns up with a new bankroll. The police in every state have tried to find the source of his money, but no dice. Many arrests, no convictions. Beat a murder rap in Frisco. Self-defense. Has a war record few can equal." Near the end of the film, Martha, the actual murderer, asks Sam to help her kill Walter: "You've killed. It says so in your record," she reasons. "I've never murdered," Sam corrects her.

Vulnerability—physical, psychological, socioeconomic, and sometimes a combination of all three—is a recurring theme in these films. Lieutenant Dixon in *The Guilty* (1947) and Buzz in *The Blue Dahlia* (1946), both subject to spells and blackouts, are convinced (or nearly so) that they have murdered someone. In both instances, the real culprits, in the former case a trusted fellow veteran, take advantage of the protagonists' suggestibility. Sometimes the frame-up involves a piece of evidence: in *Railroaded!* (1947) it is a navy scarf that lands an innocent former sailor in jail even though the detective admits that such an article can be picked up in any surplus store. The veteran's vulnerability is also political. Resentment can be exacerbated by the attitudes of civilians, which are often far from welcoming. *The Blue Dahlia* offers a party in which a veteran is derided as an "ex-hero" who is used to solving problems through violence, while in *Where the Sidewalk Ends* (1950), a friend tries to dissuade a woman from going back to her war-hero husband, who has become a violent alcoholic: "So he won the war and freed the slaves, does that give him the right to drink barrelsful of whiskey and punch girls on the nose?"

As Richard Lingeman writes, a 1947 survey revealed that more than fifty percent of ex-servicemen reported that the war "had left them worse off than before." Often naïve and in need, ex-service members were sometimes preyed upon by veteran organizations, some of which had racialist or other sinister agendas. These groups were the subject of several of Bill Mauldin's most controversial cartoons in *Back Home*; they also found their way into the movies. In *Till the End of Time*, a group of white supremacists tries unsuccessfully to recruit three marines in a bar, while the machinations of another dangerous veteran group form the central plot of *Violence* (1947), in which a racketeer, disguising his shakedown scheme as a patriotic organization called United Defenders, recruits veterans to serve as muscle by telling them he will lobby Washington for better housing, the jobs they've left behind, a general improvement of living conditions, and "the right to live as free men who deserve the gratitude of the free men you fought for." The agitator tells a group of potential recruits, "What do you think you're gonna get by being nice? If you tried that on the front lines, you'd all be dead ducks right now. You had to be tough and hard." In a telling scene, he sends these men in to break up a legitimate protest staged by another group of out-of-work, homeless veterans.

The racketeer in *Violence* counts on his ability to stoke the rage and hate already simmering within these men and encourages them to look for a new enemy. The same phenomenon is addressed in *Crossfire*. The veteran Joseph Samuels (Sam Levene) notices a troubled soldier, Arthur Mitchell (George Cooper), drinking alone at a hotel bar and falls into conversation with him: "We don't know what we're supposed to do, what's supposed to happen . . . We're too used to fighting, but we just don't know what to fight." Samuels tells Mitchell that his difficulty isn't merely personal but societal: "I think maybe it's suddenly not having a lot of enemies to hate anymore . . . You can feel the tension in the air. A whole lot of fight and hate that doesn't know where to go. Guy like you maybe starts hating himself." Samuels's words make sense to Mitchell, who can't articulate the vertigo he feels, but when Samuels is murdered by an anti-Semitic soldier named Montgomery (Robert Ryan), it is Mitchell who is suspected of the crime. The film takes care to assure the audience that Samuels, far from being the shirker Montgomery imagines, served valiantly and was wounded at Okinawa. That fact, recited by the detective in charge of the case, is meant to heighten our outrage at his murder.

At one point in the film, Mitchell asks another sympathetic soldier, Keeley (Robert Mitchum), "Has everything suddenly gone crazy? . . . Or is it just me?" Keeley reassures him: "No, it's not just you. The snakes are loose. Anybody can get them. I get them myself, but they're friends of mine." When Mitchell's wife arrives to help her despondent husband, he tries to define the "snakes" that beset him:

> I couldn't write to you because I was depressed and jittery. Samuels, the man who I was supposed to have killed tonight, he understood it . . . he said a guy like me now, with the war over, could start hating himself.

> Maybe that's what happened. Maybe I started hating
> myself because I was afraid of getting going again. Of
> trying to draw again. Of looking for a job. Of having
> you waiting all the time, after having waited four years
> already. It began to be hard for me to think about you.

Mitchell's anxieties are rooted in part in his Depression-era socioeconomic experience. The WPA supported him before the war, when things were a struggle, then the army paid him to paint signs, but there is no guarantee, despite the interlude of war, that he will be able to make a living as an artist afterward. Again, the artist who is unable to make his postwar world cohere proves a particularly attractive figure for working out postwar anxieties. He is a stand-in for all those noir veterans who, if successful during the war, are derailed by chance in wrong-man plots, the discovery of secrets in their past, or a residual instinct for self-sabotage, and who find themselves involved, willingly or not, in crimes inevitably gone awry.

The idea that the war has reshaped the home front in sinister ways becomes even clearer in *The Street with No Name* (1948). In this film, the gangster Alec Stiles (Richard Widmark) runs a criminal army modeled on the actual one: "I screen people, like the army, only I choose my own recruits." Discussing his methods with a new man, an undercover FBI agent (Mark Stevens), he asks, "What's the use of having a war if you don't learn from it?" The film's prologue features an FBI teletype warning of the rise of organized gangsterism across the country. And it is no accident that Stiles's signature weapon is a Luger. The ubiquity of ex-GIs and military weapons becomes a source of great anxiety in *The Sniper* (1952), set in a San Francisco terrorized by a series of killings with an M1 carbine. The police in that film find it extremely difficult to narrow their pool of suspects because, the detective in charge complains, every veteran "pinched" an M1 on leaving the service and there are millions more men still in uniform. With the draft still in effect—the film was released in the midst of the Korean War—this large standing army with its easy access to weapons intensifies the ambient fear of violence hanging over the city.

An even more obvious association of war and crime can be found in *Brute Force* (1947), Jules Dassin's exposure of prison barbarity. Cellmates plot an escape, the key to which comes from a veteran known simply as Soldier (Howard Duff). The prisoners' leader, Joe Collins (Burt Lancaster), gets a tip from a dying inmate to ask Soldier about Hill 633. At night in their cell, Soldier tells his war story with the aid of some chess pieces:

> SOLDIER: Well, it's a hill in Italy, not far from Rome. Why?
> COLLINS: Tell me about it.
> SOLDIER: There's not much to tell. The krauts had the hill, and we were ordered to take it.
> COLLINS: How? What'd you do, charge 'em?
> SOLDIER: Did you ever try it uphill with a few kraut 88s puttin' the blast on ya?
> SPENCER: Let me have those chessmen, will ya?
> SOLDIER: Give me some light. Here was the hill. Here was us. Mountains here, the ocean here. Stalemate.
> COLLINS: But you took it.
> SOLDIER: Yeah. We took it, all right. Give me some more light. We sent some men out in a boat. They landed up here. We covered 'em with a heavy bombardment. At "H" hour, we attacked uphill. The krauts turned all their guns to stop us. That was exactly when the other gang attacked from behind.
> COLLINS: And it worked.

SOLDIER: Yeah. We got through, all right. Most of us anyway. The rest are still there.

COLLINS: They couldn't cover both sides, huh? Thanks, Soldier.

In the ultimate parody of a sand table exercise, in which soldiers rehearse operations, the inmates thus plot their escape. They have been assigned to work in a tunnel just outside the prison gate by the sadistic Captain Munsey (Hume Cronyn), who—like the Nazi aesthetes depicted in a range of films—abuses prisoners to the strains of classical music. Collins knows that the single machine gun in the tower can cover only one side of the wall at once. Unlike the taking of Hill 633, the attempted breakout ends in utter disaster. Almost everyone ends up buried there.

The veteran killer makes a sadistic cinematic last stand in the person of John Baron (Frank Sinatra) in *Suddenly* (1954). This late noir pits a manifestly honorable veteran, in the form of Sterling Hayden's Tod Shaw, a sheriff full of duty, rectitude, and domestic inclinations, against Sinatra's chilling contract killer, who takes over a local house in order to set up for an assassination of the president of the United States. "I won a Silver Star," Baron boasts monomaniacally throughout the film. The army gave him an illusion of self-worth: "First time I got one [a rifle] in my hands and killed a man, I got some self-respect. I was somebody." We get hints of a miserable childhood and an aimless prewar life: "I drifted and drifted and ran, always lost in a big crowd. I hated that crowd . . . I'm no traitor, Sheriff. I won a Silver Star. And learned how to kill. Yeah, maybe I did. Maybe that changed everything. Maybe people began to know who I was." But the universalizing socioeconomic explanations that so often supply the real anxiety in the films of the immediate postwar period through the late 1940s are really beside the point in

Suddenly. Baron is a psychopath: the war provided an environment in which his particular talents could flourish.

The sheriff guesses, although the film never confirms it, that Baron was such a prodigious killer that he eventually committed a war crime: "You look yardbird to me." Baron had found something he was good at. "You're a born killer," Shaw tells him, and Baron understands it as a compliment. "Yeah. When you get real good at something, you're a murderer. Yeah, over there you can knock over a whole platoon, or a guy invents a bomb and kills a hundred thousand people just like that and maybe gets more medals. Here you put a slug in a double-crossing squirt that isn't even worth burying and you have to take the gas. I got no feeling against the president; I'm just earning a living." "By treason," another character objects, and Baron continues, "Don't give me that politics jazz, it's not my racket. I don't even know who's paying me and I don't want to know." In Baron, the combat soldier is distilled into a pure killing machine, without morals, without cause other than "earning a living." None of the arguments made by Shaw and the other upstanding characters held hostage in the house makes any impression on Baron: there is nothing inside to which to appeal. All comes right in the end, and the town of Suddenly carries on in its sleepy way, even if a vague sense of menace lingers in the name.

Four years later, all that menace had dissipated. Another Sinatra film revealed the degree to which the veteran's story had lost its rawness. In *Ocean's 11* (1960) Sinatra plays Danny Ocean, a former paratrooper in the 82nd Airborne who gathers his old buddies together to pull off the ultimate caper. Military service has been reduced to a simple plot gimmick: it explains how they all know one another and why they have the suite of arcane skills required to pull off the simultaneous heist of five Las Vegas casinos. Directed by Lewis Milestone, whose early career had been notable for the antiwar drama

All Quiet on the Western Front (1930), the film has the comic-suspense formula that made it such easy pickings for the recent *Ocean* franchise. It has none of the doom or fatalism of its predecessors. The integrated star power and glamour of the Rat Pack casting (Sammy Davis Jr.'s Josh Howard would not have served in a unit with the rest of this white gang in what was a segregated army); the gags and glamour; the absence of any real bitterness about the war; and the lack of any motivation beyond that of a score all combine to make harmless entertainment of what would once have been the stuff of noir nightmare. Even when the money accidentally goes up in flames, the thieves stroll down the Vegas Strip past a marquee that features the names Frank Sinatra, Dean Martin, Sammy Davis Jr., Peter Lawford, and Joey Bishop, and the whole artifice collapses into a Rat Pack romp.

Oubliette

The veteran who has forgotten—either temporarily, through intoxication or traumatic repression, or permanently, through neurological injury—is a staple of postwar noir. John Belton thinks that the "identity crises" of these amnesiacs "mirror those of the nation as a whole" in the postwar period, while Mark Osteen argues that "amnesia noirs probe the American ideals of self-reinvention and the pursuit of happiness." The world into which they, like all noir veterans, are thrown is itself unstable and ambiguous. It may be "haunted" by the past, Osteen explains, or it may simply be "shadowed" by new fears such as "atomic destruction." Amnesiacs appear in other genres, too, where the recovery of traumatic memory proves therapeutic. In the war film *Home of the Brave* (1949), for example, remembering leads to resolution. Knowing the past permits the amnesia victim—in this case an African American soldier whose best friend has been killed—finally to access a future full of integrated promise: he and a white serviceman plan to go into business together. But in noir, being cured is often as terrifying for the amnesiac as awakening to the fact of his condition in a hospital ward. In almost every instance, these films present a scenario in which the veteran who remembers might also be forced to confront the fact that he might be someone he does not wish to be: a collaborator, as in *The Clay Pigeon* (1949), or a murderer, as in *The Blue Dahlia*, *Deadline at Dawn* (1946), and *High Wall* (1947).

Those films dramatize temporary amnesia. *The Crooked Way* presents us with a permanent case. Told by a doctor that the shrapnel lodged in his brain has given him incurable, "organic" amnesia, Eddie Rice (John Payne) declares, "Doesn't leave me much of a future, does it?" Eddie, a criminal before the war, has gone straight, the army having facilitated his reinvention, but the compulsion to know who he is plunges him back into the old world, which he must navigate without the armor of identity or a legible personal history. *Somewhere in the Night* has a similar plot involving a former criminal, George Taylor (John Hodiak), who, like Rice, has tried to escape his past by enlisting in the army under a false name. Military service has theoretically wiped the slate clean for him, as it had for Eddie Rice, but because he cannot remember the past he intended to erase by joining up, he is doomed to recover it. The film opens on a hospital ward in a voice-over spoken by the lost amnesia victim, whose wallet, and the pictures and letter he finds inside it, are the only clues to his former self:

> "These are my last words to you. That's why I write them. So that I can always be sure that these were my last. But I despise you now, and the memory of you. But

I'm ashamed for having loved you. And I shall pray as long as I live for someone or something to hurt and destroy you, make you want to die, as you have me." Who writes letters like this? Who do they write them to? Men they despise, whose memories they despise. The memory I haven't got. Won't be long, and I'll have to talk. Think fast. Now they only know my name. If I tell 'em I don't remember, they'll backtrack. They'll dig up that memory and throw it in my face. I've forgotten that man. Somebody's praying for him to be hurt and want to die. I won't let them know I can't remember. I won't let them dig him up!

Taylor doesn't want to know who he was, yet he can't help trying to find out how anyone could have been so bad as to deserve this letter. He spends the rest of the film trying to solve a robbery and a murder for which he has been framed: "I'm George Taylor. New self . . . meet old. I don't need a memory to figure this one out," he announces after convincing himself that he is a murderer. But the woman George has met since his return—the best friend of the woman who had written him the damning letter—cannot believe him capable of murder and gives him sufficient faith in his new self to press on. After identifying the real murderer, George finds redemption and promises the police that he won't return to his old ways. As dark as the film has been to this point, the ending has been read as redemptive. Osteen suggests that, "contrived" as it is, the resolution "ultimately affirms the ideology of self-recreation, proposing that, rather than recovering their prewar selves, Americans are better off tossing them aside like suits of outdated clothing." *Somewhere in the Night* and *The Crooked Way*, he argues, "endorse the American Dream in which alienation gradually yields to self-affirmation and in which a life's second act may redeem an original sin."

But I don't think these films are quite that glib. They may seem to satisfy us with happy endings, but in each case, the weight of the entire film insists on the flimsiness of promised happiness. Reconstructing the past is different from remembering it: the artificial nature of the recovery is its distinguishing attribute. In the profoundest sense, these men still do not know who they are. They are, after all, permanent amnesiacs. They are forced to forget by the trauma of the war, which ostensibly purges them of the past yet fails to release them from its revenant. Ironically, amnesiacs force everyone around them to remember, often against their own inclinations to leave an unpleasant past behind. Wars are usually begun with calls to remember (and to avenge) an injustice: *Remember the* Maine! *Remember Pearl Harbor! Remember 9/11!* Nevertheless, such war cries are inseparable from an imperative to forget the way things used to be. In going to war, we commit to making the world over. And once the war is over, we work to forget it, too.

Noting that amnesia films are hardly unique to the 1940s but commonplace throughout Hollywood history, David Bordwell insists in *Reinventing Hollywood: How 1940s Filmmakers Changed Movie Storytelling* on a "cold-blooded" reading of the phenomenon "not as a symptom of audience anxieties but as a reliable narrative device. News of battle injuries . . . offered forties filmmakers a realistic alibi for stories of memory loss." Amnesia in the movies, he proposes, "is only one step above the 'magic forgetting' we find in folktales," and we can find amnesia plots throughout literary history. Nevertheless, within an American cultural context, this admittedly ubiquitous motif illuminates a very particular function of memory. The forgetting men in veteran noir pathologize the amnesia already built into the American experiment, which has always insisted on at least a voluntary erasure of lives begun elsewhere in order to succeed in American terms, to fulfill American dreams. By short-circuiting that process, the veteran forced by circumstance to forget compels the rest of us to remember the degree to which the past is but a tissue of fragile fictions, the future just as unstable.

4

WAR, WHAT IS IT GOOD FOR?

This celebration also marks the beginning of another year of your national life; and reminds you that the Republic of America is now 76 years old. I am glad, fellow-citizens, that your nation is so young . . . According to this fact, you are, even now, only in the beginning of your national career, still lingering in the period of childhood . . . There is hope in the thought, and hope is much needed, under the dark clouds which lower above the horizon. The eye of the reformer is met with angry flashes, portending disastrous times; but his heart may well beat lighter at the thought that America is young, and that she is still in the impressible stage of her existence. May he not hope that high lessons of wisdom, of justice and of truth, will yet give direction to her destiny? Were the nation older, the patriot's heart might be sadder, and the reformer's brow heavier. Its future might be shrouded in gloom, and the hope of its prophets go out in sorrow. There is consolation in the thought that America is young.

—Frederick Douglass, "What to the Slave Is the Fourth of July?" Address to the Rochester, New York, Ladies' Anti-Slavery Society (July 5, 1852)

Wild Boys

In 1852, hard at work in service of the cause of abolition, Frederick Douglass could draw consolation from the country's youth, for in youth there was malleability, the capacity for growth, the energy to change. The conceit of youth, of the new and unfettered, has animated the American imagination since the founding. Yet after World War II, it grew increasingly difficult to sustain this illusion, hypocritical to think or to speak of the country as young when it had inherited the unlooked-for responsibilities of maturity. If the political and cultural superiority of the New World had been vindicated by the outcome of the war, it was at the paradoxical price of national adolescence. How to sustain the illusion of youth while displaying the wisdom of age? One characteristic of America's newfound maturity seemed to be a renewed preoccupation with juvenile delinquency. This worry had surfaced during the Depression and intensified during the war, only to explode in the 1950s. Sociologists had begun to study the roots of delinquency and crime in earnest amid the social and economic turmoil of the 1930s, when popular culture also gave voice to anxieties about lawless adolescents as well as a concern for the inhumanity of reform schools and other institutions.

These issues fueled several pre-Code films, including *The Mayor of Hell* and *Wild Boys of the Road*, both released in 1933. That same year, the University of Chicago sociologists Herbert Blumer and Philip M. Hauser published *Movies, Delinquency, and Crime*, a book devoted to the question of whether movies themselves were contributing to the epidemic. Blumer and Hauser concluded that movies, while not a primary cause of delinquency, might indirectly "promote criminal tendencies or behavior. We have declared that by arousing desires for 'easy money,' by inducing a spirit of bravado, toughness, and adventurousness, by fostering the daydreaming of criminal rôles, by displaying techniques of crime, and by contributing to truancy, motion pictures may lead or dispose to crime." This book was only one installment in a series of volumes sponsored by the Payne Fund Studies and devoted to studying the influence of motion pictures on the young. Various sociologists examined motion pictures as something at once alien to adult understanding and immensely appealing to children. These concerns find an echo in today's anxieties about social media.

During the war, as numerous commentators have noted, the government already harbored deep concerns over the increasingly unsupervised life of adolescents—so many fathers and mothers were contributing to the war effort—and over what was perceived to be the general moral laxity of teens. The increased prosperity of the postwar years gave young people more money, independence, and leisure time than their prewar predecessors had enjoyed. Don Carpenter's 1966 novel *Hard Rain Falling* sheds some light on a generation too young to fight in World War II, adrift, and introduced early in life to a world of cruelty, violence, and institutional indifference. Part of the novel takes place in 1947, in Portland, Oregon, where Carpenter's orphaned protagonist Jack Levitt joins a gang. The gang had formed during the war and survived it by continuing to attract "hard kids" who felt left out in high school or craved "the excitement" of the city. Drifting in and out of the gang, the members all share certain qualities: "toughness, a lack of conventional morals, a dislike of adults, and a hatred of the police." Some of the boys periodically disappeared into the military, but Jack emphatically rejects that option as soon as he ages out of the orphanage in which he has spent his early years: "They said the Army would take care of you; three squares and a flop, and all you had to do was obey orders; there wasn't a war on, so no danger of getting your ass shot off; just a nice, easy life, uniforms, barracks, *chow*, and marching around with a rifle."

Nevertheless, sickened by the idea of a life given over to institutional obedience, Jack pursues a criminal career that eventually lands him in another institution, San Quentin, with Billy Lancing, a Black pool hustler he meets in Portland who likewise fears the army as a last resort but for rather different reasons. Jack's distaste for the army is personal, but Billy's represents a larger communal fear. The night school he attended had been full of frightened Black high school dropouts like him, he tells Jack: "They . . . face that tough . . . world . . . an [*sic*] when they get home they got no money . . . and up jumps the *Army* . . . and it just scares the shit out of em." Jack and Billy, who briefly become lovers in prison, look up to the slightly older men in their midst. The war generation is represented in the novel by the sinister figures of Kol Mano and Bobby Case, gamblers who roam Portland's pool halls in "leather air corps flight jackets," fancy clothes, and "highly polished cordovan shoes." Mano, who was wounded in France, is distinguished by a hole in his throat, through which he smokes cigarettes: "Keeps the enemy off balance," he tells Jack. For a long time, Carpenter writes, Mano had been "deeply enmeshed in black-market rackets, selling watches and other PX material, and even some hospital supplies." His service record reveals a potent mix of bravery, violence, and criminality: "He was given the Silver Star, released from the hospital, arrested by the MPs, and given a general court all in the same ten-day period . . . He had the dreamy eyes of a lush and the delicate fingers of a cardshark, and he was both. Everyone considered him a little crazy." Far from being crazy, Mano is "the coolest head Jack had ever met." When Mano isn't at the veterans hospital receiving continued treatments for his throat, he spends his time "making money and living his own life," something Jack never quite learns how to do.

Youth gangs like Jack's began to maraud across the screen in the late 1940s, and they continued their mayhem, in documentary and feature films, throughout the 1950s. Some depicted police and social workers, often at philosophical odds, in a determined quest to end the national scourge of juvenile violence. The following sampling of titles, ranging from major studio productions to low-budget fodder, suggests their increasingly sensational nature: *City Across the River* (1949); *The Young and the Damned, So Young, So Bad, Gun Crazy* (1950); *The Wild One, Girls in the Night* (1953); *Cell 2455, Death Row, Blackboard Jungle, Rebel Without a Cause, Running Wild, Teen-Age Crime Wave, Mad at the World, One Way Ticket to Hell* (1955); *Crime in the Streets, The Unguarded Moment, Teenage Wolfpack, Hot-Rod Girl* (1956). The contradiction dramatized by many of these films, and by Carpenter's novel, is that the protagonists are seduced by easy money and violent excitement while often longing for nothing more than domestic stability—steady work, marriage, and family.

The film *Gun Crazy* typifies this confusion in the person of Bart Tare (John Dall). Obsessed with guns yet uneasy about killing, he is sent to reform school for stealing a pistol. After years away, Bart returns to his hometown and reunites with his boyhood friends. "Four years in reform school, and then the army," he tells them. "Not getting married on that routine." When one of his friends wonders why he didn't stay in the army, Bart explains, "It gets dull. Nothing but teaching guys how to shoot." Bart, a crack shot, joins a carnival and meets the equally proficient Annie Laurie Starr (Peggy Cummins), who shares none of his scruples about killing. The pair goes on a crime spree that ends in several deaths and ultimately their own. Bart continues to insist that he isn't a killer by nature long after he has become one in fact. His love for Laurie, who craves danger and excitement, keeps them on the run in search of the one "big" job that will make them rich. His dream, expressed more than once in the film, is not to rob banks but "to settle down." Toward the end of the film, just before their plan to escape across the border is foiled, he tells Laurie, "You know what we're gonna do when we get to Mexico? Buy ourselves a nice ranch and settle down. Maybe even raise those kids we talked about once." But Laurie has no interest in that sort of life. Almost two decades later, in 1967, *Bonnie and Clyde* will reverse these gender roles: it is Bonnie (Faye Dunaway) who longs ultimately for domesticity while Clyde (Warren Beatty) simply wants to refine his modus operandi by not pulling jobs in the same state in which they live.

Ross Macdonald, in his 1951 novel *The Way Some People Die*, describes the sensibility of Bart, Laurie, and dozens like them who populate the era's films about violent youths: "There were thousands," the detective Lew Archer muses, "in my ten-thousand-square-mile beat: boys who had lost their futures, their parents and themselves in the shallow jerry-built streets of the coastal cities; boys with hot-rod bowels, comic-book imaginations, daring that grew up too late for one war, too early for another." Macdonald's phrase "comic-book imaginations" is no throwaway descriptor, but one with deep period resonance. The Senate Subcommittee on Juvenile Delinquency, established in 1953, turned its attention to comic books the following year. After the war, as David Hajdu documents in *The Ten-Cent Plague: The Great Comic-Book Scare and How It Changed America*, the comics had "shifted in tone and content. Fed by the same streams as pulp fiction and film noir, many of the titles most prominent in the late forties and early fifties told lurid stories of crime, vice, lust, and horror, rather than noble tales of costumed heroes and heroines . . . whose exploits had initially established the comics genre in the late thirties and early forties." Moreover, unlike Hollywood, which labored under the built-in censorship of the Production Code, drafted in 1930 and enforced in 1934, the comic-book industry had no limits but the imaginations of its creators until it formed a code of its own in 1954.

During the war, the comics were heavily engaged in fighting the Axis. "Comic books, an outlet for many young Jews," Hajdu explains, "were particularly zealous in their creative assault on Fascism." Superheroes, pictured battling U-boats as early as 1940, were some of the most prominent premature anti-fascists. A celebrated March 1941 cover showed Captain America punching Hitler on the nose. "After Pearl Harbor," Hajdu notes, "almost every superhero stopped fighting traditional crime, abandoning murderers, kidnappers, and bank robbers to focus on saboteurs, spies, scientists working for the Axis, and other domestic threats." This is the story told in Michael Chabon's *The Amazing Adventures of Kavalier and Clay.* This novel, published in 2000, looks back at the robust comic-book industry of the late 1930s and early 1940s, an industry catalyzed by the appearance of Superman in June 1938, in the late-Depression era "marketplace of ten-cent dreams: to express the lust for power and the gaudy sartorial taste of a race of powerless people with no leave to dress themselves." Comic books, Chabon writes, "were Kid Stuff, pure and true, and they arrived at precisely the moment when the kids of America began, after ten years of terrible hardship, to find their pockets burdened with the occasional superfluous dime." World War II, however, gave comic-book heroes specific, grown-up monsters against which to fight.

Chabon's protagonists, Jewish cousins Joe and Sam, create the Escapist, a comic-book hero whose eponymous superpower reflects their own circumstances. Joe has escaped to New York City from Nazi-occupied Europe through the miraculous conveyance of a golem's coffin, while Sam, whom polio has left with a limp and a small stature, yearns to escape his claustrophobic life and prospects and must conceal his homosexuality in a society that condemns it. The Escapist is no exception to all those comic-book heroes who began, in the years leading up to America's entrance into the war, to unleash their righteous wrath on the Axis Powers.

Once the war ended, in the absence of a foreign enemy against whom to deploy their violence, comic books moved in the direction of brutality and horror. A brief scene in *Pitfall*, a film discussed in chapter 3, shows the Forbeses' young son Tommy awakening from a nightmare his father thinks is caused by a comic book the boy had been reading before bed. Estes Kefauver's senatorial subcommittee investigation into the causes of "youth crime" turned its attention to comics in earnest in 1954. The comics' archnemesis was Fredric Wertham, whose 1954 book *Seduction of the Innocent* helped inflame hysteria about the dangers of these publications. Wertham, having begun his campaign in 1947, revved it up in the early 1950s and found in the committee an ideal audience before which to air his concerns about young readers who had no protection against "the corrupting influence of comic books which glamorize and advertise dangerous knives and the guns that can be converted into deadly weapons." Wertham warned not only of the domestic consumption of comics but also of their proliferation, as an American export, throughout the impressionable world. Robert Warshow, in a 1947 essay about his young son Paul's fascination with the comics, suggested that Wertham's proposed ban was impractical, his fixation on the medium "simple-minded." Several factors, ranging from comics to "the unceasing clamor of television and the juke boxes," had combined to create what Warshow regarded as a "juvenile underground" in which "numbers of children" existed, "out of touch with the demands of social responsibility, culture, and personal refinement" even if most of them didn't go "over the line into criminality."

It is easy to ridicule Wertham's attack on the comics on various grounds, but his critique illuminated some troubling features beyond simple violence. He believed the comics inculcated a kind of race prejudice: their heroes were always white men, their villains dark skinned. As Jill Lepore notes in *The Secret History of Wonder Woman*, comics, far from being wholly subversive, actually underwrote certain establishment beliefs, including the ambient societal disapproval regarding women's presence in the postwar workforce. "By the end of the Second World War, the number of American women working outside the home had grown by 60 percent," but, according to Lepore, in peacetime "their labor . . . threatened the stability of the nation, by undermining men . . . At the end of the war, three-quarters of working women hoped to keep their jobs," but most were dismissed to make way for returning servicemen. By the 1950s, Wonder Woman herself became "scarcely recognizable." Once a formidable crime-fighter, now "she became a babysitter, a fashion model, and a movie star . . . the author of a lonely-hearts newspaper advice column."

Paul Fussell points out that comic books were the preferred reading of many GIs during the war, and the habit survived hostilities. In 1952 *Life* reported, "The Pacific Fleet Command has banned the sale of most war comic books in ships' stores on the grounds that they are too gory for the American sailor." Naval censorship signaled a new puritanism. Government censorship didn't stop with comic books. As the Cold War began and the Red Scare warmed up, the State Department purged various magazines as well as "books by known Communists or fellow-travelers," *The New York Times* reported in 1953. Books were removed from libraries in Europe, North Africa, South America, and Mexico. Among the casualties were the detective novels of Dashiell Hammett, including *The Maltese Falcon*, *The Dain Curse*, and *The Glass Key*. Clearly, the political sympathies of the author mattered more than the content of a particular book. This was symptomatic of the worldview that had overtaken American society (its youthful naïvety challenged by war's baffling ambiguities), which now seemed to be regressing into a childlike—one might say a comic-book—simplicity.

In Hammett's case, the purge involved powerful contradictions. His involvement in left-wing political causes had begun with the Spanish Civil War and continued up until the time he was imprisoned in 1951—a five-month stretch that destroyed his health—for refusing to tell a federal judge where the Civil Rights Congress bail fund got its money. Hammett had enlisted during World War I and served stateside with the Motor Ambulance Corps until he contracted tuberculosis. When World War II broke out, he was in his forties. Nevertheless, hoping to make up for his first war, which he finished out in Tacoma, Washington, drinking whiskey when he wasn't coughing blood, he tried to enlist again despite bad teeth and the scars on his lungs. As Diane Johnson chronicles in *Dashiell Hammett: A Life* (1983), he even agreed to have all his teeth pulled, and he ended up as a sergeant on Adak Island in the Aleutians, editing the post newspaper, smoking Chesterfields in a Quonset hut, and reading Karl Marx, Bram Stoker, and the letters his partner, the playwright Lillian Hellman, sent from New York. When it was over, fed up, he dumped his gear in Puget Sound.

The State Department's removal of *The Maltese Falcon* and other of Hammett's novels, all of which predated his leftist commitments, made no sense politically or aesthetically. It was Hammett, after all, who had contributed as much as anyone, through his creation of the detective Sam Spade, to the

American ideal of hard-boiled heroism that was used to such advantage throughout the war. Writing in *The New Yorker* in 2002, Claudia Roth Pierpont proposed,

> The noble renunciation of love for wartime principle at the end of "Casablanca," made a year after "The Maltese Falcon," is unthinkable without Spade's renunciation of Brigid for far less noble motives; the plane that takes Ingrid Bergman up, the elevator that takes Mary Astor down—both leave Bogie conveniently alone with a buddy and his personal peace restored. There is a strange sort of justice in the fact that the truculent antihero brought into existence by the traumas of the first World War should have provided the materials for the most swooningly romantic (if no less truculent) hero of the Second, and Hammett, in playing his part in this complex creation, performed a national service more significant than anything he did in the Army.

Keeping Hammett's novels from overseas diplomatic personnel and protecting sailors from the comics was part of a larger attempt to ferret out dangerous influences, wherever they might be.

This campaign extended to the instructional material designed for personnel serving in new permanent or semipermanent outposts in Europe, Korea, Japan, and elsewhere. The Office of Armed Forces Information and Education (OAFIE), which produced the Cold War–era guides, attempted, as Scott Laderman writes in *Tours of Vietnam: War, Travel Guides, and Memory,* "to conjoin the pleasures of international travel with the often painful realities of overseas military service." But Laderman reports that as early as 1948, two congressional subcommittees were convening to remove evidence of pro-union sentiments and progressive stances on race from a publication called *Armed Forces Talk*. The United States should not be referred to as a democracy, one committee member insisted, but exclusively as a republic. According to Laderman, beginning in 1953, Senator Joseph McCarthy, the crusading anticommunist who served as the chair of the Committee on Government Operations of the Senate and of its permanent subcommittee on investigations, was demanding the identity of the authors responsible for various publications designed for overseas personnel. Those in charge refused to name names; nevertheless, a new restraint prevailed within OAFIE. Gone was the sophistication and nuance of many of the wartime guides; by 1954, the booklets had become rather lifeless. They were written, moreover, at an eighth-grade reading level.

Innocents Abroad

The Cold War guides reveal the effects of these national growing pains in different ways while retaining some of their original spirit. *A Pocket Guide to Alaska* (1951), the authors of which knew that the Last Frontier would seem a foreign country to many of the soldiers stationed there, reflects a new way of understanding the world bequeathed by the war so recently ended: "The defense of Alaska is a vital job. We don't want Alaska's Dutch Harbor to become another 'Pearl Harbor'!" Soldiers in Europe were apparently no clearer on the significance of their assignments, and the guides to countries ranging from Greece to Korea emphasize the struggle raging between democracy and the forces of communism. These guides all express anxiety lest their readers "spoil" America's good reputation among their various allies. Like the wartime guides before them, there are repeated injunctions against hubris. "Remember," reads a typical warning, "crossing the water doesn't make you a hero." Or, as the guide to Japan puts it, "A conquering-hero complex isn't going to help anybody." The 1950 *Guide to Korea* gives the mission new messianic overtones: "The free nations of the world look to us to lead and guide them through these tense and trying days." Everyone is "waiting," the authors insist, to see what will happen in the world, but "fortunately" the United States has a major role in shaping the future. The ambitious cultural instruction of the wartime guides disappears from later editions, even if a general spirit of discovery survives until the end of the guides' life cycle in the late 1980s, when warnings about terrorism become far more prominent than encouragements to tourism. A comparison of the 1950 and 1987 Korea guides, for example, offers evidence of this trend, with the latter shrinking the extensive "sights to see" section to a perfunctory checklist.

The political education provided in these guides is hopelessly simplistic, the history dangerously selective. Soldiers stationed in Germany are told in the 1951 guide that playing baseball with German kids might well be the best way to illustrate the value of the "American way of life." There is, moreover, a dearth of information regarding Germany's recent history. The millions who died at Nazi hands go largely unremarked; even a paragraph on the many displaced persons the GI is likely to encounter in Germany—and, the guide acknowledges, to find rather dirty and distasteful—ignores what displaced them in the first place. Indeed, the booklet provides more information on the fabulous *Auerhahn*, a sage hen beloved of German hunters, than on the Adlerhorst, or Eagle's Nest, Hitler's military bunker complex in Hesse. Victor Brombert, who had escaped from occupied France with his family and later returned as a member of the U.S. Army, described the disdain with which the Americans generally regarded displaced persons: "Surviving Jews who had been freed from the concentration camps . . . were treated like scum. Nobody wanted them," Brombert explains in his memoir *Trains of Thought: From Paris to Omaha Beach, Memories of a Wartime Youth.* "Our own attitudes in the U.S. army were at best ambiguous. We claimed to be horrified by what the Nazis had done, and to have come as rescuers. In reality, the notion that Jews were cowards who managed to get soft jobs, or to stay out of the army altogether, and had pushed America into the war was not uncommon among the soldiers." The Harrison Report, compiled in August 1945 by the delegate sent by President Truman to inspect the displaced person camps, asserted: "we appear to be treating the Jews as the Nazis treated them, except that we do not exterminate them."

The service member who found himself in Japan, the rapid democratization of which was being superintended by MacArthur, was informed that he was not simply an ambassador for but also "the salesman of democracy." This idea was satirized much earlier in Harry Brown's 1944 novel *A Walk in the Sun* in an exchange between two infantrymen marching through Italy, which was retained in the eponymous film released the following year. Rivera, who is tired of walking, tells Friedman that it's a good thing traveling salesmen can take the train. "You're a traveling salesman," Friedman tells him. "What do you mean, I'm a traveling salesman? I'm a murderer," replies Rivera. "You're a traveling salesman," Friedman insists: "You're selling democracy to the natives." When Rivera asks his buddy where he got "that crap," Friedman tells him he read it in a book.

The guide assures its readers that the Emperor Hirohito has been rehabilitated, a process detailed by the biographer Herbert Bix, and has learned how to behave "democratically." Despite the general air of condescension toward the Japanese, there is a recognition that the issue of the atom bomb requires special handling. The rather coy allusion to Hiroshima in the 1950 version is less flippant in editions produced in the wake of the 1951 peace treaty: "A smaller city on the southern coast of Honshu," teases the earlier guide, "is famous for another reason—as the target of the first atomic bomb ever used in war. Its name: Hiroshima." Also softened, or qualified, over the years is the injunction, carried over from the World War II guides, to "Be An American!" By 1952, this has been revised to "Be a *Good* American" (my emphasis).

One of the more bizarre informational pamphlets the government published during this period is *A Pocket Guide to Anywhere* (1953; reprinted 1956), at once a celebration of the postwar U.S. economic and security partnerships with countries throughout the world and a cautionary tale about American hubris. It features two fictional American soldiers, Bill and Joe, and an elaborate thought experiment crafted by Joe for the benefit of Bill, the most benighted of GIs. The notion that one handbook can suit every destination suggests that the rest of the world—Europe, South America, Africa, Asia—is pretty much the same. But that's precisely the point: peoples everywhere are alike in their commitment to fighting communism. It is a fight, the authors suggest, that transcends diversity of language, customs, religion, color: "Any way you look at it this job of holding back Red aggression is just too big for one nation." Communism is now described as a "threat of aggression even worse than the one we got rid of when we and our allies licked the Nazis and the Japanese warlords." Yet there are also contradictions. As the guide makes clear, the persistent presence of American defenders of freedom is no longer perceived as a boon throughout the rest of the world. Bill and Joe, once "welcomed warmly as allies by the native populace," have become uninvited guests: "As time went on the attitude of many of the people changed from friendliness to aloofness, sullen resentment or downright dislike."

It is Bill's typically American complaint about ingratitude—
"You'd think they'd show some appreciation of what we're
doing for them"—that prompts Joe to dispense some official
wisdom on behalf of his government. It takes the form of a
parable about the mythical nation of "Atlantis." First, he asks
Bill, "How would you like it if a lot of foreign soldiers were
camped all over the United States?" But this is too great a leap
for the rather dense Bill, who is simply incapable of imagining the United States as anything but "the richest and most
powerful country in the world." To stand in for the Marshall
Plan, Joe invents "Atlantic Aid." In his hypothetical scenario,
the United States is forced to accept, along with various other
humiliations and indignities, having troops stationed near
Bill's hometown, enduring their unintentionally obnoxious
behavior, putting up with their inability to speak English, en-
vying them for being the "sharpest and best paid," and having a huge stockpile of supplies available to them at the post
exchange. Worst of all, Joe tells Bill, "The first thing they'd
do would be to make a play for our girls."

When Bill finally catches on, Joe cautions him against
all those offenses to which an occupying force is susceptible: exhibiting bad manners; criticizing the politics of their
allies and asking why they put more money into social wel-
fare than into defense; telling their hosts who won the war
and reminding them who continues to pay the bills; failing
to understand other cultures, especially those of poor nations that "have a high degree of civilization" and value other
things over material prosperity. "Remember," the reader is
admonished, "that the shabby little man who shines shoes
for a living may know the scores of half a dozen operas from
overture to the final curtain." Americans' bad behavior, Joe
explains, plays right into the hands of the communists. Rich
with comic illustrations, the *Guide to Anywhere* for the most
part applies a light touch. But it also tries to impress upon its

readers that they are on the front lines of an existential crisis. A devious enemy is at work, the booklet warns, trying to destroy all those who believe in "the inborn dignity of *every* individual." It also displays a recognition of the various ways in which even well-intentioned protectors blunder and inspire resentment.

American Ironies

By the spring of 1950, only five years after the end of World War II, the United States was at war again. The fighting in Korea would last for three years. In the midst of it, the American theologian and liberal activist Reinhold Niebuhr, in *The Irony of American History*, attempted to make sense of the United States' newfound role in the international struggle against communist aggression. Robert Warshow had drawn a comparison between the desperate optimism of democratic and communist societies in his 1948 essay on the gangster archetype. The sternly anticommunist Niebuhr likewise attempted to illuminate certain crucial similarities between adversaries—commonalities to which Americans were blinded by their own history as well as by the suddenness with which the country had been catapulted onto the world stage.

Niebuhr's definition of irony sets the stage for a cautionary reading of the Cold War standoff. A comic circumstance is incongruous, he explains, but the comic turns ironic if the incongruity reveals a deeper transformation—"if virtue becomes vice through some hidden defect in the virtue; if strength becomes weakness because of the vanity to which strength may prompt the mighty man or nation; if security is transmuted into insecurity because too much reliance is placed upon it; if wisdom becomes folly because it does not know its own limits." When incongruities are recognized but not remedied, Niebuhr goes on to argue, irony turns to malevolence. He believed that such a transformation had already occurred in the evolution of communism, which offered a mirror to the United States and which worked to conceal the disjunction between the ideal and the real by trying "to prove its tyranny to be 'democracy' and its imperialism to be the achievement of universal peace." It was not yet too late for the United States.

The cruelty of the Soviet regime, he argued, was rooted in the communist presumption of being able to determine history, when only hubris could lead anyone to imagine that history's long and broad drama was subject to human management. Niebuhr, the theologian, was thinking of God; other worldviews might well have substituted chance, historical forces, or the laws of physics. Niebuhr feared that the United States was vulnerable to the same mistake the Soviets had made, and to the "moral complacency" that justifies doubtful "means" by ostensibly virtuous "ends." The United States, for its part, was thus involved in a "double irony": in the Soviet Union it faced dangers that seemed wholly alien but were in fact "distilled from illusions, not generically different from our own." In failing to discern a cautionary tale in its adversary, the United States remained blind to its own precarity.

In Niebuhr's eyes, several factors complicated the United States' assumption of global preeminence, among them American culture's ambivalent attitude toward power. No country, he argued, had been more hesitant to own its preeminent position in the world than the United States—there was no "strong lust of power"—but a faith in our own innocence had left us "ill prepared to deal with the temptations of power." Moreover, once acquired, a global responsibility founded on a combination of virtue and self-interest proved no guarantor of "ease, comfort, or prosperity," but instead produced endless "vexations." This discomfort infuses *A Pocket Guide to Anywhere*, which combines idealism about American power with a frustration about how the rest of the world understands it.

American innocence—a faith in the essential virtue of our society that makes any critique evidence of ill will—is arguably one of the most important ideas explored in *The Irony of American History*. As Niebuhr outlines, the concept can be traced back to Jefferson's view of an Edenic American origin, as opposed to John Adams's recognition that no political beginning can entirely shed the innate corruptions of power and ambition. Taking advantage of geographic isolation, the Jeffersonian outlook exaggerated the break between Old and New Worlds in a way that subsequent mythographers and proponents of American exceptionalism would continue to exploit. When the First World War momentarily ended the illusion of isolation, Woodrow Wilson cannily framed U.S. intervention as making "the world safe for democracy." Niebuhr insists that this was not merely sanctimonious, but an expression of a "moral paradox": nations decline "to go to war unless it can be proved that the national interest is imperiled," but persist "only by proving that something much more . . . is at stake." Niebuhr attributes the isolationism following the First World War to some glimmering recognition that there can be no guiltless exercise of power. Yet he also acknowledges that the isolationists failed to see the truth that disavowing responsibility does not save one from guilt.

World War II confronted the United States with the facts that true security was impossible in a dangerous world and that the kind of life that would be purchased by nuclear devastation could never be worth the price. The postwar situation challenged the United States to see itself the way the rest of the world did and to respond to global resentments with something more than Tocqueville's "garrulous patriotism." Crucially, global engagement called into question the fundamentally optimistic, comic American vision of life and history, as well as our faith "in happiness as the end of life, and in prosperity" as the foundation for that "happiness." Those "tragic vicissitudes of history," so familiar to Europeans, were heretofore alien to Americans, whose idealism made them not only "certain that there is a straight path toward the goal of human happiness" but also "blind to the curious compounds of good and evil in which the actions of the best men and nations abound." Stubborn idealism always comes at a price: namely, an intolerance of complexity, compromise, and ambiguity. Thus it was left to another national incongruity—a furtive pragmatism that tempered our idealistic quest for neat and happy endings—that might, in Niebuhr's view, save us in a nuclear world from "bringing our destiny to a tragic conclusion by seeking to bring it to a neat and logical one."

The Forgotten War

One of the most important casualties of the Cold War was, in Niebuhr's view, the liberal faith in the individual: not only had hundreds of thousands of Americans been killed in World War II, but many more found themselves in Korea, despite being "promised the 'pursuit of happiness' as an inalienable right." That's essentially the complaint of navy lieutenant Harry Brubaker in James A. Michener's 1953 novel *The Bridges at Toko-Ri*. When an admiral asks Brubaker why he doesn't stay in the navy, where he might have a "great future," Brubaker responds with bitterness: "You know what I think of the navy, sir . . . Sometimes I'm so bitter I could bitch up the works on purpose . . . It would be easier to take if people back home were helping. But in Denver nobody even knew there was a war on except my wife. Nobody supports this war." The film, starring William Holden as Brubaker and released the following year, was expansive in its bitterness:

> BRUBAKER: The organized reserves were drawing pay but weren't called up. I was inactive and yet I was. I had to give up my home, my law practice, everything. I'm still bitter . . .
>
> ADMIRAL: . . . The progress this world has made has always been because of the efforts and sacrifices of a few.
>
> BRUBAKER: I was one of the few at New Guinea, Leyte, Okinawa. Why me again?
>
> ADMIRAL: Nobody knows why he gets the dirty job. And this is a dirty job. Militarily, this war is a tragedy.
>
> BRUBAKER: We ought to pull out.
>
> ADMIRAL: Now that's rubbish, son, and you know it. If we did, they'd take Japan, Indochina, the Philippines. Where'd you have us make our stand, the Mississippi? All through history men have had to fight the "wrong war" in the "wrong place," but that's the one they're stuck with.

In response to the platitudes about duty and sacrifice, Brubaker reminds the admiral of his previous sacrifices in World War II, and his anger also owes to the fact that the war is largely ignored by those at home. The admiral's perspective is more complicated and contradictory. He regards the war itself as somehow compromised and tragic even as he deems it a necessary response to aggression.

It has become a commonplace to call Korea America's "Forgotten War." In a book devoted at least in part to the consequences of collective amnesia, it is worthwhile examining more precisely the nature of this forgetfulness. The body of literature that emerged from it, including Michener's *Toko-Ri* and James Salter's *The Hunters*, was small and unheralded in comparison with the World War II–era novels of Norman Mailer, James Jones, Joseph Heller, and Kurt Vonnegut. World War II continued to generate fiction and memoir over the decades. To write about the Korean War was, in a sense, to ignore the earthquake in favor of the aftershock. One of the characters in Salter's novel captures this inherent belatedness: "Abbott had been a hero once, in Europe in another war, but the years had worked an irreversible chemistry. He was heavier now, older, and somewhere along the way he had run out of compulsion. Everyone in the wing knew it."

Perhaps no author more effectively captured the idea of Korea as belated and unremembered than William Styron, whose fiction about the conflict is always set at stateside bases rather than in Korea itself. Styron joined the marines in World War II and was slated to join the invasion of Japan when the dropping of the atomic bombs ended the war. He was called up again when the Korean War broke out, trained at Camp Lejeune, and finally discharged for medical reasons without going to war. The fiction and nonfiction (the latter largely in the form of book reviews) Styron devoted to military life relies heavily on autobiography and is uniformly infused with at once a respect for the profession of arms—"I have never regarded the military profession as a villainous calling"—and a recognition of the ways in which military life can deform the individual. In a profile of Styron in *The Guardian*, the journalist James Campbell contrasts Styron's war writing with that of Mailer and Jones, "who, while exposing the brutality of battle, did so in such a way as to aggrandise it."

Styron resists any celebration of the mysteries only the soldier knows and the seductive powers of brutality that so many authors manage at once to deplore and to glorify. There is nothing grand about war or a soldier's preparation for it in *The Long March*, a 1952 novella that chronicles the fate of a group of out-of-shape reservists embarked on a field problem in the North Carolina woods. The scenario might have been the occasion for comedy—even of the coruscating kind that characterizes *In the Clap Shack*, Styron's play about a marine hospital VD ward—but the novella opens with the accidental killing of eight marines by a short artillery round, ammunition left over from the last war. Lieutenant Culver, through whose eyes events unfold, has survived Okinawa but is wholly unprepared for witnessing such carnage at a field exercise. Like Abbott, the pilot in Salter's *The Hunters*, Culver is superannuated, and he is frightened. A kind of Rip Van Winkle, he feels "as if he had fallen asleep in some barracks in 1945 and had awakened . . . to find that the intervening freedom, growth, and serenity had been only a glorious if somewhat prolonged dream." Like Michener's Brubaker, he is resentful because he had repressed the war—pushed it from "his mind entirely"—before he was recalled to duty. But war refuses to be consigned neatly to oblivion, and thus Culver finds himself in the woods.

In the wake of the fatal accident, the regular officer in charge of the battalion, Colonel Templeton, opts to carry on with the field exercise as planned. Culver is disgusted, as is his friend Captain Mannix, another reservist who, like Culver, bears the scars of his service in World War II and has had to give up his civilian occupation and leave his wife and children behind. Mannix's bitter humor expresses the sense of "futility and isolation" Culver shares. At the conclusion of the field exercise, Templeton orders a thirty-six-mile march back to base. The march is entirely punitive. "'Reluctantly,' the Colonel went on slowly, 'reluctantly, I came to this conclusion: the Battalion's been doping off.'" In truth, the battalion, especially the headquarters company of which Mannix is in charge, is entirely unprepared. "Even without packs thirty-six miles is a long way for anybody," Mannix tells the colonel, "much less for guys who've gone soft." To Mannix's reminder that his men are mostly in the reserves, the colonel gives a reply that reveals his philosophy in a nutshell: "But they aren't reserves. They're *marines. Comprend?*"

This exchange transforms Mannix's bitterness into a seething, self-destructive rage. With a vengeful tyranny that feels as if it could have come out of an Ambrose Bierce story, Mannix marches most of the way with a nail in his foot from a defective boot, yet he refuses to let any of the men of headquarters company fall out. The long night march becomes a test of wills, especially after Mannix learns that the colonel has gone to check on the back of the column in a jeep. In Mannix, Culver now sees a "great bear cornered, bloody and torn by a foe whose tactics were no braver than his own, but simply more cunning." Mannix, whose foot becomes so raw and swollen that he can put almost no weight on it, carries on regardless. More than once he refuses the colonel's suggestion that he get into one of the trucks. Eventually, in his insistence that he is going to march the rest of the way, he grows so insubordinate that Templeton actually reaches for his sidearm: "The Colonel had made a curious, quick gesture—stage-gesture, fantastic and subtle, and it was like watching an old cowboy film to see the Colonel's hand go swiftly back to the handle of his pistol and rest there, his eyes cool and passionate and forbidding. It was a gesture of force which balked even the Captain." The colonel then informs Mannix that after the march he will have him court-martialed and sent to Korea.

The Long March unspools a series of betrayals—of the body and the spirit but also of a deeper, more pervasive kind. Culver thinks of their service as a kind of bondage in which they are periodically victimized by the heartless technologies of warfare. The catastrophic, deeply ironic betrayal that dooms Mannix, however, derives from the fact that he is as much a marine, as deeply indoctrinated, as the colonel he despises. Neither has retained sufficient "free will" to give up, or give in. Culver understands this about himself as well and brings himself almost to tears by contemplating their permanent condition—"marines forever." Then his horrified thoughts turn to his friend: "Mannix was so much a marine that it could make him casually demented. The corruption begun years ago in his drill-field feet had climbed up, over-taken him, and had begun to rot his brain."

Styron's own connection to the military began in his youth. His family's tradition of military service helped to instill in him what he called a "suicidal bravado" that prompted him to enlist in the Marine Corps, in which he served proudly, for a time. His ardor quickly cooled as he progressed through combat training, but he remained glad for the "experience . . . if only because of the way it tested my endurance and my capacity for sheer misery, physical and of the spirit. If the ordeal caused me to loathe war utterly," he writes in the introduction to a collection of some of his non-fiction on military subjects, "it also has allowed me to take quick offense at any easily expressed contempt for men who dedicate themselves to fighting our battles."

The cost of such dedication is the great theme of Styron's war writing. Nowhere is this clearer than in his posthumously published short story collection *The Suicide Run*. Combat is the crucible that redeems countless ambivalent protagonists of autobiographical and fictional war stories—from Ulysses S. Grant to Henry Fleming in *The Red Badge of Courage*, from Aeneas to the Vietnam veteran Tim O'Brien. Readers of the literature of war are conditioned to wait for the moment when the soldier's anticipation becomes the lived experience in which even the most emphatic antiwar voices tend to locate their authority. *The Suicide Run* is different: these stories are all anticipation. Written over a span of decades, these five tales about the Marine Corps during World War II and Korea derive their force from the absence of battle. Styron prefers narrators who have missed the test of combat. Like Stingo in Styron's celebrated novel *Sophie's Choice*, Paul Whitehurst, the narrator of "My Father's House," the collection's longest story, arrives in the Pacific too late to see action in World War II. Like Styron, the narrator of "Marriott, the Marine" and the title story is recalled to active duty in 1951, but never makes it to Korea. When Stingo is confronted early in *Sophie's Choice* with the story of Eddie Farrell's death on Okinawa, he confesses, "I could never get over the feeling that I had been deprived of something terrible and magnificent."

In "My Father's House," Paul is plagued by "survivor's guilt" and intoxicated by his "unheroic though spellbinding escape from death." He has no similar appreciation for war's terrible beauty. In *Darkness Visible*, a memoir for which he would become unwillingly celebrated for his frank treatment of psychological pain, Styron called depressives "the walking wounded." The term seems applicable to Paul's compulsive revisiting of something described elsewhere in the collection as "the persistent ache of my dread." *The Suicide Run* relentlessly unravels a skein of "intricately intertwined fears" explored in the collection's only previously unpublished piece, "Elobey, Annobón, and Corisco." "I found myself in a conflict I had never anticipated," the narrator confesses: "afraid of going into battle, yet even more afraid of betraying my fear, which would be an ugly prelude to the most harrowing fear of all—that when forced to the test in combat I would demonstrate my absolute terror, fall apart, and fail my fellow marines." Styron's narrators know that "real fear" is something that can never be shared but must be endured alone, even within the marines' closed and "mysterious community of men." In "My Father's House," back home in Virginia, Paul Whitehurst eases "the racking misery" remembered from his time on Saipan—where he waited for the unconsummated invasion of Japan—by drinking himself into what Tidewater Virginians call a "high lonesome." Alcohol, sexual release, and physical exhaustion provide only temporary relief for a marine's "pitiless anxiety." Both "My Father's House" and the title story's account of a reckless car trip dramatize the suicidal desire Styron acknowledged as "a persistent theme" in his work.

The perspective of the loner—the participant-observer in a culture he finds at once fascinating and repulsive— dominates this collection and produces some especially fine descriptions of the military's "athletic ballet": the "almost synchronous motion" of men firing mortars, for example. This stance also yields complex characterizations of career marines, members of a "small elite fellowship." In some ways its most authentic member is Happy Halloran, Paul's charismatic battalion commander, a pure warrior. "The single feature that made tolerable my vision of D-Day," Paul announces, "was having Happy Halloran lead me into the jaws of death." Halloran displays a plausible combination of physical toughness, insouciance, intuitive authority, and hammy sentimentality, but he appeals to Paul primarily because he is "always playfully challenging the System." Nevertheless, most of Styron's marines are irrevocably coarsened, deformed, or brutalized by that system. Even the eponymous lieutenant colonel of "Marriott, the Marine," with his fluent French and love of Flaubert, finally reveals himself bound, as thoroughly as Mannix, to "the Old Corps" by sacred ties the narrator cannot share.

Even when edged with disappointment or pity, however, these portraits are scrupulously drawn. In the eyes of the marooned Colonel Wilhoite—who, having missed out on the war, commands the East River island prison that is the 1944 setting for "Blankenship"—can be discerned "specters of battles unseen and medals unwon and the slow final ooze of unlaureled retirement." The story's title character, Charles Blankenship, is a warrant officer in charge of the blockhouse where the most recalcitrant inmates are held. He may be the book's most illuminating character. Saddled with an ineffectual superior, Blankenship has a finely calibrated sense of his own abilities. A hero at Guadalcanal who shuns "swagger or parade," he is governed by "a calm and unshakable sense of order." Blankenship anticipates the periodic crises that violate this sense with the dutiful devotion and "tranquil, fierce patience of a communicant awaiting the moment of passion." Yet even this disciplined "sober professional," provoked by an intransigent prisoner named McFee, reveals his ultimate contamination by the "humiliating baggage" of the military "caste system" when his discipline and restraint give way in a moment reminiscent of the saintly Billy's almost involuntary striking of Claggart in Melville's *Billy Budd*. Blankenship, briefly "unhinged," clubs the prisoner, who, even as he slumps to the floor, tells Blankenship he, not McFee, is the real "yardbird." "Blankenship" literalizes the relationship between military service and imprisonment articulated in "Marriott, the Marine," in which the narrator likens his emotions on returning to duty during the Korean conflict to "those of an ex-convict who has savored the sweet taste of liberty only to find himself once more a transgressor at the prison gates."

Like *The Long March*, *The Suicide Run* confines itself largely to the damage done to men beyond the battlefield proper—to those who must dwell perpetually in anticipation of the horrors to come. Styron's understanding of the cruel insularity and sheer drudgery of long passages of military life prevents him from according to soldiers the kind of hero worship at the root of America's response to war. In a review of General Douglas MacArthur's *Reminiscences*, Styron brilliantly captures MacArthur's attitude and its roots in a desire "to transform the drab reality of American military life into something as rich and as mythic as medieval knighthood." In MacArthur's career, and in his shamelessly nostalgic rhetoric about the days of battle, Styron perceives not patriotism, but a very different allegiance. Most military professionals, he argues,

> far from corresponding to the liberal cliché of the superpatriot, are in fact totally lacking in patriotism. They are not unpatriotic; they simply do not understand or care what patriotism is. Most of them . . . are spiritually bound to a Service, not a country, and the homage they pay to Old Glory they could pay to anyone's flag. A true military man is a mercenary . . . and it is within the world of soldiering that he finds his only home. This is why MacArthur . . . was able to become the very archetype of an expatriate, hostile to America and understanding almost nothing of it. This is also one of the reasons why . . . he found it so easy to defy civilian authority; what did these Secretaries of the Army and fussy Presidents . . . know about the Service, which transcends all?

In few instances, perhaps, does the soldier's spiritual bond to the service take the monastic and extreme form it did in MacArthur's case, and few have the opportunity to display it at such senior levels of command. But Styron's portrait of MacArthur as "a hopeless romantic" distills the kind of devotion to military service felt by many. It works to abstract military enterprise from its political context.

A similar dynamic can be seen in Sanford Friedman's

Totempole. Corporal Stephen Wolfe, the novel's protagonist, arrives in Korea fresh from college to be greeted by his commander, Colonel Clayborn, who explains the situation to him as follows:

> I see from your records that you're a college man. Fine, fine. That makes what I'm about to say a whole lot easier for both of us. I think by now it should be obvious— even to a child—that this entire conflagration—I'm speakin' of Korea now—has nothin' whatsoever to do with *war*—at least as far as *I* understand the meanin' of the word . . . What's happenin' at Panmunjom, what's happenin' right here—just outside the window there . . . is somethin' I call politics. And politics, whatever you may think, will never be as honorable as war.

Even though the violence is just as deadly as that of "war," Clayborn believes that events in Korea are something else, and by insisting that they are "politics," he imagines that it is somehow possible to fight an ideal form of war, beyond politics, and that there the highest kind of honor might be found.

Signally, one of the emblematic stories of Korea turns out to be that of the lost platoon, which dramatizes the divorce of action from context through an exclusive focus on a small group of men who are fearful, isolated, apparently forgotten by the larger war. Jeanine Basinger offers a comprehensive history of the subgenre of war films about lost patrols in *The World War II Combat Film: Anatomy of a Genre.* She also calls attention to "a harsh new cynicism" emergent in some films of the Korean War, which otherwise share many attributes of their World War II predecessors. Two of them, *The Steel Helmet* (1951) and *Men in War* (1957), present stories of lost patrols with a similar cynicism. They depict depleted platoons that have been separated from larger commands. The isolation is absolute in *Men in War*, which it is possible to watch without knowing precisely where or why the war is being fought. The film opens on a shattered landscape: smoke drifts across the screen, periodically obscuring the view. The whole world is reduced to a small valley, in which soldiers, several of them looking despondent, even shocked, watch and wait. The men in the platoon, commanded by Lieutenant Benson (Robert Ryan), have, as David Thomson writes, "no backstory, and little chance of a future. They are figures" in the director's "beautiful landscape photography." The soldiers exist only in this moment in this valley, under orders to take Hill 465 yet unable to communicate their desperate situation to battalion.

When they finally reach the hill after a harrowing march through open country and a treacherously beautiful wood seeded with mines, Benson decides to attempt the hill with his undermanned platoon. When Riordan (Phillip Pine), his radio operator, tells him he's going to try to raise battalion on the radio, the lieutenant replies, "Well, battalion doesn't exist. Regiment doesn't exist. Command headquarters doesn't exist. The USA doesn't exist. They don't exist, Riordan, we'll never see 'em again." Only three men survive the battle: Benson, Riordan, and Sergeant Montana (Aldo Ray), whose uncompromising way of making war has been juxtaposed throughout the march with Benson's courageous and humane approach. Along the way, Montana shoots a prisoner who turns out to have a pistol concealed in his cap; once they arrive at Hill 465, he opens fire on some unidentified soldiers who are shouting in English. Disregarding the rules of war, Montana follows only his instincts, which are to mistrust everyone. This behavior repeatedly brings him into conflict with Benson, who confronts him after he kills the unidentified soldiers, who turn out to be the enemy, running downhill toward them:

BENSON: You're right Montana. You're always right. How did you know?

MONTANA: I knew.

BENSON: You couldn't see their faces.

MONTANA: I can smell 'em.

BENSON: But you couldn't see their faces. The sun was behind their back. I couldn't see their faces.

MONTANA: So what! I was right! Wasn't I?

BENSON: They might have been three Americans.

MONTANA: You're not sure, shoot first or die first!

In the end, Montana, the atavistic survivalist, assisted by Benson, takes the hill by immolating the enemy's remaining machine-gun nest with a flamethrower. The survivors then fall asleep from exhaustion and awaken in the morning to the sounds of an approaching American column.

The only significant allusion to causes in *The Steel Helmet* is made by a captured enemy officer, identified simply as "The Red" (Harold Fong), who attempts to persuade each member of an American platoon of the injustices perpetrated by their own government. One target is the Japanese American soldier assigned to guard him. Typical of Hollywood casting, in which all Asians were interchangeable, Sergeant Tanaka is played by Richard Loo, an American of Chinese descent born in Hawaii. When The Red chastises him for being a fool to fight for a country that interned his family during World War II, Tanaka dismisses his adversary as a "sloppy . . . con artist." The Red carries on regardless, telling Tanaka, "They call you dirty Jap rats, and yet you fight for them. Why?" Revealing himself to have been a proud member of the 442nd Combat Team in World War II, Tanaka replies, "Over three thousand of us idiots got the Purple Heart . . . I'm not a dirty Jap rat. I'm an American. And if we get pushed around back home, well, that's our business."

Tanaka is actually the second target of The Red's propaganda campaign. The first is an African American medic, Corporal Thompson (James Edwards), who is bandaging his enemy's wounds. "You can't eat with" white men, The Red needles him, "unless there's a war. Even then, it's difficult. Isn't that so?" Thompson agrees that it is. The major continues: "You pay for a ticket, but you even have to sit in the back of a public bus." Thompson responds calmly, "That's right. A hundred years ago I couldn't even ride a bus. At least now I can sit in the back. Maybe in fifty years sit in the middle, someday even up front. There's some things you just can't rush, buster." Expressing an inexhaustible patience that flatters white audiences, Thompson also refuses to buy what The Red is selling. The movie attempts to expose certain fundamental racial injustices within American society—injustices, for the most part, faithfully mirrored within military culture—yet puts the criticism in the mouth of an enemy officer trying to sow division among his American captors. Samuel Fuller's film thus stops short, its critique ultimately muted by the fact that the victims of the injustice are depicted as long-suffering but staunchly loyal. Acquiring nobility through their endurance, Tanaka and Thompson are victims of discrimination who will not discomfit movie audiences unduly.

Les Enfants Perdus

The story of race—in particular of racial injustice against African Americans—is inextricably intertwined with the narrative of war throughout the history of the United States. African American soldiers were promised political equality in the Revolution, when the British offered enslaved men their freedom if they would fight as Loyalists, and again in the Civil War, in which both sides, equally steeped in the Western tradition's linking of military service with citizenship, saw African American participation as a guarantor of civil rights. The Confederacy did not want slaves to serve as soldiers precisely because they recognized that such service would constitute an argument for their humanity and citizenship. Almost every history of the African American military experience begins by quoting Frederick Douglass's 1863 endorsement of the campaign for Black enlistment in the Federal Army. "Once let the black man get upon his person the brass letters US, let him get an eagle on his button, and a musket on his shoulder, and bullets in his pocket," Douglass proclaimed, "and there is no power on earth or under the earth which can deny that he has earned the right of citizenship in the United States." After the Civil War, however, the promise of full political equality was betrayed, as it would be again after World War I. In the wake of the First World War, Paul Laurence Dunbar reflected in his poem "The Colored Soldiers" on the still-withheld recompense for African American sacrifice: "They were comrades then and brothers, / Are they more or less to-day?"

The issue of race—and racial tension—is broached at the very beginning of *The Steel Helmet*. In addition to the casual racism of American soldiers toward Koreans and Chinese, the relationship between the Black Corporal Thompson and a crude and crusty white sergeant named Zack (Gene Evans) is characterized by a complex mixture of solidarity and suspicion. Both having been separated from their units for one reason or another, Thompson and Zack meet up in the middle of the woods. Fed up with amateurs, they recognize in each other an old hand:

ZACK: So you were in the last one too, huh? . . . Red Ball Express?

THOMPSON: Yeah. Till they asked for volunteers for a rifle outfit.

ZACK: Yeah, that was to prove you guys could shoot besides drive trucks. I remember . . . Did you stay in after the last one?

THOMPSON: No. Went back to school. GI Bill.

ZACK: Oh, yeah? Go to Paris? Paint any of them pictures?

THOMPSON: Nah. Took up surgery.

ZACK: Yeah? Where? In a butcher shop?

THOMPSON: You must have been hit in the mouth.

ZACK: Yeah. D-Day. Normandy. By an 88. Half my back I'm wearing on my face.

Zack's ridicule of the veteran studying art on the GI Bill is incidental, but the idea was in the air. Vincente Minnelli's musical *An American in Paris*, released the same year as Fuller's film, stars Gene Kelly as Jerry Mulligan, an ex-GI who is trying to build a career as a painter in the French capital. The real import of the exchange is racial. Zack chooses to interpret Thompson's crack about being "hit in the mouth" literally, but Thompson is of course responding to Zack's insult about taking up surgery. Yet Zack does have a grudging respect for Thompson's combat service. As a member of the Red Ball Express during World War II, Thompson convoyed supplies along a treacherous seven-hundred-mile route for Patton's Third Army in its swift advance across Europe. Most African American soldiers were assigned to support branches such as the Transportation Corps because they were not trusted to serve in combat roles. In *The Double V: How Wars, Protest, and Harry Truman Desegregated America's Military* Rawn James Jr. calculates that in 1942, when the army badly needed infantrymen, "75 percent of the army's African American soldiers were assigned to labor battalions."

Seventy-five percent of those who drove the Red Ball Express were African American. Zack's comment thus strikes at the heart of the army's policy toward Black soldiers.

During World War I, faced with the prospect of menial labor, highly trained African American units who wanted to fight were eventually assigned to the French army, which willingly employed them as combat troops. The French referred to these soldiers as *les enfants perdus*, or the lost children. During World War II, Black soldiers continued to be disproportionately assigned to labor battalions, segregated from the rest of the force, given inferior facilities, commanded by white men, and subjected to judicial and extrajudicial violence abroad and at home, especially in the South. Even in the 1940s, the service's philosophy on race was largely consistent with a 1925 study prepared by the Army War College for the chief of staff on the "employment of negro man power in war," an unambiguously racist document that baldly asserted the inferiority of African American intellect and character. "In the process of evolution," its authors declared, "the American negro has not progressed as far as the other subspecies of the human family."

The navy employed Black sailors exclusively as cooks and stewards. In his memoir *Crossing the Line*, Alvin Kernan, who joined the navy just before the outbreak of war in 1940, describes naval culture as "covertly anti-Semitic and openly racist . . . It was a lily-white navy that never gave its racism a thought." Meanwhile, the Marine Corps refused to admit Black Americans at all—the commandant insisting that African Americans had no "right" to be marines—until ordered to do so in 1942. The largest service, the army, was referred to at the time, and for years after the war, as the "Jim Crow Army" because of its policies and procedures. A 1944 War Department pamphlet, *Command of Negro Troops*, marked an advance over the 1925 study in its attribution of certain disparities between white and Black soldiers in test scores and other performance measures to educational, socioeconomic, and other external factors. Nevertheless, this guide for commanding Black soldiers, a job still left largely to white officers, delegated decisions regarding discipline and training to local commanders, even as it acknowledged that the Selective Service Act prohibited "racial discrimination in the selection and training of men for military duty." Most of the largest army installations were located in the South, and appeals to military necessity, from George Marshall on down, could always be used to justify existing discriminatory policies. The military is not, more than one official has defensively proclaimed over the years, a sociological experiment. Although no prudent commander would employ such language regarding race today, many have had no difficulty in using it to express their resistance to full equality for female, gay, and transgender soldiers.

Military culture quite naturally reflected the racist attitudes and policies of the rest of the country. It was the defense industry's refusal to hire African Americans that inspired the "Double V" campaign, launched on February 7, 1942, by the *Pittsburgh Courier*, an African American newspaper. "Double V" stood for victory abroad and at home. The paper encouraged Black participation in the war effort while simultaneously demanding full civil rights and an end to segregation. In June 1941, the labor leader A. Philip Randolph's threatened march on Washington impelled President Roosevelt to issue Executive Order 8802, which prohibited discrimination on the basis of race or ethnicity in the workplace: "There shall be no discrimination in the employment of workers in defense industries or government because of race, creed, color, or national origin." The order did not prevent segregation, however.

Chester Himes, perhaps best known for his detective fiction set in Harlem, documented the rampant racism of a Long

Beach, California, shipyard in his 1945 novel *If He Hollers Let Him Go*. The novel depicts life among African American defense workers, segregated on the ships they are refitting, denied promotion and supervisory roles despite their skill and technical expertise, deeply ambivalent, as a result of their mistreatment, about the war effort itself. Himes's wartime home front is riven by hatred and mistrust. Bob Jones is a skilled Black ship worker who runs afoul of the system. The novel opens with Jones's recognition of the "crazy, wild-eyed, unleashed hatred that the first Jap bomb on Pearl Harbour let loose." He feels in this climate as if he must look "yellow," too, and his sense of himself as the enemy infuses the entire novel. Ultimately, Bob is forced to take refuge in the city's Little Tokyo, emptied by the authorities and since taken over by the city's other disenfranchised minorities.

Everything, to Bob, is racialized, even his commute to the shipyards. The racial tensions in Los Angeles involved Latinos as well, and the novel alludes to the Zoot Suit Riots, sparked when white servicemen attacked Latino civilians. GIs, Bob notes, "were always hostile towards a Jodie," the term for a man not in uniform, "especially a black Jodie in his fine Jodie clothes." There was an uptick in racial violence throughout the country during the war. In 1942 alone, as James notes in *The Double V,* there were more than 240 riots and racial incidents across the country, from Harlem to Los Angeles, Mobile to Detroit. In "Notes of a Native Son," published in 1955, James Baldwin describes the particular tension in Harlem during the war: "It would have demanded an unquestionable patriotism, happily as uncommon in this country as it is undesirable, for these people not to have been disturbed by the bitter letters they received, by the newspaper stories they read, not to have been enraged by the posters, then to be found all over New York, which described the Japanese as 'yellow-bellied Japs.'"

Bob Jones and his fellow ship workers in *If He Hollers* regard the war exclusively as "the white man's war." When Bob first gets in trouble at the shipyard, it is by no means clear that the union will defend him. Without his protected status as a defense worker—something the management is not above threatening to remove to ensure compliance—he will be subject to the draft. During one of their shifts his coworkers discuss what it might mean to join the army. If a Black man "refuses to go," states a man named Ben, "they send him to the pen. But if he does go and take what they put on him, and then fight so he can keep on taking it, he's a cowardly son of a bitch." A fellow worker named Smitty challenges Ben: "You can't call coloured soldiers cowards, man. They can't keep the Army from being like what it is, but hell, they ain't no cowards." But Ben remains unconvinced: "Any time a Negro says he believes in democracy but won't die to enforce it — I say he's a coward . . . If Bob lets them put him in the Army he's a coward . . . As long as the Army is Jim Crowed a Negro who fights in it is fighting against himself."

The men's political discussions have something in common with the contemporaneous communist pamphlet *Jim-Crow in Uniform*, by Claudia Jones. The American Communist Party line was antiwar until Hitler violated his pact with Stalin, but the resistance to war and military service in the African American community went far beyond the Party. The historical roots are anatomized in "A Negro Looks at This War," an article in *The American Mercury*, in which the educator J. Saunders Redding's 1942 meditates on African American attitudes toward military heroism. Wars belonged to "white folks," his parents told him. They were engaged in a different kind of struggle: "a fierce, bitter, soul-searing war of spiritual and economic attrition." Redding traced their cynicism about white people's wars back to his grandmother, a former slave who used to tell her grandchildren a Civil War story about her master's son: "An' he done som'pin big an' brave away down dere to Chickymorgy [Chickamauga] an' dey made a iron image of him 'cause he got his head blowed off an' his stomick blowed out fightin' to keep his slaves." This "iron image" of one man who died "to keep his slaves" stands in for the thousands of statues and plaques throughout the country that perpetuate a carefully engineered lie, one both North and South were complicit in propounding: namely, that the Civil War, now safely in the past, amounted to a battle between honorable white brothers now reconciled.

Many of Bob Jones's ambitions are conventionally American: he dreams of owning a house with a victory garden, of becoming a lawyer and taking his place in society. But when he is wrongly accused of attacking a white woman, he must go on the run, and his belief that "the whole structure of American thought" is against him is confirmed. The novel is punctuated by Jones's serial nightmares, which eventually turn real as he is hunted by the police. In his final dream, he is tracked by a psychotic marine sergeant with a chestful of decorations who boasts that he has committed all sorts of crimes, except, as he says with regret, "I ain't killed a nigger yet." Eventually, the woman who has falsely accused him of assault withdraws her complaint. The judge, meanwhile, invites the head of the shipyard to lecture Bob about having betrayed the trust the company had placed in him by making him a supervisor: "You were selected because you were considered the highest type of Negro." But Bob is still wanted on a concealed-weapons charge, so the judge makes a deal with him—"Suppose I give you a break, boy"—and Jones is allowed to choose his branch of service. The novel ends with the following line: "Two hours later I was in the Army."

More than two decades later, in the 1969 novel *Blind Man with a Pistol*, Himes was still writing about the war and its impact on his most celebrated characters, the detectives "Grave

Digger" Jones and "Coffin Ed" Johnson. Confronting a new era of civil unrest in Harlem, Jones explains the generational divide he perceives: "These youngsters were born just after we'd got through fighting a war to wipe out racism and make the world safe for the four freedoms . . . But the difference is that by the time we'd fought in a jim-crow army to whip the Nazis and had come home to our native racism, we didn't believe any of that shit . . . Maybe our parents were just like our children and believed their lies . . . But what saves colored folks our age is we ain't never believed it. But this new generation believes it. And that's how we get riots."

The segregated miseries that awaited the more than one million Black men—more than 2.5 million registered for the draft—who served during World War II, approximately half of them overseas, have been amply documented by participants and historians. Such were the conditions created by many World War II–era post commanders that, as Baldwin suggests in his description of wartime Harlem, it came as a "relief" to many African American service members when they were sent overseas. "Perhaps the best way to sum all this up," Baldwin writes in "Notes of a Native Son,"

> is to say that the people I knew felt, mainly, a peculiar kind of relief when they knew that their boys were being shipped out of the south, to do battle overseas. It was, perhaps, like feeling that the most dangerous part of a dangerous journey had been passed and that now, even if death should come, it would come with honor and without the complicity of their countrymen. Such a death would be, in short, a fact with which one could hope to live.

Charles Gates, a veteran of the 761st Tank Battalion, told Studs Terkel in the 1980s, "I had experienced so much prejudice in Louisiana that when I got to Europe, it was a joke." At the front, however, Gates found no bigotry. He recalled, "You don't have time for prejudice in a foxhole . . . At the close of hostilities—that's when strange things started happening. They started checking the areas where Negro troops were located, and they tried to poison the minds of the people." In particular, Gates alludes to unfounded accusations of rape. As the historian Mary Louise Roberts has documented extensively in *What Soldiers Do*, Black soldiers in the European Theater were disproportionately convicted of sex crimes and executed.

Abuses at home ranged from harassment to violence. Arguments about military efficiency notwithstanding, segregation, which was time-consuming and expensive, was enforced in Pennsylvania and Massachusetts, not just south of the Mason-Dixon Line. Dempsey Travis told Terkel, "I think of two armies, one black, one white. I saw German prisoners free to move around the camp, unlike black soldiers, who were restricted." This dynamic forms the subject of Witter Bynner's poem "Defeat," in which the sight of German prisoners eating with white soldiers on a train while Black soldiers were segregated leads the speaker to conclude that the "dead South has won." Dempsey was assigned to Camp Shenango, Pennsylvania. Arriving on a segregated troop train, he found a likewise segregated post on which Black servicemen lived in a kind of ghetto, without access to the post exchange (PX), servicemen's club, or any of the five movie theaters. One night, after a Black soldier's eye was "kicked out for going into the PX to get a beer," white MPs in battle gear descended on the area in which Black soldiers were housed and starting firing into the crowd, killing several and wounding more, including Travis. Nor was this an isolated incident, as numerous historians have recorded. Linda Hervieux notes in *Forgotten: The Untold Story of D-Day's Black Heroes*, at Home *and at War* that the Southern Governors Conference of 1942 registered a unanimous objection to the "thousands of black recruits pour[ing] into army bases built to take advantage of year-round training in temperate weather." Northern Black soldiers, unfamiliar with the grosser indignities and physical dangers of life in the South, found themselves in a precarious position.

Taking the bus proved a particularly perilous experience. Sometimes drivers wouldn't let Black soldiers aboard; at other times, Black soldiers from the North refused to move to the back, and the driver had local law enforcement drag them off. This was the case in one of the war's most well-known incidents of racial violence, the blinding of Sergeant Isaac Woodard. Woodard boarded a Greyhound bus in Georgia on his way home in 1946, after serving in the Pacific as a longshoreman. He and a group of white soldiers were socializing freely and passing around a whiskey bottle, which Woodard, a teetotaler, did not share. At one point he got up to ask the driver to use the men's room at the next stop. Calling him "boy," the driver told him to sit back down and be quiet. Woodard replied, "I'm a man just like you," a retort that scandalized the driver. Assuming that Woodard must be drunk, the driver asked him to get off the bus and talk to the police at the next stop. When Woodard did so, two policemen beat him so violently that they blinded him in both eyes. Woody Guthrie commemorated the incident in his song "The Blinding of Isaac Woodard," which he sang at a benefit held at Lewisohn Stadium in Harlem, while Orson Welles made the incident the subject of several radio broadcasts.

Woodard's blinding also contributed to President Harry Truman's decision to sign Executive Order 9981, which, in 1948, began the slow work of desegregating the armed forces. It took many more years before all the services would fully comply; the army was especially recalcitrant. Isaac Wood-

ard's treatment is only the most notorious example of the
many indignities inflicted upon Black Americans in uniform
by other service members and civilians. Hervieux records a
scathing comment by Grant Reynolds—who, along with A.
Philip Randolph, formed the Committee Against Jim Crow
in Military Service and Training—on his wartime experience
at Camp Lee, Virginia: "The South was more vigorously engaged in fighting the Civil War than in training soldiers to
resist Hitler." One of the chief ironies inherent in the project
of bringing democracy to the rest of the world remained the
signal failure to practice it at home.

The correspondence of a group of African American servicemen from Brooklyn, New York, housed in the archives
of the New York Public Library's Schomburg Center, powerfully exposes the fear of homegrown enemies that stalked
them in the service. This circle consisted of relatives and
friends of Edgar Thomas (Ned) and Elnora (Nora) Williams. The Williams's son, E. T., surmises that the network
had its origins in Brooklyn's Concord Baptist Church. The
letters are addressed to Nora, who evidently circulated news
to a wide network of friends throughout the war. Her letters
do not survive.

Writing to Nora from various stateside posts and later
from overseas assignments, the men complain of inadequate
facilities. One correspondent, Mark Jackson, writes from an
airfield near Fresno, California, that there is no USO for
Black service members. "The people in town (Fresno) treat
us as if we were Japs, but I don't blame them as some of these
fellows have asked for it," he adds, alluding to heavy drinking among his peers. Although the racism is not as overt in
California as it had been in Tuskegee, Alabama, where Jackson had previously been stationed, he explains, "They have
other ways here." William J. Hammond, attending radio repair school in Kansas City in 1943, tells Nora, "Down here in

Kansas City, it is 'beat.' You know Missouri is in the South, so therefore you can imagine just what I mean." Being sent to Camp Stewart, Georgia, is the realization of a nightmare: "Well I am down here in Georgia at last," wrote Hammond. "I really do hate it here."

Part of the problem stemmed from Black soldiers' inability to leave post. Nora's brother-in-law John C. Williams reported that Fort Bragg, North Carolina, was a "hell-hole," but that he and his comrades were "sort of restricted" and unable to go into town. In May 1943 Nora's brother Herman Bing, a medic, reported from Camp Pickett, Virginia, that he had gotten into a fight on a bus after a local man told a Black GI to move to the back. He and his friend had been able to escape punishment by melting into the crowd so that no one could identify them. Other correspondents allude to incidents on buses, a run-in with a sheriff, and multiple encounters with bigots in uniform and out. Upon arrival at Camp Shelby, Mississippi, the previous fall, Herman had rendered a more succinct verdict on southern living: "The south aint s—t." Later, when he is transferred to Camp Gordon Johnston, in the Florida Panhandle, his mood turns desperate. He nicknames the post "West Hell," the "brother" to Bataan—he had seen the movie *Bataan*, released that year. "The crackers here call you nigger in a minute & we have no Service club, theater or nothing to go to. The barracks are no where the place is made up of burnt lumber & and the floors are made of sand. So far we all wish we were dead & in hell cause this place will drive the average man crazy." Later in the letter, Herman confesses to his sister, "For the first time since I've been in the Army I feel that I won't see any of you again & that's a hellva feeling to have . . . All the boys down here walk around like Zombies." Another brother, Thomas, registers his concern for Herman in the Deep South. Indeed the entire correspondence is shot through with the overwhelming fear of being sent south—in a twentieth-century reprise of the enslaved person's fear of being sold down the river—and with anxiety for those men who have been assigned there.

One of the most positive letters from Nora Williams's correspondents came from William P. Scruggs, who had been assigned to Officer Candidate School (OCS) at Fort Benning, Georgia. "We get treated just like officers," Scruggs notes. OCS was one of the military's few experiments in integration, and the successful performance of Black candidates in an integrated environment invalidated many rationales for continued segregation. Clifton Nanton attended OCS "in a mixed group" at the navy's Service Schools Command in Illinois, where he was pleased to be able to "show some of these people that they don't have any priority on intelligence." Ned's brother John also went to OCS. He deployed to England in 1944 as a second lieutenant. A letter from this period reveals how the army carried its bigotry overseas:

> All in all tho I'll certainly be glad when it's all over if for no other reason than so that I can get out of this uniform and stop having to swallow some of the insults that I've swallowed . . . I think that since I've been over here I've stood for more than I ever have or expect to stand for in life. Not from the British but from our own white countrymen. The British resent the American white man's attitude and don't bite their tongues about saying so.

Elsewhere, John told Nora he was "staying out of trouble . . . quite a job when you are colored and in this man's army." The U.S. Armed Forces exported segregation to Britain, France, Germany, New Guinea, Japan, and elsewhere. Discrimination ruled the day overseas, especially in Germany, well into the 1960s.

The authors of the government's pocket guides were highly attuned to racial issues, and they were acutely aware that the ambient racism of the armed forces might hamper the war effort. *A Short Guide to Iraq* (1943) exhorts GIs, "Avoid any expression of race prejudice. The people draw very little color line." The *Guide to Alaska* emphasizes the differences between "white" and other Alaskans, but it also sees fit to remind readers that indigenous peoples are not freeloaders: "They have the obligations of citizenship, including service in the Armed Forces and payment of Federal income taxes." In the *Guide to Hawaii*, Hawaiians are described as "just as American as you. And just as proud of it." Japanese Americans in particular—who were not interned in Hawaii, because it proved impractical and they were needed for the war effort—are praised for their loyalty. Discussions of race prove extremely awkward in the guides. The authors work to dispel prejudice but can't always navigate the terrain without recourse to inappropriate humor or clumsy analogies. For example, although the *Guide to Hawaii* praises the bravery of Japanese American soldiers (who fought in North Africa and Italy as members of the 442nd Infantry Regimental Combat Team), it stumbles badly in suggesting that what really makes them American is their enthusiasm for Bob Hope.

The subject of race becomes most complicated in the *Pocket Guide to West Africa*, produced by the army's Special Service Division in 1943 for distribution to soldiers and sailors deployed to the region to guard supply lines. This was in many ways a typical guide: it offered practical advice, reassured personnel of the significance of their contribution to the war effort, and emphasized the need for humility and goodwill toward their hosts. The guide also advises readers not to expect Hollywood's West Africa. "There are no men like Tarzan there and no Tarzan mates in leopard skins. You probably won't see any steaming jungles, or herds of wild animals either; and certainly no naked cannibals." Unlike the guides produced for European countries, however, this one has few tourist recommendations and more details about the physical attributes of the inhabitants: "The population is almost completely African," the authors explain, "and varies in color from jet black to golden brown . . . The point is," they continue, "that though darker than most peoples you know, and differing considerably in the way they eat, dress, and live, the West Africans are pretty much like people all over the world." Africans are, the guide cheerfully reassures its American readers, "no lazier than other people in tropical climates."

It becomes increasingly clear that the authors are writing not simply for a white audience but for one that harbors a virulent color prejudice. To dispel it, they link racial hostility toward Black people to the Nazis. The guide reminds readers that "educated West Africans are fully aware of . . . the Nazi scorn for the black people. They know of the false Nazi theory of 'master' and 'slave' races." In the book's assurance that the educated African knows all about the Atlantic Charter and the Four Freedoms and "that the United States considers men as equal," there is a remarkable cognitive dissonance at work. At great pains to preempt racial incidents, the guide emphasizes the difference between West Africans and Black Americans and warns, "The educated African of the town is even more sensitive about racial issues than the American Negro, and admires dignity and reserve."

The book's mandate to suppress race prejudice is nowhere more apparent, however, than in the following injunction: "Race prejudice against the African or against American Negro troops in Africa would be a good way to turn the African against us. Everyone is entitled to his own prejudices but it would be only sensible for those who have them to keep them under cover when such high stakes as the war and men's lives are on the table. None of us wants to aid Hitler." This purely practical argument sits side by side with the clear acknowledgment that Africans not only understand freedom, dignity, and equality but also identify these values with the United States, the same country that has to warn its soldiers repeatedly to conceal the prejudices they openly display at home—the same country in which, as Stouffer's *The American Soldier* documents, a 1943 government survey of American enlisted men revealed that only thirteen percent of those surveyed could name three of the Four Freedoms. The guide never resolves this jumble of contradictions. Revealingly, it cautions white GIs not to be flattered by servile behavior of Black Africans: "Keep it in mind that when an African calls you 'Massa' (master) he usually hopes to get something from you."

Throughout the war, there were protests large and small against the racist practices and policies dominating army life. At Fort Devens, Massachusetts, Black WACs who had been trained as medical technicians were restricted to menial labor and ordered to wear a special blue smock, which made them look like maids rather than the authorized uniform. The WACs struck in 1945, demanding to meet with the hospital commander—a colonel from Maine—who insisted that "black girls" were "fit only to do the dirtiest type of work." The four technicians who refused to return to work after the meeting were court-martialed, but their convictions were ultimately overturned after a public outcry. The full story can be found in Sandra M. Bolzenius's *Glory in Their Spirit: How Four Black Women Took on the Army During World War II.* Similar incidents occurred elsewhere. At Indiana's Freeman Field, the commander used bureaucracy to deny officers of the 477th Bombardment Group, a unit of Black bomber pilots-in-training, access to the post club by restricting it to "permanent officers" and simultaneously designating the

477th "temporary officers." When officers of the 477th attempted to enter the white club on several occasions, they
were arrested. A series of peaceful protests, which came to
be called the Freeman Field Mutiny, helped to call national
attention to the army's systemic problems.

James Gould Cozzens used this incident in his 1948 novel
Guard of Honor, but he moved it to the South. The novel documents the ongoing struggle at a Florida base. One morning Lieutenant Edsell offers a satirical account of a violent
incident that occurred a few nights before: "You may have
heard that a special group of colored officers was brought in
this week on a new project," he tells another lieutenant: "The
unreconstructed Confederates and other poor white trash,
some of it from West Point, got all hot and bothered. Next
thing, people might start treating a Negro like a human being! Can't have that! So, a lot of them decided to strike a blow
for White Supremacy . . . and when a colored medium bomb
crew came in and landed, they jumped them . . . It got hushed
up of course." When the other officer expresses disbelief,
Edsell scoffs: "That's the reason a lot of sadistic sub-morons
down in dear old Dixie can do whatever they want to any
Negro, any time. When you're told about it, you don't believe
it. Those charmin', romantic Southern boys couldn't be that
unkind, could they, sugar?"

This history is often elided from the myth of the war. Stephen Ambrose's failure to incorporate a meaningful discussion of this pervasive racism into his narrative is most obvious
in his account of the Ardennes Offensive in *Citizen Soldiers*.
There Ambrose devotes enthusiastic attention to the exploits
of Major Otto Skorzeny, "the most daring commando in the
German army, world-famous for his exploits," who was attached to Lieutenant Colonel Jochen Peiper's Panzer brigade
during the offensive. Ambrose's admiration for their audacity
distracts him from his argument about the natural superior-

ity of democratic armies, leading to a simpler consideration of battlefield prowess. And indeed, we know that the undemocratic German army was much more effective, at least in the first years of the war, than our own. Lavishing attention on Skorzeny and Peiper, Ambrose ignores another story altogether, a story about African Americans that goes a long way toward revealing the contradictions endemic to the army of the liberators. The Ardennes Offensive marked the first time Black and white American troop units were at least partially integrated. So urgent was the need for replacements that the army set aside its stated policy of segregation. Military necessity, the justification always used to argue against integration, was, in an emergency, suddenly being used for it. This was a watershed moment in American military history, one that would be forgotten once the war ended and segregation resumed. Serving in the area of the Hürtgen Forest during the Battle of the Bulge, Victor Brombert remembered the emergency appeal for African American infantrymen: "The call for volunteers was presented as a singular opportunity to fight side-by-side with the white brothers-in-arms . . . We had no contact with black soldiers . . . To be honest, we had not given this much thought—that's the way it was. But now suddenly we were shocked by the spuriousness of this call for black volunteers, simply because they were needed in battle."

Ambrose largely confines his discussion of African American soldiers in the European Theater to a later chapter called, astonishingly, "Jerks, Sad Sacks, Profiteers, and Jim Crow." Into these pages Ambrose lumps all the undesirable elements of what he regards as an otherwise magnificent army: "The Army was so big . . . and put together so quickly, that thousands of sharp operators and sad sacks, criminals and misfits, and some cowards made it through." Jerks sit atop this hierarchy of outcasts. By way of illustrative comparison, Ambrose offers the following assessment of the enemy: "Next to Hitler himself, the biggest jerks in Germany" were Göring and Himmler. Having also catalogued the chickenshits, shirkers, profiteers, sadists, and drunks, Ambrose concludes, "At the bottom of the list were the cowards, and Jim Crow." This is apparently an attempt to ventriloquize the attitudes of the day, but precisely because they were the attitudes of the day, they complicate the book's oversimplified paean to decency and democracy. Ambrose alludes to the army's policy of segregation and Eisenhower's endorsement of it in the European Theater of Operations, but he mutes its severity by illustrating it with a "little incident" involving discrimination at a stateside lunch counter. The chapter concludes on a characteristically optimistic note: "After the experience of World War II, by the end of 1945 the ground had been prepared for Jim Crow's grave." But Jim Crow survived the war, and racism in the army was still thriving as late as the Vietnam War. The Double V was postponed, just as it had been after the Civil War and World War I, when African Americans who imagined their military service would lead to full citizenship were betrayed as soon as the national emergency ended. The suppression of these details is part and parcel of the most popular myth of the war.

A slightly different problem is to be found in Brokaw's *The Greatest Generation*, in a chapter titled "Shame." Brokaw introduces it by acknowledging, "Any celebration of America's strengths and qualities during those years of courage and sacrifice, however, will be tempered by the stains of racism that were pervasive in practice and policy. As it was an era of great glory for America and its people, it was also, indisputably, a time of shame." Brokaw insists that shame and glory don't "cancel" each other out, but instead of the ambiguity seemingly promised, the profiles that follow, including one woman and representatives of different racial and ethnic minorities, all conform, as John Bodnar observes, to a particular plot deter-mined by hope, endurance, and socioeconomic achievement. Each sketch is prefaced with an uplifting epigraph highlighting the resilient attitude of these veterans regardless of the treat-ment they received. It is their capacity for patient suffering that earns them membership in the Greatest Generation.

For example, the story of the African American soldier Johnnie Holmes, "a ready volunteer," chronicles many of the abuses suffered by Black service members during the war and acknowledges that Holmes had to fight a "two-front battle . . . Germans in front of him, racial bigots at his back." But the sign of Holmes's greatness is that he prefers not to dwell on such unpleasantness: "He's much more inclined to help out at his church or take his Lincoln Town Car on long driving trips than to sit around and remember the bad old days." Community participation and economic achievement—the Town Car—produce a kind of amnesia that conforms to the book's agenda. The chapter concludes with Holmes's confirmation: "It is my country, right or wrong . . . None of us can ever contribute enough." It is this story of a Black man possessed of an undoubtedly heroic positive attitude—a man who marched with Martin Luther King Jr., yet "decided he wouldn't personally bow to the inherent frustrations of discrimination"—that holds the book's golden age together. Underreported in the book, however, are the stories of Black World War II veterans whose lives did not conform to the pattern: men like the civil rights leaders Charles and Medgar Evers, for example. Medgar was assassinated by Byron De La Beckwith of the White Citizens' Council in 1963. In the wake of his brother's murder, Charles, a complex figure who had made his postwar living as a racketeer involved in pros-titution, numbers, and bootlegging, devoted himself to a life of outspoken political activism while never quite leaving his controversial reputation behind.

The Tuskegee program, in which Black Americans were trained as pilots, is often described as one of the great successes of the war, cited by anyone wishing to find an uplifting story about race during the period. In *A-Train: Memoirs of a Tuskegee Airman*, Charles W. Dryden suggests that this "historical drama" reveals not only the heroism of African Americans but several other dramas as well: the ongoing resistance to the program, the pervasive influence of Jim Crow, and the villainy of "various 'ugly Americans.'" When the pilots stopped at bases in the South on training flights and were refused service at flight line snack bars, they often preferred to fly home hungry "rather than submit to Jim Crow" by eating elsewhere on the base. In 1944, Dryden's frustrations exploded. He was court-martialed and ultimately acquitted for flying low—"buzzing"—a tower in South Carolina. Dryden describes the welter of emotions, the "simultaneous pride and bitterness" that motivated his decision. He was proud of his abilities and resentful of the army's lack of faith, and he wanted to show everyone that the Tuskegee men were "damn good pilots." It had been an expression of "folly and unbridled anger," and "a half century later," he wrote in his memoirs, "the tears of hurt and rage still flow!"

In a 1944 article in *The New Republic*, Lucille B. Milner reported evidence of increasingly poor morale among Black servicemen. They were "patriotic," Milner wrote, and "eager to get into the fighting areas," but they were "excluded from the mainstream of military service" and thus prevented from expressing "their patriotism, their democracy, and their militancy freely. They have fought bravely in every war . . . but still they are not treated like Americans." The article relied heavily on the flood of correspondence from service members to the NAACP and other organizations. Military service in World War II contributed to a political awakening among African Americans and helped spur the civil rights movement. It gave Northern Blacks a clearer sense of conditions in the South; it gave Southerners the courage to demand their rights as citizens. In 1946, in order to vote in the primary election, more than a hundred veterans from Birmingham, Alabama, presented their discharge papers at the county courthouse as proof of their literacy. "The vast majority was rejected," Jack H. Pollack reported in *The American Mercury*. "Among those turned down were Negro officers, many with high school and college training, property owners and operators of successful businesses." A few months later the Alabama legislature, fearing, in the words of the outgoing governor, "a flood of Negro registration," passed an amendment that made the existing literacy test even more stringent.

Change in the military was also slow. When the army desperately needed troops for Korea, A. Philip Randolph, one of the leaders of the Committee Against Jim Crow in Military Service and Training, informed Truman that he was prepared to tell African Americans to boycott the draft unless the force was integrated. In 1950, once the army doubled in size, segregation became increasingly unfeasible, and at least one commander at a training center independently declared that he didn't have time to sort recruits by color. Segregation also proved impractical in the Korean theater, where there was a manpower shortage, but it took MacArthur's replacement, Matthew Ridgway, formally to desegregate the command.

As Maria Höhn and Martin Klimke argue in *A Breath of Freedom: The Civil Rights Struggle, African American GIs, and Germany*, by reproducing structural discrimination at foreign bases, "the postwar occupation of Germany—even more than the struggle against Nazi Germany during World War II—*nationalized* America's race problem, making it an *American* rather than merely a *Southern* issue, at last impelling momentum for change." That change did not come until the late

1960s, after race relations in the army exploded during the Vietnam War. White GIs burned crosses in Germany, Höhn and Klimke report; Black GIs joined various Black Power groups and began to give Black Power salutes instead of conventional military ones; and there were numerous disturbances at off-base bars and clubs designated whites only. Racial tensions also simmered throughout the Vietnam theater. White supremacist symbols became commonplace after the assassination of Martin Luther King Jr. in April 1968, when white service members prominently and provocatively displayed a Confederate flag at Cam Ranh Naval Base and burned crosses elsewhere. Jim Crow had become one of the American liberators' most visible and incongruous postwar legacies.

Slouching Towards Twenty-Five

The year 1968: assassinations, riots, burning crosses, Confederate flags, Tet, My Lai, and Khe Sanh; the twenty-fifth anniversaries of Guadalcanal, the Warsaw Ghetto Uprising, and the Allied invasion of Sicily, all of which took place in 1943. Nowhere, perhaps, was it easier to see the ways in which the wars bled into each other than in Hawaii, and no one chronicled that phenomenon more perceptively than Joan Didion. In 1968 she published *Slouching Towards Bethlehem*, a collection of essays concerned with the decade's various dislocations. In these essays, as in all of Didion's work, the interpretation of current events is rooted in the deeper history of the United States. Several provide anatomies of American exceptionalism, in addition to more topical insights. "Letter from Paradise, 21° 19′N., 157° 52′W.," originally published two years earlier in *The Saturday Evening Post* as "Hawaii: Taps over Pearl Harbor," surveys the island landscape to discover the traces of three wars.

As a child, Didion had first associated Hawaii with a place in an atlas "that meant war and my father going away and makeshift Christmases in rented rooms near Air Corps bases and nothing the same ever again." That childhood also introduced her to John Wayne, whose movies she watched in a theater in a Quonset hut at Colorado's Peterson Field during the summer of 1943. The essay "John Wayne: A Love Song" proposes that Wayne's image on the screen offered Americans a glimpse of some primal national myth. "In a world we understood early to be characterized by venality and doubt and paralyzing ambiguities," Didion writes, Wayne "suggested another world, one which may or may not have existed . . . a place where a man could move free, could make his own code and live by it; a world in which, if a man did what he had to do, he could one day take the girl and go riding through the draw and find himself home free." If the myth's hold in 1943 was already loosening, by the 1960s, it was in the wind, irretrievable. The American dreams that form the subject of so many of the essays in *Slouching Towards Bethlehem* no longer resemble those conjured by John Wayne, into whose ideal form the directors John Ford and Raoul Walsh had "poured the inarticulate longings of a nation wondering at just what pass the trail had been lost." The dreams had become instead the crooked nightmares of film noir: "A belief in the literal interpretation of Genesis," Didion writes in "Some Dreamers of the Golden Dream," an essay about a domestic murder in the San Bernardino Valley, "has slipped imperceptibly into a belief in the literal interpretation of *Double Indemnity*."

In Hawaii, Didion visits the *Utah* and *Arizona*, submerged memorials in Pearl Harbor, in order to discover what the site signifies twenty-five years on. She doesn't find out, however, because she is overwhelmed by her own response, which is to cry. When a near contemporary expresses mystification about her reaction, telling her that the Kennedy "assassination, not Pearl Harbor, was the single most indelible event of . . . 'our generation,'" she tells him, "We belonged to different generations." She goes on to tell the reader about her subsequent visit to the National Memorial Cemetery of the Pacific, where, high above Honolulu, nineteen thousand graves occupy a volcano crater named Punchbowl, where the dead all seem to be twenty years old, and where they have rested for longer than they were alive.

Four years later, Didion returns and meets Punchbowl's superintendent, Martin T. Corley, an experience she writes about in an essay called "In the Islands," which appears in *The White Album*. Corley processes the bodies and administers the burials of those killed in Vietnam: 1,078 in the first three months of 1970. Didion describes a cemetery where the dead of three wars—World War II, Korea, and Vietnam—now mingle. In this setting, Vietnam "seemed considerably less chimerical than it had seemed on the Mainland for some months, less last year's war, less successfully consigned to that limbo of benign neglect in which any mention of continuing casualties was made to seem a little counterproductive." Among the graves, the chimerical becomes real; the "nonexistent" war, palpable; statistics, individual human lives. The graveyard collapses the nominal distinctions between wars, reducing them all to a harvest of the dead. When, toward the end of the essay, Didion visits Schofield Barracks, it seems to her that nothing has changed across the years since the time of James Jones's *From Here to Eternity*: "A foursome on the post golf course seemed to have been playing since 1940, and to be doomed to continue." Watching the perennial rhythms of Schofield, Didion reveals the solipsism of military life, miraculously unbroken across the decades.

An elision of the intervals between wars, an expression of the continuity of military life, also characterizes Tim O'Brien's description of what it meant to end up in Vietnam.

"I grew out of one war and into another," O'Brien writes in his memoir *If I Die in a Combat Zone, Box Me Up and Ship Me Home*, reflecting on the ways in which the World War II service of his parents shaped his relationship to his country and, more precisely, to his own military service. "I was the offspring," he explains, "of the great campaign against the tyrants of the 1940s." Vietnam destroyed the romance of war per se, but it intensified the particular romance associated with World War II, the romance on which O'Brien grew up. Styron notes the ways in which Vietnam somehow "degraded each person . . . touched by it." As World War II "recedes, and the Pacific battlefields become merely palm-shaded monuments in the remote ocean," Styron writes in a review of Philip Caputo's Vietnam memoir, *A Rumor of War*, "there is a tendency to romanticize or to distort and forget. Bloody as we all know that conflict was, it becomes in memory cleaner and tidier—a John Wayne movie with most of the gore hosed away for the benefit of a PG-rated audience. The Marines in that war seem a little like Boy Scouts, impossibly decent. Could it be," Styron muses, "that the propinquity of the un-speakable horrors of Vietnam forces us to this more tasteful view?"

A Rumor of War also links the two wars. Born into the sub-urbia that was a by-product of the postwar housing shortage, Caputo dreamed of a "savage, heroic time . . . before America became a land of salesmen and shopping centers." This long-ing, coupled with the patriotic fervor of the Kennedy years, induced him to join the marines in 1960, a decision that would ultimately rob him of all "of the optimism and ambi-tion a young American is supposed to have." Caputo's ideas about war and heroism were shaped by World War II, spe-cifically by the movies. Like thousands of boys, he imagined himself performing heroic feats in the style of John Wayne. Caputo had no need of the recruiter's "sales pitch." Seduced by what Styron refers to as the Marine Corps's "fatal glamour," Caputo submitted himself wholly to the mob psychology of basic training. Likening the mood to a *"Bund* rally," he explains that an indoctrinated recruit eventually "begins to believe that he really does love the Marine Corps, that it is invincible, and that there is nothing improper in praying for war, the event in which the Corps periodically has justified its existence and achieved its apotheosis." The service is all, while the country it theoretically exists to serve disappears from view.

Veteran marines regale Caputo with tales of their first commands in World War II or Korea. A first command, he explains, was "supposed to be like first love," yet his own experience has already faded into a vague memory. He can't even remember the members of his platoon clearly. Caputo's first command comprised the kinds of young men who have always wielded violence in the ostensible defense of our dreams—"to a man thoroughly American, in their virtues as well as flaws: idealistic, insolent, generous, direct, violent, and provincial in the sense that they believed the ground they stood on was now forever a part of the United States simply because they stood on it." Yet the majority of Caputo's marines "came from the ragged fringes of the Great American Dream." They hadn't finished high school, they were often fatherless, and they were the victims of urban or rural poverty. "They were volunteers, but I wondered for how many enlisting had been truly voluntary." These marines prepare for Vietnam by undergoing two weeks of intensive counterinsurgency training in Okinawa, where Caputo's instructors attempt to inculcate a set of "antisocial attributes" necessary for survival. The jungle fighter "has to be stealthy, aggressive, and ruthless, a combination burglar, bank robber, and Mafia assassin." This description calls to mind the British *Handbook of Modern Irregular Warfare*

(1942), quoted by Fussell in *Wartime*: "Every soldier must be a potential gangster."

There is no ennobling cause demanding this violence, no grand strategy it serves, no goal it can possibly achieve: "In the patriotic fervor of the Kennedy years, we had asked, 'What can we do for our country?' and our country answered, 'Kill VC.'" The longer Caputo and his men are in Vietnam—the more fruitless searches they conduct, the more villages they destroy, the more death they witness and impose—the more like gangsters they become. They pass through several stages of degradation, arriving at a state "of moral and emotional numbness" before moving past "callousness into savagery." Eventually, one of the soldiers kills two prisoners on a "pretext," an action that results in a court-martial. In Caputo's eyes, the act of killing the prisoners was inseparable from the character of the war. Yet the defense counsel will not make this argument; to do so would have been to cast doubt on the whole American military action.

Styron suggests that what ultimately saved the marines in World War II was the fact that they had been sent "to kill purposefully and with a reasonably precise goal in view—not as in Vietnam to produce mere bodies for General Westmoreland's computer . . . Thus," he concludes, "the Pacific war may be viewed in retrospect as a discussible moral enterprise. It was an awful war, one of the worst . . . Tarawa, Peleliu, Iwo Jima—arguably the most satanic engagements in which men have been pitted against one another since the birth of warfare. But those who fought in the Pacific war, whatever the nature of their wounds or their diminishment, could emerge undefiled." Lyndon Johnson may have dusted off the old rhetoric of World War II to burnish the war in Vietnam—"We have declared war on tyranny and aggression"—but the latter conflict succeeded only in drowning its participants in what Styron calls "a moral swamp." Lieutenant William Calley, who presided over the massacre at My Lai in 1968, became for Styron, as for so many others, the war's most important object lesson. "Few of us may be enamored of the military," he writes in his review of Calley's autobiography, but "war is still steadfastly a part of the human condition, and . . . our very survival as human beings continues to depend on accommodating ourselves to ancient rules of conduct."

The trouble with appealing to ancient rules and codes, however, is that they are, at bottom, a fiction. Looking at honor "afresh," observes Eugen Weber in "The Ups and Downs of Honor," "we will discover that the *Iliad* . . . presents two gang-leading thugs, Achilles and Agamemnon, facing each other down, trading threats and insults over loot and women, and that the whole poem turns on plunder and pride and the sport of killing." Weber charts the destructive glamour of this kind of honor in literature as in history: "So honor is renown, glory, riches, power; but these have to be won and preserved by valiance—valor, bravery." Small wonder, Weber points out, "that when George Armstrong Custer . . . led a cavalry charge near the Little Bighorn River from which not one man came out alive, the *New York Herald* extolled the charge as 'mad' and praised the catastrophic Custer's 'strong impulses, greathearted friendship and bitter enmities, nervous temperament, undaunted courage, will and determination.'" Military culture is steeped in a tradition that defends honor and reputation by achieving dominance through destruction. Even when a war's cause is just and its actors infused with ideals of decency, its means are always violent.

Vietnam, Styron concludes, "disgraced the name of bravery." The search for a kind of honor amid the ruins, a need for redemption, burns through much of the literature of Vietnam, as it does through that of our more recent wars in Iraq and Afghanistan. It infuses Robert McNamara's astonishing 1995 book *In Retrospect: The Tragedy and Lessons of*

Vietnam, and it is what makes Errol Morris's documentary on McNamara *The Fog of War* (2003), such a strange and terrifying film. McNamara's story reveals not only the insidious and irresistible nature of war's momentum but also the ways in which a commitment to data-driven decision-making ultimately yielded a strategy of conspicuous illogic. McNamara's fascination with statistics—especially statistics substantiating the destructive capacity of strategic bombing—seems entirely to eclipse the truth. It had been no secret since World War II that "strategic bombing" had little "strategic" value. Summarizing the U.S. government's Strategic Bombing Survey, commissioned to assess the role of targeting Japanese and German cities in shortening the war, committee member John Kenneth Galbraith recalled in his memoir *A Life in Our Times,* "Our patiently gathered data on the disastrous failures of strategic bombing were extensively ignored." As the historian Gian Gentile notes, even the final report contained the "disturbing conclusion . . . that strategic bombing, during 1943 and into early 1944, might have helped streamline, rather than injure, the German war economy." One of the most well-known poems of the war, "The Fury of Aerial Bombardment," by Richard Eberhart, concludes that the devastation (strategically effective or not) wrought by this strategy was a human enormity not even "History" itself could understand.

Near the end of *The Fog of War,* McNamara sums up the tragedy of Vietnam as follows: "We all make mistakes . . . We are rational, but reason has its limits." *In Retrospect,* as its subtitle suggests, is a "tragedy," but it is a tragedy with a happy ending in which the "lessons" of Vietnam give McNamara reason "to view the future with new hope." His story illustrates many things: the slipperiness of beginnings and ends, the refusal of war to stand still long enough to be shaped into a coherent story, the ambient fog that obscures causes and consequences as well as ends and means. It also testifies to the dubious efficacy of the quest for resolution or absolution.

Refusing such absolution is central to Tobias Wolff's Vietnam memoir, *In Pharaoh's Army: Memories of the Lost War*, published at about the same time as McNamara's book. Wolff is always learning "lessons," but they are seldom what they seem, often conceived in ignorance and resentment, and rarely teach what they are designed to impart. One of the most important of Wolff's parables occurs toward the end of the book in a chapter called "Souvenir," an account of one of his final acts in Vietnam while working as an artillery liaison with a Vietnamese battalion headquartered in a village. An officer new to the country, Captain Kale, has just arrived to take over temporarily for the departing Wolff until an artillery officer can be located. In his spare time, Kale orders cheap "reproductions of Bavarian artifacts" made in Singapore, with which he plans one day to decorate his house: "There was no way you could tell they weren't German," he tells Wolff. When he isn't ordering ersatz souvenirs, Kale, an infantry officer unhappy in his assignment, lectures Wolff on his slackness and manages to insult the Vietnamese battalion commander and alienate the rest of the soldiers.

The story hinges on Kale's decision to stage a helicopter sling-load operation too close to the small huts of the nearby village. Wolff knows better, but because Kale refuses to listen to his suggestions, he behaves with a form of resentment common to military life: a rebuffed subordinate determines to obey even to the point of rejecting an opportunity to change his commander's mind and thereby avert disaster. (The American Civil War writer Ambrose Bierce tells such a story in "One Kind of Officer," where resentment has lethal consequences.) When the helicopter pilot informs Wolff that he thinks the space might be too tight to perform the operation, Wolff has the opportunity to change course. He doesn't take it. "That's what he wants," he tells the pilot. In the end, the helicopter's rotor wash tears up the huts, which are left in ruin. As the two officers survey the wreckage, they find an old sepia photograph of a woman, clearly a precious possession. Kale tries to give it back to one woman after another as the villagers return to collect what's left of their lives. No one will take it from him. Wolff predicts that it will "end up in his Bavarian trophy case, with his Chicom rifle and VC flag and all the medals he was going to write himself up for, but Captain Kale didn't know that yet." In trying to teach Kale a kind of lesson, Wolff ends up with a souvenir of a very different kind. "This was my work, this desolation had blown straight from my own heart," he recalls. "This was, I understood, something to be remembered, though I had no idea what that would mean. I couldn't guess how the memory would live on in me, shadowing my sense of entitlement to an inviolable home; touching me, years hence, in my own home, with the certainty that some terrible wing is even now descending, bringing justice."

But the story, crucially, does not end here with confession, remorse, or recognition, or with the neat coincidence of poetic and existential justice. Not long after returning to the States, Wolff finds himself telling the story of Captain Kale to two other veterans and a date with whom he has just seen Renoir's *Grande Illusion*, even though he knows he should remain silent. Searching for the right way to tell the story, Wolff first tries "somber and regretful," but that sounds "phony." Next, he goes for "clinical . . . exposition," which is worse because it is dull and untrue. Finally, because a particular detail elicits laughter from one of the veterans, he settles on brutal comedy, an approach that so thoroughly disappoints his date that she doesn't even reproach him. As a result, he finds himself full of anger and shame. "How do you tell such a terrible story?" he demands. Although he knows the story ought to remain untold, for reasons of memory, tone, and ethics, he also knows "it will be told." He is reluctant to judge the man he was, even as he knows he must, because he was lucky enough to escape, and that man's "fears and desires" have been almost forgotten. In the end, it isn't judgment but the very act of confessing that causes Wolff the greatest ethical problem. "But isn't there, in the very act of confession, an obscene self-congratulation for the virtue required to see your mistake and own up to it? And isn't it just like an American boy, to want you to admire his sorrow at tearing other people's houses apart?" Watching Robert McNamara in tears at the end of *The Fog of War,* one senses that same obscene need for admiration.

Return of the Comic-Book Heroes

In a 2019 *New York Times* editorial, the film director Martin Scorsese offered a critique of the superhero franchises that have come to dominate mainstream cinema throughout the world. Today, he argues, there are two distinct branches of moviemaking: global "entertainment," which encompasses Marvel movies and their ilk, and "cinema," populated by practitioners who believe that film is art with a rich history and a capacity to realize "the complexity of people and their contradictory and sometimes paradoxical natures." Cinema is about the surprising, the ambiguous, and the confounding, Scorsese contends, whereas superhero movies, the evident talents of their makers notwithstanding, are akin to "theme parks." They don't take the risks required to explore the human condition. The fact that mainstream cinema today presents us with a seemingly endless series of superheroes suggests something important about contemporary American concepts of heroes and heroism.

National mythologies hinge on their heroes. As I explored in chapter 1, there is no more important part of the myth of World War II—no element that generates more passion, confusion, and distortion—than the figure of the American soldier as an agent for good in the world. Today, in an era of murky wars and elusive peace, we keep searching for a hero as satisfying and uncomplicated as those favorite images of the GI distributing Hershey bars to children or receiving bouquets of flowers from grateful women. Despite the public's profound lack of interest in the actual wars the country has continued quietly to wage in recent years, America's worship of the soldier seems as devoted today as it has ever been. With the heroic status zealously accorded to the police (among other first responders) after 9/11 shaken in recent years by events in Ferguson, New York City, Baltimore, and elsewhere across the country, the soldier remains securely enshrined as a national icon. The novelist Ben Fountain captures the hysterical quality of today's civil-military encounters in *Billy Lynn's Long Halftime Walk*, his account of a group of Iraq veterans feted at an NFL game. Today's cult of the soldier invests heavily in a white, masculine, and heteronormative ideal. Despite surface-level changes over the years, American military culture remains deeply inhospitable to other values, wedded to an outmoded honor culture, still confused about the diversity it claims to celebrate. In 2020 the U.S. Army began phasing in new service uniforms that looked rather old: they are modeled on the "pinks and greens" of the World War II era. Even the cropped "Ike" jacket has been revived.

In a 2014 article in *The Atlantic*, James Fallows suggested that one by-product of the all-volunteer military and the shrinking number of citizens who serve in uniform can be seen in the profound "difference between the earlier America that knew its military and the modern America that gazes admiringly at its heroes." But when America did know its military, it liked it much less; this is especially true of the regular army, which has been regarded with suspicion and disdain since the founding. "Americans have in many ways been a bloodthirsty people," Styron observed, "but except in odd spasms they have never been militaristic." In the present century, by contrast, America's admiring gaze has persisted largely undiminished throughout institutional military failures such as Abu Ghraib and the sexual violence against women in uniform at Fort Hood and elsewhere. That gaze—only in part the result of a national desire to atone for the treatment of service members during Vietnam—also works to keep soldiers at arm's length and preserve their armor-clad anonymity. The soldier as archetypal American hero is apparently here to stay. With President Trump's 2019 pardoning of military personnel accused of war crimes, adulation turned grotesque.

How did we get here? Heroes, anthropologists tell us, reveal something fundamental about a culture. Yet soldiers were precisely the prospective heroes against whom founders such as Thomas Jefferson and John Adams warned their fellow citizens just a few centuries ago. Both men noted the ease with which the people tended to fall under George Washington's spell: "Instead of adoring a Washington," Adams wrote in 1785, "mankind should applaud the nation which educated him." The success of the political system would depend, according to Adams, on the people's ability to "consider themselves as the fountain of power." The people "must be taught to reverence themselves, instead of adoring their servants, their generals, admirals, bishops, and statesmen." In the eyes of many political commentators of the age, military excellence grew naturally into tyrannical vice. "There is no trusting of liberty," insisted the eighteenth-century British Whig pamphleteers John Trenchard and Thomas Gordon, "in the hands of men, who are obeyed by great armies." Napoleon's rise to power at the beginning of the nineteenth century only confirmed for many observers the enduring danger posed by military saviors to the young American republic. The central problem for the founders was the commanding general—the man on horseback—not the common soldier. Yet a fear persisted that any sort of hero worship, irrespective of its object, suggested something fundamentally at odds with the kind of political and social self-reliance in which Adams placed his hopes.

In the 1850s Ralph Waldo Emerson sounded the danger in *Representative Men*. "It is natural to believe in great men," he granted, but there is a "limit" to their uses and "a new danger" in their excessive "influence." In "The American Scholar" Emerson suggested the danger involved in surrendering to a hero: admirers "sun themselves in the great man's light, and feel it to be their own element. They cast the dignity of man from their downtrod selves upon the shoulders of a hero, and will perish to add one drop of blood to make that great heart beat, those giant sinews combat and conquer. He lives for us, and we live in him." Emerson was writing in an era in which heroes and hero worship were all the rage, especially in Victorian England, where it was fashionable to celebrate history's heroic exemplars: its generals and statesmen, its captains of industry. "No nobler feeling than this of admiration for one higher than himself dwells in the breast of man," Thomas Carlyle declared in his first lecture "On Heroes" in 1840. Heroes are "the modellers, patterns, and in a wide sense creators, of whatsoever the general mass of men contrived to do or to attain." They are, in short, the emphatically masculine motors of history and society—the motors propelling civilization into the modern future. Emerson's critique extends far beyond military heroes, who are only the most visible and readily understood instance of the great man. His concern is that our thirst for heroes prevents us from achieving the independence of thought and action required to reach our full potential. To put it another way, heroes should be understood as inherently undemocratic. If Americans were to defy the patterns of the Old World, they would have to reconceive both heroes and their relationship to them.

From the first, America's heroes were of a rather different cast. Like the nation that produced them, they seemed an antidote to European models: defiant rebels, frontiersmen who in hard intrepidity made up for what they lacked in soft manners, underdogs who placed their hopes in a Declaration of Independence from the Old World's chains. Our original great men—Abraham Lincoln called them the "iron men" of revolutionary days—were castaways first of all, washed up on the wild shores of liberty. It should come as no surprise that the descendants of these original antiheroes should populate American culture: from Ethan Allen to Davy Crockett; from *Casablanca*'s Rick Blaine to *Unforgiven*'s William Munny; from the early bluesman Robert Johnson, who was said to have sold his soul to the devil for the gift of making music, and the balladeer Woody Guthrie, whose guitar bore the message THIS MACHINE KILLS FASCISTS, to twentieth-century folk poets like Bob Dylan and Tupac Shakur. Sometimes our love of rebels ensnares us in uncomfortable allegiances: witness the cult status of Robert E. Lee, which still endures in certain quarters.

World War II gave birth to the transcendent heroism of the American soldier, yet the legend did not immediately obliterate his humanity. The journalism of Pyle and others delivered the dogface, the common soldier, the GI to home-front audiences. For a time, however, as the literature and film of the late 1940s and 1950s reveal, America wrestled with rather than fully embraced him. If wartime America needed straightforward comic-book heroes, the postwar nation struggled to absorb millions of complicated ex-GIs. Only gradually did the worship of the veterans of World War II begin to reflect the antidemocratic impulse Emerson insisted lay behind hero worship, by allowing us to celebrate an archetype of stoic humility rather than a readily identifiable individual. The practice of making soldiers larger than life dominates our culture today and effectively prevents true empathy. World War II veterans gradually became objects of veneration who no longer needed the reality, the complexity, the ambivalence—in short, the humanity—that Pyle and others bestowed on them during the war. This is the real erasure of the fiftieth-anniversary mythology, which cannot account for the kind of revelation the poet John Ciardi experienced once he got to the Pacific: "I thought war was raucous and close mouthed and rigidly exact and that all men close to the fighting and dying were obscene as Marine Sgts. and hard as Hollywood desperadoes. I believed that in my fearful innocence. I never dreamed that there was gentleness and tenderness and confessed fear everywhere in it."

Is it any wonder that the fear and confusion of the post-9/11 era have prompted the resurrection of the comic-book heroes of old? Our theatrical celebrations of veterans in arenas and stadiums are complemented by our obsession with comic-book movies: according to some estimates, there have been more than fifty of them in the last several years. Those fantastic agents of American power appeal to an enduringly boyish national sensibility that has over the centuries produced presidents as otherwise dissimilar as Theodore Roosevelt and George W. Bush. In 2009, Captain America, who in 1941 was pictured on his first cover punching Adolf Hitler, was reawakened to fight new villains. Captain America has a catholic appeal: "All liberals want Captain America to be standing on a soapbox outside the White House bashing President Bush," Ed Brubaker, who in recent years helped revive the comic originated by Joe Simon and Jack Kirby, declared in an interview on NPR. "All right-wingers want Captain America to be . . . over in Afghanistan punching Osama in the face." The recent films have given Steve Rogers the requisite ambivalence and darkness to satisfy an America too knowing to worship heroes in quite the old way yet too sentimental to give them up. Rogers is the fictional apotheosis of the reigning heroic archetype, the American Soldier, whom we persist in mythologizing while his or her real analogue continues to commit to service in a murky world in which postwar exhaustion competes with the slow boil of global terrorism. These are the heroes we have claimed. The question is whether we have done them any favors and whether, in our mindless worship, we have disrupted the calculus that determines when and how to risk their lives.

Tocqueville is the writer so many Americans invoke when they wish to make the claim for national exceptionalism, but while Tocqueville thought the geographic and historical "situation of the Americans . . . entirely exceptional" and judged it unlikely that any "democratic people will ever be put in the same situation," he did not invest it with a mystical aura, particular destiny, or moral superiority. A careful reading also suggests that creating heroes may be a satisfyingly romantic occupation, but it is no way to sustain a democracy. "If your object be not to stimulate the virtues of heroism," Tocqueville writes,

> but to create habits of peace; if you had rather witness vices than crimes and are content to meet with fewer noble deeds; . . . if, instead of living in the midst of a brilliant state of society, you are contented to have prosperity around you; if, in short, you are of the opinion that the principal object of a Government is not to confer the greatest possible share of power and glory upon

the body of the nation, but to ensure the greatest degree of enjoyment and the least degree of misery to each of the individuals who compose it—if such be your desires, you can have no surer means of satisfying them than by equalizing the conditions of men, and establishing democratic institutions.

If one were to reverse engineer Tocqueville's formulation, one might end up with a maxim like this one: If you would like your democratic institutions to flourish and your citizens to enjoy a maximum of equality, you can have no surer means of securing your desires than in knowing your heroes but refusing to worship them.

5

GIDDY MINDS AND FOREIGN QUARRELS

> . . . Therefore, my Harry,
> Be it thy course to busy giddy minds
> With foreign quarrels; that action, hence borne out,
> May waste the memory of the former days.
>
> Henry IV's advice to his son Prince Hal, Shakespeare,
> *2 Henry IV*

The Confederate Air Force and Other Southern Myths

FIFI was the world's only airworthy B-29 Superfortress for almost fifty years, until the restoration of a second plane, *Doc*, in 2016. A sleek World War II relic still flying today in air shows across the United States and Canada, *FIFI* was saved by the Commemorative Air Force (CAF), a Texas 501(c)(3) devoted to preserving and restoring World War II combat aircraft. The CAF originated in 1961, coincident with the Civil War centennial, under a different name: the Confederate Air Force. By 1968 its founders had taken up headquarters in Texas on a part of the old Harlingen Air Force Base that they renamed Rebel Field. Dan Jenkins's August 12, 1963, *Sports Illustrated* feature, "The Confederate Air Force Flies at Last," presents a cheerful profile of this group of former World War II pilots, all of them "commissioned colonels" in the CAF, dressed in gray, suffused with nostalgia, and relying "heavily on the Confederate whimsy as an excuse for social rallies. The Rebel air militia has become one of the most elite clubs in the valley." Apparently, there were no difficulties about all this "Confederate whimsy" until 2001, when members voted to rename the organization. The group's website does not discuss the change beyond noting the date it went into effect. It does offer as its motto a quotation from the science-fiction writer Robert Heinlein: "A generation which ignores its history has no past and no future."

Our national problem has not been ignoring the Civil War, but turning it into a kind of theme park in which nostalgia and mendacity have eclipsed the raw and unpleasant truth that one army fought, and lost, a battle for the liberty to enslave other human beings, while the other, full of imperfect men fighting for a variety of motives, secured the emancipation of those human beings and thereby preserved a political experiment underwritten by the idea of equality. That experiment, as this book has attempted to show, entered a new phase with the Second World War, a conflict in which the United States, despite domestic divisions and an initial reluctance to enter the war, sided with the forces of liberation and became a symbol of enduring freedom for the rest of the world. It would become a triumphalist narrative perhaps ultimately most persuasive to Americans themselves. The countries the United States helped to liberate and subsequently occupied inevitably tired of it before we did. In this case, our "garrulous patriotism" expressed itself, as the pocket guides warned, as a belief that the world should be grateful for American military might, which was exceptional because it was always applied in the name of freedom.

Remembrance of the Civil War tends, in contrast to that of World War II, to submerge causes in a celebration of honor on the battlefield and fraternal reconciliation. Yet there is a special relationship between the nation's two watershed conflicts. It textures various World War II narratives, official and unofficial. On May 29, 1945, after nearly two months of fighting on Okinawa, Marines broke through the main line of Japanese defenses in what marked a turning point in the battle for the island. Atop Shuri Ridge sat the ruins of Shuri Castle, a relic of the Ryukyu Kingdom, conquered by Japanese troops during the late-eighteenth-century Meiji Restoration and destroyed by American artillery in the battle. The castle's capture had both strategic and symbolic importance, as E. B. Sledge reveals in *With the Old Breed*:

> Earlier in the morning Company A, 1st Battalion, 5th Marines had attacked eastward into the ruins of Shuri Castle and had raised the Confederate flag. When we learned that the flag of the Confederacy had been hoisted over the very heart and soul of Japanese resistance, all of us Southerners cheered loudly. The Yankees among us grumbled, and the Westerners didn't know what to do.

This uncharacteristically lighthearted passage follows Sledge's graphically detailed depiction of the marines' battle on a slope below the ridge, where the brutalizing work of killing and dying was exacerbated by the pains of surviving amid mud, filth, and rotting corpses—"things . . . too horrible and obscene even for hardened veterans" to discuss. Sledge admits that what he witnessed there brought even "the toughest I knew almost to the point of screaming." Sledge's description of A Company's planting of the Confederate flag atop the rubble— "over the very heart and soul of Japanese resistance"—comes to seem like a culmination of all their labor, the closest this grim book gets to a triumphant moment, almost the only whiff of romance in an otherwise notably cold-eyed narrative of war. That Sledge, with some amusement at the consternation of the Northerners and bemusement of the westerners, yet with no irony, should link victory first with the planting of the Confederate flag, and only later with the Stars and Stripes that was raised afterward, calls attention to a fault line in American history—a line linking the mythology of World War II, the country's defining foreign conflict, to that of its cataclysmic civil war.

That link is even more pronounced in Charles W. Cawthon's memoir *Other Clay: A Remembrance of the World War II Infantry*. As a member of the 2nd Battalion, 116th Infantry Regiment (known as the Stonewall Brigade), 29th Infantry Division, Cawthon drew an explicit connection to the earlier war. The nickname of this Virginia National Guard regiment comes from the storied brigade led by Thomas "Stonewall" Jackson and known for its participation in First Bull Run, Spotsylvania, and other Civil War engagements. In 1948 Congress authorized guard units to fly streamers commemorating these battles, and together with other symbols of Confederate lineage they continued to be displayed even in Afghanistan and Iraq. For Cawthon, whose book was inspired by the memoirs of two members of the original brigade, the wars resonated. The nostalgia that infused his introduction to war can be heard in this passage, which describes the ritual commemorations of the Battle of Stones River in Murfreesboro, Tennessee:

> The battle was still a presence in the town when I was a boy, its memory revived annually at reunions of the county's Confederate veterans. My father, born and reared in Murfreesboro during the Reconstruction, was active in organizing these gatherings of shrunken and palsied old men who huddled in their gray uniforms under the great oaks at the fairgrounds each spring to hear themselves lauded once again for long-lost battles . . . This, and a pastime of wandering over the half-century-

old battlefield, hunting the conical lead slugs . . . with
which the North and South had argued their differences, constituted my military background in 1940.

If stories of old battles informed Cawthon's understanding
of war, however, there is also an important sense in which he
regarded World War II as different not only from the Civil
War but also from the more recent Spanish-American War
and World War I: "There was no lack of patriotism, or of that
young men's spirit of adventure in which war-fever germi-
nates so readily, but these emotions were not hyperstimulated
as in 1861, 1898, and 1917." Indeed, he suggests that by the
time of the Second World War, "the whole business engendered more distaste than fervor" in all save a passionate few.

The work of uniting North and South against a foreign
enemy had begun in earnest during the Spanish-American
War, one of the country's most explicitly imperialist under-
takings. Stephen Kinzer explains in *The True Flag: Theodore
Roosevelt, Mark Twain, and The Birth of American Empire*:
"Expansionists . . . succeeded in promoting their cause as a
genuinely national project that would, once and for all, end
the regional division that had culminated in the Civil War."
Kinzer notes that newspapers published countless stories
about former Union and Confederate officers now serving together against a common enemy. President William McKinley, a veteran of the horrors of Antietam, made the most of
the new foreign war as a means of defusing the sectional
antagonisms that had plagued the preceding century. In a
speech at Cedar Falls, Iowa, on October 16, 1899, McKinley
cast the war in progress as a fight for national ideals rather
than the nakedly imperialist gambit it was:

On ship and on shore the men of the South and the
men of the North have been fighting for the same flag

and shedding their blood together for the honor of the country and the integrity of its institutions. Lawton and Wheeler in the Philippines are fighting side by side to-day. [Applause.] This is the Union we have now, and the North and the South are vying with each other in loyalty, and are marching side by side in the pathway of our destiny and the mission of liberty and humanity.

Among those men of the South who volunteered for the Spanish-American War and once again donned federal blue were the West Point graduates and former Confederate generals Joseph Wheeler, whom McKinley mentions, and Fitzhugh Lee. The pair coauthored a book about the war, *Cuba's Struggle Against Spain*, which begins with a diatribe against Spanish colonialism and its abuses of liberty and property rights that sounds a lot like antebellum Southern complaints about federal tyranny. Portraits of Lee and Wheeler joined the other paintings of whiskered men in federal blue that adorn the walls of West Point's memorial hall. Built with the bequest of the staunchly Unionist George W. Cullum, who had served on the staff of Henry W. Halleck, Union Army chief of staff during the Civil War, Cullum Hall was intended to memorialize those who had died fighting for their country. By fighting in a foreign war, Lee and Wheeler could be rehabilitated, their treasonous pasts effectively erased. They are the only former Confederates so honored in the building.

In *The Legacy of the Civil War*, written on the eve of the war's centennial in 1961, the poet and novelist Robert Penn Warren reflected on the ways in which the nation's nineteenth-century insurrection continued to shape its twentieth-century history. Toward the end of the book, Warren illuminates an intimate connection between the Civil War and World War II:

> No, simply piety and blood connection do not account for the appeal, and certainly not for the fact that the popular interest has been steadily rising, and rising for nearly twenty years before the natural stir about the approaching centennial. We can remember that during World War II, the Civil War, not the Revolution, was characteristically used in our propaganda, and that it was the image of Lincoln, not that of Washington or Jefferson, that flashed ritualistically on the silver screen after the double feature; and in classrooms for young Air Force specialists (and perhaps elsewhere), it was sometimes pointed out that the Founding Fathers were not really "democratic," that democracy stemmed from the Civil War.

Examples of this appeal to the Civil War include a quotation from the Gettysburg Address ("we highly resolve that these dead shall not have died in vain"), which appeared on the Office of War Information's 1942 "Remember Dec. 7th!" poster, and the use of Lincoln's image and words to sell Liberty Bonds. The connection was drawn in unofficial contexts as well. Robert Sherwood's 1938 Pulitzer Prize–winning play *Abe Lincoln in Illinois*, for instance, turned the story of Lincoln's own internal struggle over the issue of slavery into an allegory of anti-isolationism.

John Ford's *Young Mr. Lincoln*, made in 1939, that momentous year, likewise offers a portrait of Lincoln before the war and a potent American myth for a world on the brink of chaos. David Thomson speculates that Ford's turn to Lincoln emerged from society's increasing anxiety about the coming of war and ambivalence about the possibility of Roosevelt's running for a third term. The film is centered on Lincoln's defense of two brothers accused of murder, a case he wins with a combination of common sense, cleverness, and charisma. Played by Henry Fonda with a preoccupied air and a casual loose-limbed gait suggestive of a wandering poet, this Lincoln is a folksy trickster who is nevertheless the soul of rectitude. He ends disputes and disperses a lynching party with rhetorical appeals, but also by means of his towering presence and by the promise of physical violence flickering beneath his ostensible gentleness. He is a figure right out of myth—part rail-splitter, part confidence man, part saintly peacemaker—and the film, in Thomson's words, is "a sublime dream" in which Ford can indulge "every treasured feeling for a past he would have loved to inhabit." Thomson provocatively anatomizes the problem created by this mythologizing of Lincoln: "To the degree that Lincoln is a legend and film a dream, this is nearly perfect. But because Lincoln was real, actual, and made out of difficult thought, this film is a travesty and deeply antidemocratic. For it wants to believe that democracy does not rely on the steady application of human effort and compromise."

Ford foreshadowed his hero's destiny in the film's final shot by showing Lincoln walking alone up a hill under a storm-brewing sky to the strains of the "Battle Cry of Freedom." But if the idea of Lincoln proved useful to the war effort in the early 1940s, it was the ideal of the South's Lost Cause that continued to exert enormous popular appeal and to texture the ways in which many Americans understood wars past and prospective. This narrative had been nurtured during the First World War, which overlapped with the Civil War's fiftieth anniversary. It was endorsed by President Woodrow Wilson, whose multivolume *A History of the American People* offers as unreconstructed a vision of U.S. race relations as one can find. In 1913 Wilson presided over the fiftieth-anniversary reunion of veterans at Gettysburg, when sentimental remembrance of the Civil War reached its zenith in the photographs of white-bearded, rheumy-eyed old men, medals dangling from their chests, shaking hands on the very ground over which once they tried to kill each other. The cult of the Lost Cause, stoked by the United Daughters of the Confederacy and other powerful interest groups, remained strong throughout the 1930s.

In 1936 Franklin D. Roosevelt unveiled a statue of Robert E. Lee in Dallas, Texas. Like many contemporaneous memorials, this one has recently become a subject of contention. In 1936, there was little controversy. The South was crucial to Roosevelt's reelection bid. Cynical or heartfelt, his speech tapped into the popular interpretation of the Civil War and of Lee. "All over the United States of America we regard him as a great leader of men and a great General, but also all over the United States I believe we recognize him as something even more important than that," Roosevelt proclaimed, considerably raising the stakes of the celebration: "We recognize Robert E. Lee as one of the greatest American Christians and one of our greatest American gentlemen." To make a case for Lee as a great military leader and general is at least plausible, if far from airtight, but to make a claim for him as a saintly American gentleman is quite another. *The Dallas Morning News* described Roosevelt's presence at the unveiling as a tribute to all those "warriors in the lost cause of the Confederacy."

Such tributes remained the order of the day in the Jim Crow South, also home to the army's largest posts. One obvious reminder of the ongoing affinity between the U.S. military and the Lost Cause is the number of those posts named for Confederate officers during the great boom in military installations occasioned by both world wars. In addition to the ten posts now extant, there were several camps established in 1941 or 1942 (and since decommissioned) named for Confederate officers. Initially, naming was at the discretion of local commanders. During the interwar period, that authority was transferred to the Department of the Army, which made its decisions in consultation with local commanders, who were naturally keen to maintain good relations with civilian leaders in the surrounding communities. The wording of the regulation emphasizes the potential impact of naming decisions on a given region. The extent to which the army bowed to local prejudices, especially in the South, is clear from the list of names. In addition to the World War I–era installations Bragg, Lee, Gordon, Wheeler, Battle, and Beauregard, some of which were closed and then reopened in the 1940s, there were the newly established Fort A. P. Hill, Virginia (1941); Fort Polk, Louisiana (1941); Camp Van Dorn, Mississippi (1942); and, arguably the most egregious, Camp Forrest, in Tullahoma, Tennessee, an existing installation renamed in 1940 for Nathan Bedford Forrest, the commander of a massacre of Black soldiers at Fort Pillow and a leader of the postwar Ku Klux Klan. The camp was deactivated in 1946. The contortions required for some of these decisions can be readily perceived in the official history of Fort Pickett, Virginia, now a National Guard site:

> At its inception, Fort Pickett was originally named Camp Pickett. The name was chosen to honor Richmond, Virginia native Major General George F. Pickott, whose Ill-fated charge at the Battle of Gettysburg in Pennsylvania during the US Civil War, holds a unique place in the history of warfare. Situated just east of the town of Blackstone, Virginia, the location of Camp Pickett was chosen for its central location and access to natural resources. Approximately 46,000 acres were acquired and cleared, and construction began in January 1942. The camp was formally dedicated in ceremonies

at 3 p.m. on July 3, 1942, exactly 79 years to the day
and hour of Pickett's Charge in Gettysburg.

Pickett's charge does indeed hold "a unique place in the
history of warfare." It is the quintessential example of bad
decision-making, something akin to the Charge of the Light
Brigade. The enshrinement of such a colossal failure by an
institution equally enamored of Douglas MacArthur's claim
that "there is no substitute for victory" is a mystery explained
only by the lingering tyrannies of willful misremembrance.
Dedicating a fort to the man who led that charge signifies
a desperate commitment to the romance that makes defeat
bearable.

Robert Penn Warren understood that it was quite normal
during "a period of crisis" for Americans, as for any people,
to "look back upon their past and try to find therein some
clue to their nature and their destiny." But he discerned that
the Civil War's haunting of the Second World War was a
symptom of a more enduring political and cultural obsession:
"World War II merely initiated the period of crisis through
which we are passing, and it is only natural that the Civil War
looms larger now than ever before," not only in the South but
across the country. That preoccupation, chronicled so thoroughly by the historian David Blight in *American Oracle: The
Civil War in the Civil Rights Era,* has not abated in the years
since the war's 150th anniversary.

In *South and West,* a notebook documenting her travels
in the American South in the 1970s, Joan Didion observed
that this region of the country seemed to her what the West
did to most Americans: "I had only some dim and unformed
sense . . . that for some years the South . . . had been for
America what people were still saying California was, and
what California seemed to me not to be: the future, the
secret source of malevolent and benevolent energy, the psy-

chic center." This chapter examines the ways in which the enduring power of the South as "psychic center"—an idea, a bridge, a way of imagining the future of the United States through a particular thread of its past—foreshadows the development of the myths that constitute this book's central subject. In other words, to understand the mythology of World War II, one must understand that of the Civil War, which continues to bleed freely across the national imaginary.

Honor at the Stake

John L. O'Sullivan's essay "The Great Nation of Futurity," published in *The United States Democratic Review* in 1839, constitutes the first and arguably the most influential articulation of the idea that would come to be known as Manifest Destiny. O'Sullivan divorced the United States from the Old World and even from history itself:

> The American people having derived their origin from many other nations, and the Declaration of National Independence being entirely based on the great principle of human equality, these facts demonstrate at once our disconnected position as regards any other nation; that we have, in reality, but little connection with the past history of any of them, and still less with all antiquity, its glories, or its crimes. On the contrary, our national birth was the beginning of a new history, the formation and progress of an untried political system, which separates us from the past and connects us with the future only; and so far as regards the entire development of the natural rights of man, in moral, political, and national life, we may confidently assume that our country is destined to be the great nation of futurity.

Here and in the later essay "Annexation" (about the annexation of Texas), published in the *Democratic Review* in 1845, O'Sullivan attempted to exonerate the young nation of the crimes of the past—not only Europe's but its own. O'Sullivan at least initially appears to leave room for a discrete American past, but just a few clauses later he claims that the country's birth "separates us from the past and connects us with the future only." Disconnecting the country from time altogether, he goes on to link its progress with space—with movement across a continent that he, together with so many others, regarded as open and empty. Imagined as inviting or hostile (or both together), figured as garden, wasteland, or halcyon plantation, this continental expanse is always characterized as available to those new settlers destined to claim it. The antebellum embrace of Manifest Destiny committed many Americans to an ideal: a country without a past.

Instead of the conventional freight of history, the novel weight of expansive futurity helped to license the Mexican War, energize the erasure of indigenous peoples, and ultimately underwrite the late-nineteenth-century recasting of the Civil War's achievement from African American emancipation to white reconciliation. The reconciliationist narrative obscured an earlier understanding of the war that was articulated, for example, by Ulysses S. Grant in his 1885 memoir. There Grant forcefully identified the cause of the war as slavery, which he called the "worst for which a people ever fought, and one for which there was the least excuse." The revised history cultivated by Southern apologists for the Lost Cause—and, after Reconstruction, by many in the North—emphasized manners over morals, an anachronistic chivalry over the brutal realities of increasingly mechanized warfare, states' rights over slavery. It invested both sides of the conflict with a moral authority by celebrating a disembodied concept of battlefield honor at the expense of a complex discussion of the war's origins and consequences.

The myth of the Lost Cause also gave the nation of futurity a new history. The postwar canonizing of Southern heroes, together with the cultivation of the plantation myth, which conjured an antebellum golden age, effectively destroyed the narrative of emancipation, which had been written in the blood of war and sealed with the ink of three constitutional amendments. In the historian David Blight's words, "romance triumphed over reality, sentimental remembrance won over ideological memory." Mark Twain diagnosed this condition in *Life on the Mississippi* as "Sir Walter disease," his shorthand for a dreamy infatuation he identified with the postbellum South—with the "dreams and phantoms; with decayed and swinish forms of religion; with decayed and degraded systems of government; with the sillinesses and emptinesses, sham grandeurs, sham gauds, and sham chivalries of a brainless and worthless long-vanished society." Walter Scott, the once wildly popular Scottish poet and historical novelist, served Twain as a useful straw man, but an infatuation with the world Twain delineates still holds sway in explicit and insidious ways throughout the United States today.

What we might call a sham-chivalric interpretation of the American Civil War won out over the nineteenth-century version of history expressed eloquently by Frederick Douglass and Abraham Lincoln, the two most capacious political thinkers of the age. Both understood the particular brutalities of civil insurrection and the slippery promises of peace; each offered Americans an expansive reading of the nation's past, present, and future. From his first publication, the 1845 *Narrative of the Life of Frederick Douglass, an American Slave,* through the postwar period, Douglass refused to understand an American future without reference to its past, even as he was willing to let go of those parts of the past that proved constricting rather than liberating. As early as the 1830s, Lincoln began to cultivate a similar understanding of the nation's limitless "futurity" as contingent on its past. His vision found fullest expression in the Second Inaugural Address in 1865. The reading of the United States crafted by Douglass and Lincoln continues to offer a poetics of American identity that circumvents apology, revisionism, and triumphalism. At least in part, it is a vision also illuminated by the plays of Shakespeare, which offered Lincoln, Douglass, and other nineteenth-century Americans an alternative account of civil war and of political violence more generally. What might it have meant for our history had some other vision of civil war—namely, the kind that Shakespeare repeatedly dramatized and that Lincoln and Douglass subsequently articulated in their own forceful modes—taken root in a country that has so often liked to claim the playwright as its own?

Frontier Shakespeare

Released in 1946, the year the film historian Scott Simmon calls a "dynamic turning point" in the evolution of the Western, John Ford's *My Darling Clementine* replaces the wide-open expanses typical of the genre with a series of claustrophobic interiors. Simmon proposes that the film reflects a shift from the epics about "grand historic processes and Manifest Destiny" that dominated the Western's prewar phase to more intimate examinations of individual self-definition "within the confines of small communities." *Clementine*, infused with a new darkness of visual style shared by film noir, presents a version of one of the central legends of the American West: the gunfight at the O.K. Corral. Embedded within it is also a seemingly gratuitous subplot that might be described as "frontier Shakespeare."

Tombstone's new marshal, Wyatt Earp (Henry Fonda), is out to avenge the death of his brother at the hands of the Clanton gang. Earp has made an odd alliance with the consumptive gambler Doc Holliday (Victor Mature)—a surgeon in Ford's version but historically a dentist—who hails from the East. When an English actor named Granville Thorndyke (Alan Mowbray) arrives for an engagement at the local theater, Holliday sighs wistfully, "Shakespeare in Tombstone," and invites Earp to go to the theater with him. That the placard out front advertises not Shakespeare but something called *The Convict's Oath* doesn't end up mattering because Thorndyke, already a bit drunk, fails to materialize on the stage. To forestall a riot, Earp and Holliday go looking for the actor and find him in the saloon, where he is at the mercy of the Clantons, who are forcing him to recite while standing on a tabletop. To the uncomprehending disappointment of the Clanton gang, Thorndyke chooses the "To be or not to be" soliloquy from *Hamlet*. Befuddled by drink, he falters midway through, but Holliday picks up where he leaves off until a fit of tubercular coughing makes him leave the saloon.

Hamlet, a play rife with suspicion about violence, is perhaps an odd choice for an audience so quick on the draw. Presented with the problem of avenging his father's murder, Hamlet looks around him to behold a world in which "honor" is everywhere "at the stake." The thirst for it galvanizes his peer, the Norwegian prince Fortinbras, who marches across Denmark on his way to conquer Poland. After a captain in Fortinbras's army confides that he is about to risk his life for a piece of land he wouldn't pay five ducats to farm, Hamlet concludes that this is precisely the sort of violent expedition that breaks out—an "impostume," or abscess—in times of "wealth and peace" to kill without warning. This military spectacle prompts Hamlet to soliloquize about honor, but what spurs the belligerent Fortinbras remains alien to him.

Sounding martial honor's hollowness, Hamlet cannot but fail to find inspiration in Fortinbras's willingness to bury twenty thousand men to secure his own glory and fame.

In *John Ford: The Man and His Films*, Tag Gallagher suggests that the speech "is not out of place" within the film's "muddle of duty, vengeance, right, and doubt" and struggle between civilization and violence, but this rather long interlude really has little bearing on the central plot of Ford's film. Force, not poetry, ruled the West, and even when characters wrestle with responsibility, this is a genre of action not words. The educated Holliday may be able to finish an actor's lines, but his deftness with a gun, mitigating the taint of East Coast sophistication, is the unambiguous source of his power in Tombstone. Earp, the real westerner in Ford's film, is respectful of Holliday's display of learning but, in truth, nonplussed. He likes Doc, and anything that displeases the Clantons naturally suits him. The scene suggests that while you don't have to know Shakespeare—only obsolete emissaries from the Old World or dying easterners seem to do so in this film—you should at least listen politely. In the process it turns the quintessential action genre inward into the realms of melancholy introspection. Thorndyke chose *Hamlet*, after all, not *Henry V* for his recitation.

The Clantons, of course, respect nothing. "Look, Yorick," one of them demands, "can't you give us nothin' but them po'ms?" The scene showcases the hecklers' ignorance, even if they do understand that they are being insulted when the defiant actor announces, "Shakespeare is not meant for taverns nor for tavern louts." Yet there is something in the Clantons' question, a demand made of the Old World by the New, that is deeply suggestive, for "them po'ms" offer Americans a version of history, and of the phenomenon of civil war in particular, that we have long rejected at our peril. Shakespeare's plays, especially yet not exclusively the English history cycle, contain a civil war historiography radically different from the one manufactured in the United States during the period in which Ford's film is set and during which Northern and Southern veterans joined together to build the Union Pacific Railroad and settle the West under the provisions of the Homestead Act. That deeply and dangerously sentimental vision, not Shakespeare's, continues to captivate us in ways large and small. In understanding the damage it has done, we might also come closer to a recognition of the damage being done by the memory of that comparatively recent conflict: World War II.

Shakespeare performances were commonplace in the nineteenth-century American West. Memoirs, stories, poems, and newspapers of the period confirm what observers of national life since Tocqueville have insisted: namely, that many Americans (the Clantons excepted) have manifested a great enthusiasm for Shakespeare over the years, even if, as James Shapiro notes in *Shakespeare in a Divided America*, they have diverged wildly in their interpretation of his works. Arguably, the two most well-known national associations with Shakespeare in the nineteenth century were violent ones: the May 1849 Astor Place Riot, sparked by rival productions of *Macbeth*, and the April 1865 assassination of Lincoln by the actor John Wilkes Booth, a member of the country's most celebrated acting family. The Astor Place Riot was less about aesthetics than class antagonism: Shakespeare was simply a convenient catalyst. But the assassination, an event lying at the core of our national mythology, bears a substantive link to a writer for whom political murder proved a central preoccupation. We know from correspondence and other evidence that Booth identified himself with Shakespeare's Brutus, a connection provocatively explored in David Stacton's novel about the actor, *The Judges of the Secret Court*, published in 1961, at the beginning of the Civil War centennial. Stacton exploits the degree to which the Booth family's American Dream is bound up with Shakespearean tragedy. John Wilkes Booth, whose character in the novel is a pastiche of dramatic costumes and gestures, seeks to dignify a real-life existence occasionally approaching farce by embarking on the high tragedy of assassination. "Tomorrow," Booth thinks on the eve of his crime, "he would be a hero and a tyrannicide."

As period newspapers from across the country attest, typical nineteenth-century American engagements with Shakespeare were for the most part less sensational than Booth's and less thoughtful than, for example, Lincoln's own deep communion with the tragedies. Theater listings featured performances in East Coast cities and remote western towns; booksellers regularly advertised new editions; quotations of (and references to) the plays and poems were unremarkable, detailed explanation of their significance largely unnecessary. Allusions to Shakespeare—not just to *Hamlet* but also to the comparatively obscure poem *The Passionate Pilgrim*—appear in a broad range of contexts, from crime blotters and abolitionist orations to murder-trial summations and congressional debates to serious features on literature and frivolous columns on handsome celebrity authors.

Inaugurating the myth of frontier Shakespeare in *Democracy in America*, Tocqueville recalled reading "the feudal drama *Henry V* for the first time in a log cabin" in 1831. "The literary genius of Great Britain still shines his rays even to the farthest reaches of the New World forests," Tocqueville declared in 1840. "There is scarcely a pioneer hut where one cannot find the odd volume of Shakespeare." Whether that odd volume served as an object of study or a status symbol remains unclear. Many of the readers drawn to this episode in *Democracy in America* tend to ignore its context in a chapter asserting the poverty of homegrown literature in the United States. There must be something deeply flattering and affirming—else why would we regularly quote it?—either in the actual scene Tocqueville depicts, that of a Frenchman reading an English author in an American log cabin, presumably because the occupants are too busy doing important things, or in another scene that must be imagined into being: that of the pioneer taking time by the light of a brief candle to read a little Shakespeare after an exhausting day of hacking through the forest and taming the virgin land (to say nothing of violently removing any Native Americans standing in the way). Armed with our muskets by necessity but our odd volumes of Shakespeare by choice, we are not perhaps so uncultured and untutored after all. What we have actually gleaned from this "feudal drama," or from Shakespeare's meditations on war and peace more generally, remains an open question.

Pointing out that Shakespeare was everywhere in America—from New York City to the western frontier, from *McGuffey's Reader* to the popular stage, in the heads (and hearts) of private citizens and public figures (even presidents and generals)—is not the same thing as asking what this phenomenon might have meant. In her essay "Eloquent Shakespeare," Sandra Gustafson has argued persuasively for the political significance of the playwright during the antebellum period, when excerpts from the plays "were incorporated into the growing body of American oratory and used to contest major ethical and political issues such as slavery" as well as to teach elocution. This cultural possession has further implications, especially for the way Americans rewrote their history in the latter part of the century and understood their twentieth-century global preeminence. Despite the fact that so many Americans knew Shakespeare, it was not his understanding of war, civil war in particular, to which they were primarily drawn.

The Skulls of Men

The antebellum U.S. Army could hardly be described as a hotbed of literary study, but allusions to Shakespeare's work were as common and casual among soldiers as among civilians: Ulysses S. Grant's unremarkable use of the phrase "ocular proof" in his memoirs, for instance; or his staff officer Horace Porter's suggestion that one general's "intensely dramatic" response to the sound of distant firing ("My horse! My horse!") "recalled vividly to the bystanders the cry of Richard III on the field of Bosworth." Grant's West Point friend James Longstreet reveals in his memoir *From Manassas to Appomattox* that, while waiting for the beginning of the Mexican War in their camp in Corpus Christi, Texas, officers amused themselves by staging dramatic performances, including *Othello*. Grant, in Renaissance fashion, was originally cast in the role of Desdemona, but when the actor playing Othello protested against "male heroines," a professional actress was recruited from New Orleans. According to his son Frederick, Grant "had no special fondness for the theater except as a form of amusement and relaxation from the cares of life. He enjoyed Shakespearean representations when they were well played, and was a great admirer of the elder Booth."

William T. Sherman's appropriations of Shakespeare tended to be more pointed, as when he railed against the elitism of staff officers with an allusion to *1 Henry IV*. They are, Sherman writes in his 1875 *Memoirs*, like "the young lord in 'Henry IV,' who told Harry Percy . . . that 'but for these vile guns he would himself have been a soldier.'" Like Hotspur, Sherman was a soldier of the line, impatient with politics, acutely sensitive to slights. His love of Shakespeare was well known among his contemporaries. In *Personal Recollections of President Abraham Lincoln, General Ulysses S. Grant and*

General William T. Sherman, fellow Union general Grenville
M. Dodge describes an evening at the theater in Sherman's
company in December 1863 in Nashville, Tennessee, where
Grant had gathered his subordinates for a conference. At
Sherman's insistence, the party went to see a performance of
Hamlet, followed by an oyster supper:

> You all know what a fine Shakespearean critic Sherman
> was. The play was simply being butchered—to the great
> amusement of a theater full of soldiers, who were either
> coming from leave of absence or going upon one. No
> one in the audience seemed to recognize us, and we sat
> there quite a while. Sherman, who was sitting next to
> me, talked so loudly about the play that everybody could
> hear him. He said: "Dodge, that is no way to play Ham-
> let!" and he went on so excitedly that I said to him two
> or three times, "General, don't talk so loud, some of the
> boys will discover us, and there will be a scene." But
> he was so indignant at the butchery of the play that he
> could not keep still. During the grave-digger's scene,
> where Hamlet picks up the skull of Yorick and solilo-
> quizes upon it, a soldier in the back part of the audience
> rose up and halloed out at the top of his voice. "Say
> pard, what is it, Yank or Reb?" Of course the whole
> house came down, and Grant said, "We had better get
> out of here." We left, and no one knew that the two
> great soldiers of the age had been listening.

At first blush, Dodge's vignette seems to be of the frontier
Shakespeare variety found in *My Darling Clementine,* but
one should not allow the raucous atmosphere of Dodge's an-
ecdote to distract from its actual revelation. Those soldiers
watching *Hamlet* were not at all confused about what was being represented onstage. They were entirely attuned to the

badness of the performance—and the license it gave them to ridicule—but the idea of death on which the play meditates was the ever-present theme of their lives.

The Ohioan John Beatty, who fought at the Battle of Chickamauga in September 1863, recorded an actual encounter with a skull on that Tennessee field three months after the battle:

> To day we picked up, on the battle-field of Chickamauga, the skull of a man who had been shot in the head. It was smooth, white, and glossy. A little over three months ago this skull was full of life, hope, and ambition. He who carried it into battle had, doubtless, mother, sisters, friends, whose happiness was, to some extent, dependent upon him. They mourn for him now, unless, possibly, they hope still to hear that he is safe and well. Vain hope. Sun, rain, and crows have united in the work of stripping the flesh from his bones, and while the greater part of these lay whitening where they fell, the skull has been rolling about the field the sport and plaything of the winds. This is war.

The Nashville theater audience had spent a good deal of time actually contemplating skulls, and they met this dramatic representation with the gallows humor typical of soldiers and the irreverent, rough-hewn practicality associated with westerners at the time. What is really at stake here is a way of understanding war and mortality. As Sherman would tell a reunion of veterans in Columbus, Ohio, in 1880, in a descriptive claim often misread as normative: "There is many a boy here to-day who looks on war as all glory, but, boys, it is all hell."

The two modes of understanding war that Sherman contrasted—all glory and all hell—clashed on February 16,

1862, at Fort Donelson, on Tennessee's Cumberland River. Union troops under Grant's command had surrounded the fort on February 13. Three days later, Simon Bolivar Buckner became the first rebel general to surrender in the Civil War. His immediate superiors having decamped in the night along with a cavalry detachment, Buckner elected to yield the fort rather than risk a breakout. His letter to Grant proposing "the appointment of Commissioners" to discuss terms was met with the following terse reply: "No terms except an unconditional and immediate surrender can be accepted. I propose to move immediately upon your works." Buckner was taken aback, but he had no choice. "The distribution of forces under my command," he replied frostily, "and the overwhelming force under your command, compel me . . . to accept the ungenerous and unchivalrous terms which you propose."

Buckner and Grant were, as the latter explains in his memoirs, "quite well acquainted." They had met at West Point, fought and traveled together in Mexico. Buckner had lent Grant money in New York City in the 1850s, when the latter was unable to pay either his hotel bill or his passage home. I am not telling a sentimental story of brother fighting brother here—others have wanted to read it that way—but trying rather to establish the unsettling intimacy of civil war, something Shakespeare dramatizes in *3 Henry VI*, when the king beholds the twinned griefs of a father who has killed his son and a son who has killed his father at the Battle of Towton, by some accounts the deadliest battle ever fought in England. In language befitting this gentle witness to slaughters conducted in his name but in which he plays no active part, Henry pledges the only thing in his power to give: "Weep, wretched man, I'll aid thee tear for tear; / And let our hearts and eyes, like civil war, / Be blind with tears, and break o'er-charged with grief."

Grant became a hero in the North for his victory at Donelson—the papers nicknamed him "Unconditional Surrender" Grant—but Buckner was not alone in resenting his ungenerous, unchivalrous behavior, which marked a radical shift from the courteous precedent established less than a year earlier by P.G.T. Beauregard, whose troops removed their caps as a sign of respect for the defeated Federal garrison at Fort Sumter, commanded by Beauregard's former West Point artillery instructor Robert Anderson, as it marched out under arms. The correspondence between Beauregard and Anderson had been exceedingly cordial throughout the siege; Beauregard even sent his former instructor brandy and cigars. Anderson politely returned the gift and would not yield at first, but he wrote in his initial refusal, "Thanking you for the fair, manly and courteous terms proposed, and for the high compliment paid me." In the end, his troops were permitted to salute the flag, and no one, winner or loser, mentioned the word *surrender*.

Two months after Donelson, having presided over the shocking carnage of the two-day Battle of Shiloh in April 1862, Grant claims to have given "up all idea of saving the Union except by complete conquest. Up to that time it had been the policy of our army . . . to protect the property of the citizens whose territory was invaded, without regard to their sentiments . . . After this, however, I regarded it as humane to both sides to protect the persons of those found at their homes, but to consume everything that could be used to support or supply armies," he writes in his memoirs. "Their destruction was accomplished without bloodshed and tended to the same result as the destruction of armies . . . This policy I believe exercised a material influence in hastening the end" of the war. Even then, of course, it didn't end before the grinding campaign from the Wilderness to Appomattox produced a stunning number of casualties on both sides.

Grant's businesslike approach is perhaps all the more remarkable given his adolescent reading of romantic tales of
adventure. "Much of the time" at West Point, he reported,
"I am sorry to say, was devoted to novels, but not those of a
trashy sort. I read all of Bulwer's then published, Cooper's,
Marryat's, Scott's, Washington Irving's works, Lever's, and
many others that I do not now remember." In his way of
both making and writing about war, Grant departed from the
dominant nineteenth-century mode. His style differs radically from that of most of his contemporaries. In its rejection
of sentimentality and expression of a clinical attitude toward
war, it is closer to the fiction of John William De Forest and
Ambrose Bierce than it is to the many memoirs written by
Civil War veterans in the latter part of the nineteenth century. But Grant lacks Bierce's bitterness, and his swift narrative has little room for De Forest's novelistic embellishment
or interiority. Grant's account of his second battle in the
Mexican War typifies the general tenor of his war writing:

> There was no resistance, and we captured a Mexican
> colonel, who had been wounded, and a few men. Just as
> I was sending them to the rear with a guard of two or
> three men, a private came from the front bringing back
> one of our officers, who had been badly wounded in ad-
> vance of where I was. The ground had been charged over
> before. My exploit was equal to that of the soldier who
> boasted that he had cut off the leg of one of the enemy.
> When asked why he did not cut off his head, he replied:
> "Some one had done that before." This left no doubt in
> my mind but that the battle of Resaca de la Palma would
> have been won, just as it was, if I had not been there.

Grant took particular delight in deflating the tall tales that
grew up around the war: "That much talked of surrender-

ing of Lee's sword and my handing it back," he wrote of his
adversary's surrender at Appomattox, "this and much more
that has been said about it is the purest romance." Few authors were as singularly committed to demythologizing war.

Most contemporaneous accounts were infused with the
romance Grant was busy puncturing. They are characterized
by medievalism and frequent archaisms, full of knights, paladins, chargers, and steeds. The following description of the
Battle of Chancellorsville in 1863, contributed by Confederate officer James Power Smith to the Century Publishing
Company's landmark series of essays by Union and Confederate veterans, *Battles and Leaders of the Civil War*, is representative of the style that predominated, complete with an
allusion to Shakespeare's *Julius Caesar* in the phrase "dogs
of war." Nearly contemporaneous with Grant's book, this account could not be more different stylistically:

> For a moment all the troops seemed buried in the
> depths of the gloomy forest, and then suddenly the
> echoes waked and swept the country for miles, never
> failing until heard at the headquarters of Hooker at
> Chancellorsville—the wild "rebel yell" of the long
> Confederate lines.
>
> Never was assault delivered with grander enthusiasm.
> Fresh from the long winter's waiting, and confident
> from the preparation of the spring, the troops were in
> fine condition and in high spirits. The boys were all
> back from home or sick leave. "Old Jack" was there
> upon the road in their midst; there could be no mistake
> and no failure. And there were Rodes and A. P. Hill.
> Had they not seen and cheered, as long and as loud as
> they were permitted, the gay-hearted Stuart and the
> long-bearded Fitz Lee on his fiery charger? Was not
> Crutchfield's array of brass and iron "dogs of war" at

hand, with Poague and Palmer, and all the rest, ready to
bark loud and deep with half a chance?

This style was arguably strongest in Southern writers, but
similar passages can be found throughout the work of Northern veterans as well. Moreover, it survived well into the
twentieth century, perhaps most notably in Shelby Foote's
self-consciously epic history, *The Civil War*, a project Foote
himself described as "my *Iliad*." Here, for example, is his
account of Stonewall Jackson in the hours before his fatal
wounding at Chancellorsville: "Every time Jackson heard the
wild yell of victory . . . he would lift his head and smile grimly,
as if in thanks to the God of battle. Conversely, whenever he
came upon the bodies of his own men, lying where panicky
shots had dropped them, he would frown, draw rein briefly,
and raise one hand as if blessing the slain for their valor."
The romance informing this portrait of the doomed Jackson
is signaled by the archaic diction ("God of battle," "slain for
their valor") as well as by the attribution of an almost sacred
aura to Jackson, a devout Presbyterian who once told his wife
that he prayed his troops might constitute "an army of the
living God, as well as of its country."

Twentieth-century Americans confronting their second
global conflict in two decades were conditioned to imagine
war in particular ways. Memories of the Revolutionary War
were regional and distant, while memories of World War I,
although they may have been bitter—they certainly were to
the Bonus Marchers—involved a great geographical remove.
Memories of the Civil War, the only other major war to take
place on home soil, were still alive, however. And it was politically expedient, especially in the Jim Crow South, to keep
them sharp. The wild success of Margaret Mitchell's 1936
novel *Gone with the Wind*, to say nothing of the ensuing film
adaptation, revealed the degree to which Americans warmed

to the Confederacy's Lost Cause and to the memory of Reconstruction as an oppressive tyranny. In the years before World War II, it was the Civil War, to a greater degree than any other national conflict, that preoccupied Americans, and their image of it was largely shaped by sentimentality and romance. This was not the way World War II would initially be remembered, but in the ensuing three-quarters of a century, with the influential model of Civil War remembrance before us, we have developed a similarly misleading mythography.

Return of the Cattle Rustlers

As the headlines testify, the sentimental school of Civil War remembrance, bordering at times on the mystical, endures today. It continues to animate various defenses of the Southern cause and nostalgic laments for a lost world of honor and chivalry effaced by a callous, chaotic modernity. Southern memorial engines forged the myth of the antebellum South as an Edenic green world and sold the doctrine of white supremacy in poetry, song, history and literature (written for adults and children), school textbooks, and statuary. If the Lost Cause appears to have been rendered largely innocuous through the eccentricities of living historians who reenact Civil War battles, as well as through pop-culture expressions such as the television series *The Dukes of Hazzard* (1979–85)—or, more recently, through the removal of a very small percentage of the country's thousands of Confederate memorials—the original animus remains available for periodic weaponizing. Witness the revival of the Confederate battle flag during the civil rights movement and the flag's resurgent popularity today as a white-supremacist symbol.

The normalizing of such sympathies is notable in Hollywood cinema. *My Darling Clementine* is unusual among

John Ford Westerns in not using the Confederacy as a moral touchstone. Ford's cavalry trilogy—*Fort Apache* (1948), *She Wore a Yellow Ribbon* (1949), and *Rio Grande* (1950)—all celebrate the Confederacy in one way or another while casting doubt on Union methods. The only competent recruit in *Fort Apache* is a veteran of Forrest's cavalry, which a sergeant lauds as "the greatest cavalry force that ever lived." The Yankee Kirby York (John Wayne) must atone for the burning of his wife's Shenandoah Valley plantation in *Rio Grande*. *She Wore a Yellow Ribbon* elevates rebel honor and principle over postwar federal power. Indeed, the only thing that tends to unite Northern and Southern veterans in these films is a commitment to extirpating Native Americans. Cavalry Westerns of the postwar period often feature Civil War veterans, whose experience was vital historically in a force of new recruits and green West Point lieutenants ill-equipped for the rigors of frontier fighting. In *Yellow Ribbon*, Yankee captain Nathan Brittles (John Wayne) relies heavily on the capable Sergeant Tyree (Ben Johnson), a defiantly proud Southerner who takes orders from Brittles but, to the end, remains suspicious of the "Yankee War Department." After a battle with Indians, Brittles's troop buries an old soldier killed in the fighting. Known as "Trooper Smith," the soldier turns out to be a former Confederate general, Rome Clay, who had been serving incognito under an assumed name. The funeral provides an occasion for the reconciliation of old foes: Smith is buried with a Confederate battle flag, lovingly made for him by the wife of another cavalryman. Brittles, sounding rather like Roosevelt at the dedication of the Lee statue in Dallas, eulogizes Smith as "a gallant soldier and a Christian gentleman."

If the memory of the Civil War is an occasion for nostalgic remembrance in *She Wore a Yellow Ribbon*, it becomes a source of lasting gall to Ethan Edwards (John Wayne) in *The Searchers* (1956). At the beginning of the film, Edwards comes home belatedly from the Civil War, suspiciously well provided with gold. When his old comrade Reverend Sam Clayton (Ward Bond) muses that he didn't see Ethan at the surrender, Ethan replies, "Don't believe in surrenders. Nope, I still got my saber, Reverend. Didn't turn it into no plow-share neither." The implication is that Edwards has turned to thieving—"You fit a lot of descriptions," Clayton notes—and he refuses to be sworn in to the posse Clayton is forming to rescue Ethan's niece Debby from the Indians who have kidnapped her. "Figure a man's only good for one oath at a time. I took mine to the Confederate States of America. So did you, Sam," he reproaches Clayton. The rest of the film offers a complex portrait of a man consumed with hate, one who has simply replaced Yankees with Indians as the object of his violence. Even at the end of the film, having expended his rage and returned his niece home safely, he does not cross the threshold of his brother's house. Instead, in the film's iconic last shot, he walks away, a disaffected Odysseus con-demned to wander, refusing or unable to be reincorporated within home and society. There will never be room in the Union for this committed rebel.

Ford's Westerns were part of a postwar resurgence of the genre, which had been a staple of cinema since the silent pe-riod before falling on hard times in the 1930s. In *Gunfighter Nation: The Myth of the Frontier in Twentieth-Century America* Richard Slotkin divides the evolution of the Western into several eras: the early epics of 1923–31 were followed by a period of decline throughout the 1930s, when Westerns were largely relegated to low-budget B pictures. In 1939, however, the genre enjoyed a renaissance, which "established as a basic given of the form that the Western is 'about' American his-tory, and it developed a range of approaches that facilitated both celebrations and critiques of that history." It was during this period, Slotkin asserts, that Westerns became a site for "the active fabrication and revision of public myth and ideology," in some instances seeming to analogize the battle between cowboys and Indians to that between Americans and Nazis. Later, of course, Native Americans would stand in for the Vietnamese. With World War II, Slotkin writes, "it became possible to see the mythic space of the Western genre as an appropriate field for the projection of real questions about the state of the nation and for the cultivation of fictions embodying possible answers to those questions."

Technology and politics complemented each other in the 1950s, when the widespread use of Technicolor and the proliferation of wide-screen systems made the Western an even more attractive subject for filmmakers. The wide-open spaces of many of these films provide a home to disaffected Civil War veterans who find themselves embroiled in contests similar to those of their counterparts in film noir, where they drift through a world of unpredictable violence. Slotkin sees a stylistic connection with noir beginning in 1947, with the advent of the Cold War, when the Western grew more sinister, its heroes "psychologically damaged and alienated," its plots dominated by vengeance.

Slotkin, together with many other critics, often reads these films as Cold War allegories. He interprets the postwar Western's treatment of the intertwined themes of violence, justice, and nation as a reflection of anxieties about the international situation. Such interpretations tend to shortchange a different—domestic—point of connection for postwar audiences. These films offered the twentieth-century veteran a historical mirror in the figure of the alienated Civil War veteran. Like noir, the Western anatomizes the war veteran's relationship to American civil values and examines the nature and extent of society's debt to the veteran. It is also the case that commentaries on these films simply accept their Southern sympathies at face value rather than reading them as symptomatic of a larger trend in the country's attitude toward war.

Fort Defiance (1951) dramatizes a postwar West made unsafe and uncertain by veterans roaming the landscape, stealing cattle and making trouble: "Look here, mister, I ain't hostile to veterans," a modest rancher, rifle in hand, weary of rustlers, tells a stranger in Union blue, "but the best you can get here is feed and water for your horse and a hunk a bacon for the trail. And don't let any of our herd attach themselves to you on the way out." When two more veterans ride by on their way to the California goldfields trying to buy some cattle dirt cheap, gunplay breaks out almost immediately. After the men ride away, one of them wounded, the rancher declares, "There never was much law here 'fore the war, even less now. Men keep coming through, don't know where they're going, or no notion of what they're gonna do. Got so used to killin' that killin's the only thing they sure of."

In a plot echoed by many other films, disgruntled veterans turn to cattle rustling in Budd Boetticher's *Horizons West* (1952). Three Confederate veterans come home to a Reconstruction South dominated by unscrupulous carpetbaggers and assorted profiteers. Brothers Dan and Neil Hammond (Robert Ryan and Rock Hudson) return from the war to their parents' Texas ranch together with their foreman, Tiny McGilligan (James Arness). While Neil and Tiny seem content to resume their peacetime lives, working hard to make a go of ranching, Dan is seized by impatience and the ambition to make it big. He refuses his brother's plan "to pick up right where we left off." "I don't like to lose," Dan declares, still wearing his faded Confederate gray, adding that he feels compelled to make up for "four stolen years." Westerns such as *Horizons West* simply transplant the typical noir plot to a new setting: the veteran, cheated out of his best years by the war—this time the Civil War—determines to steal something for himself. And Dan is not alone. Riding the range with their father, the Hammonds come upon a camp of drifters in a valley. The elder Hammond explains that the men are "ex-army deserters and renegades . . . the dregs of war." It is to that camp that Dan Hammond will return to recruit an army of cattle rustlers to prey on the local ranchers. The campaign begins as one of vengeance against a single carpetbagger who has humiliated Dan over a gambling debt, but greed ultimately consumes him, and he enlists a squad of violent veterans (Union and Confederate) in an unscrupulous land-grab scheme. He dies ignominiously in the dark street of an unnamed Mexican town, his quest to build an empire having come to nothing.

If veterans aren't rustling cattle in these films, they are the victims of thieves. The plot of the cheated veteran is a very old one in American cinema. Slotkin cites *The Patriot*, a 1916 film in which a Spanish-American War veteran returns home to become the victim of dishonest politicians who cheat him out of his homestead. In *The Naked Spur* (1953), one of the five Westerns that James Stewart made with the director Anthony Mann after World War II, Stewart's Howard Kemp has become a bounty hunter in order to earn enough money to buy back the ranch that was sold out from under him. The man he has captured, Ben Vandergroat (Robert Ryan), ridicules Kemp: "You know what he done? When he marched off to preserve the union, he signed over his ranch to this gal so she could work it legal. Guess what? Come back to find out she'd sold it, used the money to run off with another fella!" Kemp must repeatedly come to terms with his own violent desires over the course of the film, until he finally renounces the bounty and vows to start fresh in California with the woman he has met while hunting his quarry.

The other Mann-Stewart collaborations are *Winchester '73* (1950), *Bend of the River* (1952), *The Far Country* (1954),

and *The Man from Laramie* (1955). In four of the five Stewart is a Civil War veteran. If the veteran in these films is not
redirecting his violence against Native Americans, he is often simply trying to outrun his past in a fashion similar to
the amnesia victims of noir. This is the case with Stewart's
Glyn McLyntock in *Bend of the River*. McLyntock is an erstwhile Missouri-Kansas border raider wrestling with his own
propensity for violence and struggling to remake himself as
he guides a party of settlers through the lawless frontier. He
bets that he can triumph over his past and make a new life
with the settlers. He eventually does so, at the cost of tracking
and killing several men using the same skills he had honed
as a guerrilla. Stewart's anguish in this film is typical of the
work he did with Mann. In each case he is driven to take vengeance, often nursed for years, for a crime. David Thomson
thinks the roles tapped into Stewart's "suppressed neuroses
as the adventurer hero." The films also implicitly seized on
Stewart's own status as a war veteran. As a bomber pilot with
the Eighth Air Force in England, he had flown twenty combat missions.

   In the richest of the postwar Westerns that engage with the
Civil War, and Mann's are certainly among them, the veteran
is neither pathologized nor sentimentalized, extremes favored
by many of the post-Vietnam films that depict returning veterans. His repatriation may be unfinished—it may even be a
total failure—but the films insist on the complexity and depth
of the veteran's character as he navigates his own transformation and the expectations of a changing society. These films
provide oblique commentary on the World War II veteran
and the society to which he returned by transposing the story
to an earlier period. They are valuable today because they
dramatize difficult truths about the violent histories of individual and nation. They are also part of a more widespread
enterprise, conducted by journalists, historians, novelists, and

others during and after the war, to examine the myth of the frontier and the place of the West in shaping national identity. Their work ranges from Bernard DeVoto's frontier trilogy—*The Year of Decision: 1846* (1943), *Across the Wide Missouri* (1947), and *The Course of Empire* (1952)—which celebrates the story of westward expansion essentially as a romance, to Richard Drinnon's reinterpretative *Facing West: The Metaphysics of Indian-Hating and Empire-Building* (1980), which traces the idea of the West and American expansion from colonial days through the debacle in Vietnam.

General Lee's Broken Heart

If Civil War mythology finds a natural home in the Western, it also appears in some unexpected places. Frank Capra's fable *Mr. Deeds Goes to Town* (1936) offers an important example. Longfellow Deeds, played by Gary Cooper, is an amateur poet from Mandrake Falls, Vermont, whose rural bliss is interrupted by news that an inheritance awaits him in New York City. His uneasiness at visiting the metropolis is mitigated only by the fact that the trip will satisfy a long-cherished desire to see Grant's Tomb. All the New Yorkers he meets think Deeds is daft, and his wish becomes one of the film's running gags. In fact, by 1936, the tomb had become a neglected pile, while Grant's reputation lay in ruins. When Deeds's guide, a newspaper reporter played by Jean Arthur, suggests that most tourists find the tomb "an awful letdown" and "a washout," Deeds responds with wonder: "Oh, I see a small Ohio farm boy become a great soldier. I see thousands of marching men. I see General Lee with a broken heart, surrendering, and I can see the beginning of a new nation." It is telling that Deeds, in whom Capra means us to see old-fashioned rural American values endangered by the money and corruption of the modern city, should look at Grant's Tomb only to discover a brokenhearted Lee.

To understand how we got to this point, it is instructive to return to the period of transformation after the Civil War. On July 5, 1875, near the end of Reconstruction, Frederick Douglass delivered a lecture on "The Color Question" in Washington, D.C. Independence Day was Douglass's great occasion; in 1852 he offered one of his most searing indictments of the nation's betrayed ideals and a simultaneous celebration of their redemptive force in "What to the Slave Is the Fourth of July?" Sandra Gustafson suggests that Douglass "appropriated Shakespeare's cultural authority in defense of the abolitionist cause" in this speech, in which his quotations from *Julius Caesar* and *Macbeth* "reinforced the 'scorching irony' that he identified as his central and necessary trope" in exposing the "profound failing of the early American republic." Commentators have also called attention to the use of *Macbeth* in the 1875 speech, where Douglass expresses the need for "a man . . . who will boldly climb high enough to hang our banner on the outer wall," by which he means a figure who would speak for Black Americans and assert their independence. Douglass allies himself with Macbeth by turning the tyrant's final defiance into a statement of liberation.

As important as the image of the banner was to Douglass, this allusion seems ultimately less central than his invocation of *Richard III* in revealing the full extent of his unsentimental understanding of civil war. *Richard III* is a particularly provocative choice for several reasons. First, it was the most frequently performed and one of the best-known plays in America. It was also the first play staged by William Brown's African Theatre in New York City on September 17, 1821. This was right around the time that the city's most prominent theater, Stephen Price's Park, was scheduled to reopen after a fire, with a production of the same play. As Errol G. Hill and James V. Hatch document in *A History of African American Theatre*, Price encouraged a campaign of police and public harassment of the successful African Theatre, which was forced to move several times. At the Park, Black audiences were segregated at the rear. Brown's theater accommodated white audiences, but in a reversal of custom, it was they who were required to sit in the back. When Brown rented space in a hotel next door to the Park and performed scenes from *Richard III*, Price sent ruffians to disrupt the performance. He subsequently incited a riot at Brown's newly built theater on Mercer Street on August 10, 1822, and the evening ended with police arresting the actors.

With this history in mind, Douglass's invocation of Richard III's opening soliloquy in the 1875 speech becomes even more provocative than his use of *Macbeth*. Douglass begins "The Color Question" by incorporating Black Americans into the warp and woof of national history: "Colored people have had something to do with almost everything of vital importance in the life and progress of this great country." He places Black men at the forefront of "resistance" during the Revolution, the War of 1812, and the Civil War. At the same time, he reminds his auditors, Black Americans' "progress and present position are due to causes almost wholly outside of our own will and our own exertions. We did not make or control the issues of our destiny . . . The white people of this country quarreled and came to blows, and it was our lot to be on the side of the victorious party." The Civil War therefore both is and is not the Black man's war. It is, emphatically, the white man's war, and the imminent centennial of the Revolution will, Douglass predicts with his usual clarity, bring about a white man's peace. He forecasts what will happen as the carnage of the Civil War continues to recede in American national memory, and he does so by his subversive use of *Richard III*, a play about the cozening peace that occasionally punctuates civil war:

> Now when this mighty quarrel has ceased, when all the asperities and resentments have gone as they are sure to go, when all the clouds that a few years ago lowered about our national house, shall be in the deep bosom of the ocean buried, when this great white race has renewed its vows of patriotism and flowed back into its accustomed channels, the question for us is: in what position will this stupendous reconciliation leave the colored people? What tendencies will spring out of it, and how will they affect us? If war among the whites brought peace and liberty to the blacks, what will peace among the whites bring?

Douglass's choice of Richard III, rather than some forthright character sincerely invested in brokering an honest peace, seems deliberately provocative, for it links the postwar period directly with the antebellum in its emphasis on deceit and fraud—the very foundations of slavery, as Douglass had argued as early as his 1845 *Narrative*. Here the allusion is to the soliloquy that opens the play. A Yorkist victory has seemingly ended the civil wars between the Houses of Lancaster and York by placing the crown on the head of Edward IV, Richard's brother. Richard, whose signally bloodthirsty contributions to the earlier insurrections were documented by the previous play in Shakespeare's tetralogy—comprising the three parts of *Henry VI* and *Richard III*—is as disgusted by the ascendant peace as everyone around him seems to be delighted by it:

> Now is the winter of our discontent
> Made glorious summer by this sun of York;
> And all the clouds that loured upon our house

In the deep bosom of the ocean buried.
Now are our brows bound with victorious wreaths;
Our bruised arms hung up for monuments;
Our stern alarums changed to merry meetings,
Our dreadful marches to delightful measures.
Grim-visaged war hath smoothed his wrinkled front;
And now, instead of mounting barbed steeds
To fright the souls of fearful adversaries,
He capers nimbly in a lady's chamber
To the lascivious pleasing of a lute.
But I, that am not shaped for sportive tricks,
Nor made to court an amorous looking-glass;
I, that am rudely stamped, and want love's majesty
To strut before a wanton ambling nymph;
I, that am curtailed of this fair proportion,
Cheated of feature by dissembling nature,
Deformed, unfinished, sent before my time
Into this breathing world, scarce half made up,
And that so lamely and unfashionable
That dogs bark at me as I halt by them;
Why, I, in this weak piping time of peace,
Have no delight to pass away the time,
Unless to spy my shadow in the sun
And descant on mine own deformity:
And therefore, since I cannot prove a lover,
To entertain these fair well-spoken days,
I am determined to prove a villain
And hate the idle pleasures of these days.

Douglass's allusion to Richard, the breaker of the peace, underscores the perils of peace among the whites: "Has justice so deep a hold upon the nation," he demands, "has reconstruction of the basis of liberty and equality become so strong that the rushing together of these mighty waves will not disturb its foundations?" Douglass has here managed to turn peace itself into a violent action: a rushing together of waves that can destroy the foundations of a Reconstruction won by war. It is, in other words, a peace that will erase rather than fulfill a victory. The subsequent history of the country suggests the accuracy of Douglass's prophecy.

Before the war, in his 1853 novel, *The Heroic Slave*, Douglass had quoted not only *Richard III* but also an earlier play in the series, *2 Henry VI*, which chronicles the vicissitudes of civil war. Its opening lines appear as the epigraph to the novel's second part, which narrates the enslaved Madison Washington's escape to Canada. They are spoken by an unnamed lieutenant who finds in the dead of night appropriate cover for the bloody business of negotiating for the lives of his captives, who will either be ransomed or have their throats slit:

> The gaudy, blabbing, and remorseful day
> Is crept into the bosom of the sea,
> And now loud-howling wolves arouse the jades
> That drag the tragic melancholy night;
> Who, with their drowsy, slow, and flagging wings,
> Clip dead men's graves, and from their misty jaws
> Breathe foul contagious darkness in the air.

Predating the war, Douglass's affinity for Shakespeare's depiction of insurrection as tragic, melancholy, foul, and contagious reveals at once a recognition of war's grim necessity as well as a resistance to gilding it with romance. This was an understanding shared by Lincoln and Grant, but not by the majority of Americans who would come to write about the Civil War or—as Stephen Ambrose's enthusiastic embrace of the chummy "band of brothers" motif implies—about World War II.

Peace That Is No Peace

Taking my cue from Douglass, I would like to amplify my earlier suggestion that Shakespeare's vision of civil war might serve as a kind of antidote to the ongoing misreading of our history. If Shakespeare serendipitously fell in on the *Henry VI* plays and then logically advanced his chronicle up to the advent of the Tudors in *Richard III*, he nevertheless, by offering a kind of prequel in the second tetralogy, capitalized on the material that England's long history of civil war provided. This organization works a vertiginous effect. Shakespeare's violation of chronology—his going back in time to the beginnings of the English civil war—serves to illustrate the very phenomena he apprehended: the uncontrollable force of war, which bursts the boundaries of genres and kingdoms alike, and the illusory nature of peace, especially in the context of civil war. Orwell once described the Cold War as a "peace that is no peace." It is a phrase equally suited to Shakespeare's dramatization of the fragility of this condition. At the end of *Richard III*, Richmond, the future Henry VII, announces, "Now civil wounds are stopped, peace lives again." He asks God: "Abate the edge of traitors . . . / That would reduce these bloody days again, / And make poor England weep in streams of blood!" The traitor of course will be Shakespeare himself, his bloody instruments *Richard II* and the three plays that follow. Peace is often an ambiguous, inconvenient thing in Shakespeare. It is, at different moments, soft, false, and sleepy; its "fat ribs" sit ready for the hungry to feed on in *King John*; it is good for "nothing, but to rust iron, increase tailors, and breed ballad-makers" in *Coriolanus*; it is a "comma" of amity bought by execution in *Hamlet*; it is easily "frighted" and short of breath in *2 Henry IV*. The slimness of peace's chances is signaled perhaps nowhere more emphatically, however, than in Edward IV's summoning of his violent and duplicitous brother, the future Richard III, to make its "perfect period."

But if peace is unstable and deceptive, war proves no more comforting. Shakespeare seems to regard it with deep suspicion even as he acknowledges it to be the engine of many of his plots. Martial honor, bankrupt though Hamlet and Falstaff persuade us it is, ordinarily has at least the advantage of calling a soldier "hence." Honor demands a rejection of the peaceful pleasures of Egypt for the warlike business of Rome, the security of Dunsinane's fortifications for the hazards of the field. Arguably this is the root of Othello's crisis: he brings his home to war. Civil wars do the reverse: they bring war home. Shakespeare communicates the particular dangers of "civil strife" in the comedies and romances no less than in the histories and tragedies, but whereas the former's green worlds permit a magical politics and a largely bloodless resolution, the latter present us with "civil dissension" as a deadly "viperous worm" that Henry VI tells us "gnaws the bowels of the commonwealth."

Civil strife is simultaneously domestic in origin—Romeo and Juliet's "two households," "alike" but divided by an "ancient grudge"—and cosmic in consequences, as when, near the beginning of *Julius Caesar*, that play so rich with omen and portent, Casca finds in the skies a mirror of terrestrial politics and attributes the literal storms besieging Rome to "civil strife in heaven." Civil war is "domestic fury," Antony tells us after Caesar's death. It is proximate, intimate, personal, familial, shocking in the way it forces us to see ourselves in our enemy and thus to be assaulted by our own capacity for violent betrayal. In a comparison made by *King John*'s casuistic Cardinal Pandulph to the French king, "civil war" serves as the vehicle to describe the state of mind that makes "faith an enemy to faith," "set'st oath to oath," and "tongue against . . . tongue." Soldiers can never really come home from civil war: they have never left the home they have just destroyed.

It is Henry IV who devises a cure for civil war in busy-
ing "giddy minds / With foreign quarrels." In the United
States, that cure would come first in the form of the Spanish-
American War and later in the two world wars. In the opening speech of *1 Henry IV*, wonderful in the way it reveals the
physiological toll of usurpation, the "shaken" and "wan" king
proposes his first solution in the form of a Crusade in order
to heal the "intestine shock" of the civil war he started. Miraculously, Henry believes, the chaos of the recent "furious
close of civil butchery" will resolve itself into an orderly military progress to Jerusalem. Soldiers formerly opposed, but
in truth "of one nature," he wishes, "Shall now, in mutual
well-beseeming ranks, / March all one way and be no more
opposed / Against acquaintance, kindred, and allies: / The
edge of war, like an ill-sheathed knife, / No more shall cut
his master. Therefore, friends, / As far as to the sepulchre of
Christ." Henry can barely get these words out of his mouth
before news arrives that the rebels are in arms again. Later, an
angry Henry will harangue one of the rebels by likening war
to a knot: "Will you again unknit / This churlish knot of all-
abhorred war?" We must look back to *Richard II*, of course,
for the beginning of Henry's troubles. There it is Richard
himself who intuits before everyone, including Bolingbroke,
that his cousin cannot stop—the momentum of unleashed violence will not let him—until the crown is his. Shakespeare
gives us no access to Bolingbroke's inner thoughts in this play,
in part because they are not material. We need not sound his
rebel depths, because we see him returning home in arms.
There's no turning back from such a course.

As Stephen Greenblatt's *Tyrant: Shakespeare on Politics*
demonstrates, the histories do not lack for contemporary
commentary, but they seem of less interest to twenty-first-
century criticism than Shakespeare's other plays. I would
like to turn back briefly to an earlier twentieth-century critic,

Harold Goddard, because his chapters on the two English history cycles in *The Meaning of Shakespeare*, published posthumously in 1951, were signally haunted by "foreign quarrels," specifically by World War II and by the false peace of the 1938 Munich Agreement that served as its prologue. Goddard discerns a similarly contradictory peace that is no peace in Richard's decree banishing two difficult noblemen, his cousin Bolingbroke and Thomas Mowbray, for attempting to engage in a trial by combat at the beginning of *Richard II*:

> For that our kingdom's earth should not be soiled
> With that dear blood which it hath fostered;
> And for our eyes do hate the dire aspect
> Of civil wounds ploughed up with neighbors' sword;
> And for we think the eagle-winged pride
> Of sky-aspiring and ambitious thoughts,
> With rival-hating envy, set on you
> To wake our peace, which in our country's cradle
> Draws the sweet infant breath of gentle sleep;
> Which so roused up with boisterous untuned drums,
> With harsh resounding trumpets' dreadful bray,
> And grating shock of wrathful iron arms,
> Might from our quiet confines fright fair peace
> And make us wade even in our kindred's blood,
> Therefore, we banish you our territories.

Goddard points out the hopelessly convoluted nature of this speech, which purports to be about preserving the peace but actually warns against awakening it: "Obviously, when peace sleeps, war and domestic turmoil have their chance. Don't awaken peace, says Richard, lest she frighten out of our land . . . and to our logical consternation we discover that what this aroused infant peace is to scare into exile is, of all things, peace itself!" This elemental confusion

reflects, according to Goddard, Richard's fundamental du-
plicity and his complicity in the violent event (the murder
of the king's uncle Gloucester, which has taken place before
the play begins) that is the ostensible cause of the trouble.
Subsequent events, Goddard goes on to argue, turn "Richard's rhetoric—falsehood, cowardice, mixed metaphors, bad
grammar and all . . . into truth . . . 'Peace' [and by this Goddard means Richard's frightened deferral of war] will indeed
frighten peace out of England. It did for a century on this
occasion. It did in our own day," he adds, "when an English
leader [Neville Chamberlain] in a difficult position thought
he had purchased 'peace in our time' by a similar act of fear."
Goddard joins many readers in seeing political disorder as a
special Shakespearean preoccupation. However, he observes
that while a great deal has been said "of Shakespeare's love
of unity and order," it was in truth "harmony and peace, not
unity and order, that Shakespeare loved." To Goddard, the
"order" enforced by "strong" men—for example, the peace
that Henry V forces on France—is but a "forgery." Goddard's
recognition of the difference between "harmony and peace,"
on the one hand, and "unity and order," on the other, helps to
illuminate the true tragedy of Douglass's "peace among the
whites," which enforced "unity and order" through the state-
sponsored violence of Jim Crow.

Henry V is as apt a pupil as any father could wish. He follows Henry IV's advice to busy "giddy minds / With foreign
quarrels" to the letter by redirecting all that English violence
onto France. I could enumerate all those actions—from his
illicit war to his purchased peace and wife—that make me
want to place Henry among the most dangerous of Shakespeare's villains, but the soldier Pistol's determination after
the decisive Battle of Agincourt to "steal" away to England
where he'll "steal" is as nice an expression as one could wish
of Henry's own enterprise. This king is no prince of peace; he

is the very incarnation of war, as he confesses in the wooing scene, when he tells Katherine that his ambitious father "was thinking of civil wars when he got me." The sense of uneasiness intensifies in the epilogue, which explicitly returns the audience's attention—we spectators, like Henry's subjects, have been distracted by foreign quarrels—to the brevity of Henry's life, the instability of his infant son's reign, the loss of France, and the civil bleeding of England, "which oft our stage hath shown." In vain, it now appears, did a royal councilor summon Henry V's ghost at the beginning of *1 Henry VI* to "keep" the realm "from civil broils." Here we are plunged right back into them again.

Thus Shakespeare's dramatization of civil war presents no deliverance from history, no possibility of looking into the future without reference to the past. That is what "them po'ms" offer us, inheritors as we are of a history badly in need of fresh understanding. We have successfully suppressed the interpretation of the Civil War that operated in its immediate aftermath—that of deliverance from a tragic world into a new birth of freedom. The potential "harmony and peace" of that resolution, because of the way it forced Americans to regard their antebellum past as tragically corrupt rather than idyllic, was quickly revised into a narrative in which the war itself became an avoidable tragedy—the result of failed compromise that worked the destruction of the plantation's green world and delivered the South into a chaos the filmmaker D. W. Griffith described in *The Birth of a Nation* (1915) as "the anarchy of black rule." What Douglass called "peace among the whites" would grow into the false and tyrannical order of Jim Crow. It repudiated the Reconstruction that forced us to remember in favor of a reconciliation that enabled us to forget. This stubborn amnesia about the Civil War has crucial implications for our remembrance of World War II, a war only half as old.

Even if the overt racism of the early myth of the Civil War has gone largely underground, a tendency to make moral equivalents of North and South endures—in popular culture, in political speeches, in defenses of Confederate memorialization. Its tenacity in military circles owes in part to a desire to view the military profession in old-fashioned chivalric terms but also to the refusal to acknowledge that the defection of numbers of military officers, many of them trained at West Point, constituted a colossal failure of the system. Not long ago, in the context of a course on American exceptionalism, my students and I encountered yet another trace of the myth in a speech Douglas MacArthur delivered to the Corps of Cadets in 1962, one hundred years after Shiloh. Given just two years before his death, MacArthur's speech is a valedictory to West Point, the institution that shaped him and of which he had been a pivotal superintendent. It is characterized by overheated prose and by all the immodesty of a man who had been for years the de facto ruler of Japan and whose insubordination as commander of U.N. forces in Korea led to his firing in 1951. Paul Fussell dismissed MacArthur's rhetoric—typified by the phrase "the witching melody of faint bugles blowing reveille"—in this way: "The troops may have talked and sung dirty, but they never uttered anything as offensive as that."

MacArthur exhorted the aspiring army officers of the early 1960s to live according to the institutional motto *duty, honor, country.* Should they fail, he warned, "a million ghosts in olive drab, in brown khaki, in blue and gray, would rise from their white crosses, thundering those magic words." MacArthur elsewhere claims (as Lee did) to have hated war, but the speech's closing paragraphs reveal how much he actually loved it. He spoke of "the dreams of things that were . . . wondrous beauty, watered by tears and coaxed and caressed by smiles of yesterday . . . the witching melody of faint bugles blowing reveille, of far drums beating the long roll . . . the crash of guns, the rattle of musketry, the strange, mournful mutter of the battlefield." When I asked my students what they thought of MacArthur's language, one volunteered that it sounded Shakespearean, which of course it doesn't at all. I don't mean to single out my student; he is by no means alone in his misreading.

American Alchemy

I close this chapter with one final strange meeting of Shakespeare and Hollywood. It occurs in Howard Hawks's 1941 comedy *Ball of Fire*, in which Gary Cooper plays a clueless English professor named Bertram Potts, who together with several other charmingly unworldly academics has devoted years to a grand encyclopedia project. On discovering that his entry on slang is hopelessly outdated, Potts ventures out into New York City to learn how regular people talk. At a nightclub he encounters a singer and gangster's moll named Sugarpuss O'Shea (Barbara Stanwyck). He wants to study the way she talks, and she needs to go on the lam, so she hides out with the professors, leading them in a conga line and other adventures that enliven their dusty routine, while Potts falls in love with her. Part of the humor of the nightclub scene (and of the film) is that characters who speak at cross-purposes nevertheless come to understand each other's hearts.

Potts proposes to O'Shea with a ring on which he has inscribed the act, scene, and line numbers (the words won't fit) of Richard's duplicitous wooing of Lady Anne, whose father and husband he has killed: "Look, how this ring encompasseth thy finger. / Even so thy breast encloseth my poor heart; / Wear both of them, for both of them are thine." Trying to decipher the inscription, in which Potts has included the play's title, *Richard III*, O'Shea asks, "Who's Richard ill?" There seems no irony intended in this transformation of Richard's wooing of Lady Anne over the coffin of her father-in-law, which we know does not end well, into a proposal that leads to the marriage with which the film ends happily. Clearly, Sugarpuss is insufficiently familiar with Shakespeare to interpret the quotation Potts has had inscribed on the inside of the ring as anything but a straightforward declaration of love from a man she describes to her gangster friends as a "jerk" and a "giraffe," but whom she nonetheless can't help loving.

Nor does Potts intend that she should read it any other way. He has no motivation for cruelty. He worries only that she'll think him "corny." So the characters aren't in on the joke. Whether most moviegoers are—whether the screenwriters Charles Brackett and Billy Wilder intended such a joke (on us)—is uncertain but also slightly beside the point, for in transmuting tragedy into comedy, *Ball of Fire* makes an emphatically American mistake. The moment underwrites the pursuit of happiness that the late philosopher Stanley Cavell identified with Hollywood comedies of remarriage—a genre he also described in *Pursuits of Happiness* as "an inheritor of the preoccupations and discoveries of Shakespearean romantic comedy." *Ball of Fire* partakes of an unrelenting drive toward reinvention, a drive that expresses an American conception of history.

The Irony of American History, Reinhold Niebuhr's attempt to make sense of America's newfound role in a world of foreign quarrels, was published in 1952, a century after Douglass's "What to the Slave Is the Fourth of July?" As I discussed in chapter 4, Niebuhr insisted that the United States' commitment to beginning anew, by blinding it to the "tragic vicissitudes" so familiar to the Old World, made the country all the more susceptible to them. James Baldwin, whose own trenchant insights into America's troubled relationship with history were likewise a product of the early 1950s, similarly refused to interpret American history as a self-contained New World comedy. When, for example, he perceived a crisis of identity among the American veterans studying in Paris on the GI Bill, he concluded that they had been confronted for the first time with the impossibility of considering a "person apart from all the forces which have produced him" and with the recognition that American identity is, myths of futurity to the contrary, inextricably bound up with history: "It is the past lived on the American continent, as against that other past, irrecoverable now on the shores of Europe, which must sustain us into the present." Slavery was the primal horror of that American history, and Baldwin insisted that the past would "remain horrible for exactly as long as we refuse to assess it honestly."

Baldwin's meditations on America's uneasiness with the very idea of history—and with the civil butchery at the core of the country's own past—were occasioned by a foreign quarrel, but these illuminations were overshadowed by the long series of misguided foreign quarrels that ensued. The United States' turn inward under the Trump administration, and its signature lament for lost greatness, reflected the enduring appeal to many voters of a vanished green world together with a repudiation of all those connections—the hostility toward NATO and other organizations constituting the postwar liberal international order—to the very real Old World of Europe. This retrograde fixation on isolated greatness also expresses a fundamental generic confusion. It is an impulse to deny our domestic tragedy in the relentless pursuit of comedy and the happy endings it provides.

In his 1999 book *Sentimental Democracy* the historian Andrew Burstein presents what he calls the "emotional history" of the United States. Burstein "charts transitions in the

language used to express America's romantic self-image."
One of the most important of those transitions occurred in
the nineteenth century, when the vision of a republic animated by "the culture of sensibility was overtaken by a
more overtly aggressive consciousness" better able "to cope
with an expansive capitalistic society bent more than ever
on shows of strength. The restraining values of the culture
of sensibility were supplanted by the language of manifest
destiny," Burstein argues, "while chivalric male protection
of female delicacy and honor was reinforced . . . Sentiment
and coercive power, long seen in opposition, merged into the
attractive combination that sentimental democrats have pa-
raded at home and abroad ever since." This is a dangerous
brew. Expressions of sentiment, or genuine human feeling,
in American political life have all too often degenerated into
sentimentality, a quality the poet Wallace Stevens once described as "a failure of feeling."

Nowhere is this more apparent or more dangerous than in
the contemplation of American wars. This chapter has been
devoted to illuminating the dishonest sentimentality that has
washed over the Civil War and has made its myth so resistant
to all subsequent attempts to undo it, the removal of a few
statues and the renaming of a few buildings notwithstanding.
In many respects, especially with regard to the subject of
race, the damage wrought by sentimentality is incalculable.
The Civil War is twice as old as World War II. Now, more
than seventy-five years on, frail old men in ball caps meet
together at Normandy as their aged forebears once did at Gettysburg to commemorate their role in a war that is drifting
out of history and into legend. Before World War II is sealed
away forever, like the Civil War before it, within an epic past
that we can no longer retrieve, before we transform utterly
those who fought it into symbols of an erstwhile greatness
bought by blood, perhaps there is still time to reckon with the

myths that mask a far more complex truth. As a teacher of aspiring military officers who will likely be veterans of future wars, I don't think we can afford to shirk that responsibility. The so-called greatness of the Greatest Generation is a fiction, a sentimental fiction, suffused with nostalgia and with a need to return to some finest hour. In a nation once billed as the great nation of futurity, there's a particular irony in dwelling so stubbornly in the past.

EPILOGUE: AGE OF IRON

> It's all because they cannot stand the fact that the America First movement is the most powerful movement in American political history.
>
> —Representative Matt Gaetz (Republican, Florida), speculating about Democratic motives in calling for the impeachment of Donald J. Trump, House Judiciary Committee Hearings (December 12, 2019)

"When a man is plunged up to his neck into the cauldron of war," Vasily Grossman writes in *Life and Fate*, his epic novel of the Russian experience in World War II, "he is quite unable to look at his life and understand anything; he needs to take a step back. Then, like someone who has just reached the bank of a river, he can look round: Was he really, only a moment ago, in the midst of those swirling waters?" Rooted in its author's own experience as a Red Army war correspondent, *Life and Fate* was written during the latter part of the 1950s, after Grossman had taken that step back and endured the various indignities of postwar Soviet life. The power of the book owes something to its belated and precarious birth: a child of defiance eluding a totalitarian state. In 1961, the KGB seized the manuscript and everything associated with it, including the typewriter ribbons. Fortunately, Grossman had secreted two copies with friends, and the text was eventually smuggled out of the USSR. The book was published in the West in the 1980s and, finally, in Russia itself in 1988. English speakers know it through Robert Chandler's translation, reprinted in 2006, and in 2011, BBC Radio 4 further popularized the book by presenting it in the form of a serialized drama.

What Grossman observes in *Life and Fate* about the psychological state of the individual in war might also be said of nations. Pericles posited something similar about the Athenians in the middle of their war with the Spartans millennia ago. We might say it of the United States today, still enmeshed, directly and by proxy, in persistent violence in the Middle East and Afghanistan and, after two decades, caught between the Scylla of maintaining influence in the region and the Charybdis of complete withdrawal. These wars loosed us onto an indefinite river with inhospitable shores, but their nature—limited war fought at a great geographical remove by a small professional force—has perhaps given Americans a false sense of perspective amid the "swirling waters." Grossman's novel reminds us how elusive the achievement of any kind of equilibrium during wartime really is. A natural response to such dislocation is to create a myth, and World War II offered the temptations of myth to every country that endured it. In Russia, of course, it was not the Good War but the Great Patriotic War. Yet Grossman was less interested in perpetuating myths than in penetrating to the essence of violent conflict.

Grossman interpreted his war through the lens of another one, just as the journalist W. C. Heinz read the Allied advance on Mons in the Second World War through the lens of the British retreat in the First, William Styron read Vietnam through World War II, and George H. W. Bush read the Gulf War through Vietnam. When Grossman was in the middle of World War II, he read only one book: Leo Tolstoy's *War and Peace*. From its title to its voracious scope, *Life and Fate* is explicitly indebted to, yet never overwhelmed by, Tolstoy's saga of Napoleon's invasion of Russia. Grossman paid tribute to his predecessor in his notebooks (selections from which were published in *A Writer at War* in 2005) after visiting Tolstoy's grave during the war: "Roar of fighters over it, humming of explosions and the majestic calm autumn. It is so hard. I have seldom felt such pain." Yet Grossman rarely grants his characters Tolstoyan luxuries of redemption, recognition, or reformation. Nor, unlike *War and Peace*, does his novel conclude with a lengthy theory of history. *Life and Fate* instead commits fully to many divergent and irreconcilable voices. In this way, it has perhaps an even more audacious sweep than that of *War and Peace*. We are now with a soldier enduring the siege of Stalingrad; now with an Old Bolshevik imprisoned in Stalin's gulag; now with Eichmann pausing during an inspection of a newly constructed gas chamber to enjoy hors d'oeuvres and wine; now with David, a young Jewish boy walking toward his death in such a chamber. Few characters are spared deformation, corruption, or destruction by the totalitarian state, Nazi and Stalinist, or by the autonomous violence of war. Grossman's anatomy of the Soviet system's corrosive nature—and its resemblance to the enemy's—is the reason, as commentators have noted, that the book itself became a political casualty.

Various interpretations of the post-9/11 passage in American history—competing "political fictions," to borrow Joan Didion's phrase—have already begun to emerge and will no doubt continue to be written in the decades to come. One of the most popular story lines has to do with the liberation of Afghan women from the repressive tyranny of the Taliban. This liberation is inarguably one of the more palatable outcomes of our invasion, and the protection of women's rights has been invoked on the right and the left as an argument for staying the course in Afghanistan. How easily consequence is becoming justification. How flattering it will be one day to reimagine it as original objective.

Some are now reading our recent wars as a tragic coda to the American Century, a coda that betrayed the identity, earned by signature initiatives such as the Marshall Plan, of the United States as a global force for good. Subscribing to the post–World War II faith in the exceptional purposes of American force, others may well cast our war on terror as a valiant crusade betrayed, like the war in Vietnam before it, by a lack of political will or perhaps by journalists and an indifferent public. Still more will seek to interpret our twenty-first-century military adventure, again, like Vietnam, as an exception or an aberration rather than a true expression of national principles. The specter of Vietnam is never far from view. Whenever the invocation of World War II becomes an uneasy fit, it is the shadow comparison lying in wait: the twin poles of American military adventure abroad. The language of one war bleeds through to another, even though somewhere we know that echoes can be false, that analogies may not hold. Grossman knew this, too. He knew that wars are seething struggles, not object lessons. That's why his novel ends with a tentatively hopeful vision of the future that its characters greet only with ambiguous silence.

The longer war stories go on, the more difficult they are to listen to. Instead of needing to know how they will end, we simply want them to stop. I'm not talking here about stories of the imagination—about the *Iliad* or *War and Peace* or *Life and Fate*. In the hands of an expert storyteller, war proceeds at precisely the right pace. It accelerates when we need it to, before slowing down so that we can catch our breath. It relaxes us with irony before hurling us back into gore and grief. Real wars don't work that way, although we like to pretend they do. In fact, they resist the shapely plots and satisfying conclusions we try to impose on them. Authorizations, declarations, agreements, and treaties give an impression of neatness, but these are ephemeral measures of strength and weakness, of victory and defeat. Grossman understood this. One of the uneasy truths revealed by his encyclopedic account of the Soviet Union's struggle against the Nazis—and ultimately against itself—is that the old dichotomy of war and peace in fact no longer holds. "The war had given way to peace," Grossman observes in a description of Stalingrad after the siege, "a poor, miserable peace that was hardly any easier than the war."

In the midst of a miserable peace, the pains of war are quickly forgotten while its imagined glories grow. Causes are retrofitted, participants fondly recall heroic gestures. As happens to all wars, the deep ambiguities and complexities of World War II, so amply documented and taken for granted in the war's immediate aftermath, continue to recede. In addition to the Berlin Airlift, the Marshall Plan, the United Nations, and NATO, the generation that fought the Second World War subsequently brought us the worst excesses of the Cold War: the Red Scare at home and irresponsible military expeditions abroad, all of them cloaked in the rosy glow and the atomic fallout of World War II. As that generation passes away—to be frozen within the pantheon of heroes, walled off from the present, larger than life, untouchable, not quite of this world—the real and deeply ambivalent legacies of the Second World War risk becoming lost forever. So what? What harm, after all, can there be in telling exclusively, in Stephen Ambrose's words, "all the things that are right about America"? Isn't America First, after all?

Speculating about Democratic motives in calling for the impeachment of Donald J. Trump, the Florida Republican Matt Gaetz declared before the House Judiciary Committee hearings in the fall of 2019, "It's all because they cannot stand the fact that the America First movement is the most powerful movement in American political history." Factual inaccuracy aside, this celebration of a movement that shares its name with a fascist organization of the 1930s might be an expression of genuine ignorance or, given that Gaetz is the same man who invited a Holocaust denier to the State of the Union address, it could be an example of the dog whistler's specialty: the feigned ignorance that permits plausible deniability.

Donald Trump, the man Gaetz was defending, traffics in the same kind of rhetoric, suffused with vitriol in service of disruption; its frequent logical incoherence never interferes with the message. It is nevertheless telling that one of the few occasions to which Trump responded with any kind of restraint while he was in office was the seventy-fifth anniversary of D-Day in 2019. At Normandy, Trump participated in what Reagan established as a presidential rite. His speech earned praise from many quarters; some listeners, evidently dazzled by the solemnity of the occasion, perceived in the speaker a sudden capacity for statesmanship. Somehow, the sacred aura attaching to the event managed to cow even the disrupter-in-chief, something that had not happened on an earlier visit to France to commemorate the centennial of the end of World War I, during which Trump reportedly bickered over his America First foreign policy with Emmanuel Macron.

The world will not long remember what Trump said at Normandy. This is in part a function of the degree to which he did what is expected of heads of state on such occasions. In truth, it was a pedestrian speech—what passes for oratory in a tin-eared age of tweets—full of platitudes, hyperbole, and recycled phrases: "Great Crusade" (Eisenhower), "Freedom's Altar" (a Civil War song), "consecrated to history" (bastardized Lincoln), "new frontiers" (misappropriated Kennedy), "heat of battle," "fires of hell," "Nazi fury," "awesome power," "breathtaking scale," "cherished alliance," "undying gratitude" (clichés), and "tough guy" (ad lib). And there are generous helpings of greatness: "great," "greatest," "very greatest." Even when a traditional rhetorical move is made, as in the parallelism of the sentence, "The full violence of Nazi fury was no match for the full grandeur of British pride," there is none of the precision or economy that makes such a device effective. Most of the sentences don't bear the weight of careful reading; this one makes little grammatical sense: "After months of planning, the Allies had chosen this ancient coastline to mount their campaign to vanquish the wicked tyranny of the Nazi empire from the face of the Earth." But the emphasis throughout is entirely consistent with the fiftieth-anniversary mythology, as in this explanation of why soldiers persisted under fire on the beach:

> They were sustained by the confidence that America can do anything because we are a noble nation, with a virtuous people, praying to a righteous God.
>
> The exceptional might came from a truly exceptional spirit. The abundance of courage came from an abundance of faith. The great deeds of an Army came from the great depths of their love.

Only by the magic alchemy of American exceptionalism can war be made to seem an act of love.

How did we get here? Part of the answer, as I have tried to show, can be found in World War II, while another, more distant part can be found in the Civil War, misremembered now for a century and a half. That misremembering has left a landscape littered with the stone relics of a Lost Cause and a society not yet recovered from the structural inequities of Jim Crow. The best teacher of that war, Abraham Lincoln, was also the best reader of another war, the Revolution, which overshadowed his youth. Antebellum America had to reckon with its own "Greatest Generation," which had forged a nation and left it with a compromise that would need to be resolved by the deaths of what is now estimated to be more than 750,000 Americans in the Civil War. These founders— Lincoln called them "iron men"—were much on his mind as he embarked on his political career in the 1830s. In an important early speech to the Young Men's Lyceum of Springfield, Illinois, in 1838, Lincoln meditated on the theme of "the perpetuation of our political institutions." Horrified by the racially charged mob violence that had broken out in St. Louis, Missouri, and elsewhere, he looked back in this speech to the founding generation with a curious mixture of respect and impatience. Those "deep rooted principles of hate, and the powerful motive of revenge" against the British may have been necessary to founding a nation, Lincoln told his audience, but they were no longer the best resources for perpetuating the republic. The revolutionary "state of feeling must fade, is fading, has faded, with the circumstances that produced it," Lincoln asserted without nostalgia or regret. He then went on to describe the proper place of these iron men in the national memory:

> I do not mean to say, that the scenes of the revolution are now or ever will be entirely forgotten . . . In history, we hope, they will be read of, and recounted, so long as the bible shall be read;—but even granting that they will, their influence cannot be what it heretofore has been. Even then, they cannot be so universally known, nor so vividly felt, as they were by the generation just gone to rest. At the close of that struggle, nearly every adult male had been a participator in some of its scenes. The consequence was, that of those scenes, in the form of a husband, a father, a son or a brother, a living history was to be found in every family—a history bearing the

indubitable testimonies of its own authenticity, in the limbs mangled, in the scars of wounds received, in the midst of the very scenes related—a history, too, that could be read and understood alike by all, the wise and the ignorant, the learned and the unlearned. But those histories are gone. They can be read no more forever . . . They were a forest of giant oaks; but the all-resistless hurricane has swept over them, and left only, here and there, a lonely trunk, despoiled of its verdure, shorn of its foliage; unshading and unshaded, to murmur in a few more gentle breezes, and to combat with its mutilated limbs, a few more ruder storms, then to sink, and be no more.

Those "lonely trunks" were the last survivors of the greatest generation the young country had yet known, and the passage offers at once a powerful homage and a recognition that every age demands new virtues. The founders may have seemed "giant oaks," but they were not giants. They were only men. They were heroes for their own time, but not for all time. The men of the Revolution were men of passion. Passion declared and won independence, but in 1838 violent passion threatened the very rule of law they had established with the violent chaos of mob rule. Lincoln recognized that a different attribute altogether was required if the Union were to be sustained:

They were the pillars of the temple of liberty; and now, that they have crumbled away, that temple must fall, unless we, their descendants, supply their places with other pillars, hewn from the solid quarry of sober reason. Passion has helped us; but can do so no more. It will in future be our enemy. Reason, cold, calculating, unimpassioned reason, must furnish all the materials

for our future support and defence. Let those materials be moulded into general intelligence, sound moral-
ity and, in particular, a reverence for the constitution
and laws; and, that we improved to the last; that we
remained free to the last; that we revered his name to
the last; that, during his long sleep, we permitted no
hostile foot to pass over or desecrate his resting place;
shall be that which to learn the last trump shall awaken
our WASHINGTON.

Lincoln respected the past without being paralyzed by it;
he understood the ways in which improvement must temper
veneration and reason moderate passion. He recognized that
only truth could conquer the dangerous distortions of myth.

Twenty years later, on the Fourth of July, during the senatorial debates with Stephen Douglas, Lincoln returned to
the theme of generations. He alluded to the ways in which
people gathered to think about the country's development,
over the course of eighty-two years, into a prosperous land
of thirty million inhabitants: "We find a race of men living
in that day whom we claim as our fathers and grandfathers;
they were iron men, they fought for the principle that they
were contending for," Lincoln declared. "We hold this annual celebration to remind ourselves of all the good done in
this process of time of how it was done and who did it, and
how we are historically connected with it; and we go from
these meetings in better humor with ourselves—we feel more
attached the one to the other, and more firmly bound to the
country we inhabit." Lincoln once again explores, as he had
done in the Lyceum speech, the relationship between the
men of the Revolution and the present generation. At first,
he seems to be arguing for an enduring connection between
one generation and the next—between the heroes of the past
and his present-day listeners, who presumably see in those

"iron men" their own ancestors and a source of strength. But then Lincoln reveals a new development in the national family tree:

> But after we have done all this we have not yet reached the whole. There is something else connected with it. We have besides these men—descended by blood from our ancestors—among us perhaps half our people who are not descendants at all of these men; they are men who . . . have come from Europe themselves, or whose ancestors have come hither and settled here, finding themselves our equals in all things. If they look back through this history to trace their connection with those days by blood, they find they have none, they cannot carry themselves back into that glorious epoch and make themselves feel that they are part of us, but when they look through that old Declaration of Independence they find that those old men say that "We hold these truths to be self-evident, that all men are created equal," and then they feel that that moral sentiment taught in that day evidences their relation to those men, that it is the father of all moral principle in them, and that they have a right to claim it as though they were blood of the blood, and flesh of the flesh of the men who wrote that Declaration; and so they are. That is the electric cord in that Declaration that links the hearts of patriotic and liberty-loving men together, that will link those patriotic hearts as long as the love of freedom exists in the minds of men throughout the world.

Lincoln replaces a false history of blood—the kind of history that once produced aristocracies and that is still capable of producing nativists, white supremacists, and America Firsters— with a vital one of moral sentiment and principle embodied in the phrase that all are "created equal." Tolstoy once wrote that the military "greatness of Napoleon, Caesar or Washington is only moonlight beside the sun of Lincoln." The peculiar "greatness" of Lincoln, according to Tolstoy, lay in the fact that he "was a universal individualist who wanted to see himself in the world—not," as Napoleon had done, "the world in himself." No chaser of ghosts, no Aeneas trying vainly to grasp the shadow of the past only to embrace an empty present, Lincoln knew that the superstitious veneration of iron men and the backward-looking search to recover their illusory greatness can never sustain a republic. To do that, one must stretch an "electric cord" capable of energizing future generations.

RECOMMENDED BOOKS AND FILMS

On Thursday, June 1, 1944, A. J. Liebling, a correspondent for *The New Yorker*, boarded a landing craft that would participate in the imminent D-Day landings. On another craft berthed alongside, he found members of the First Division, veterans of the North African and Italian campaigns, sprawled everywhere, the majority reading Armed Services Editions (ASEs), oblong-shaped paperbacks printed by the millions and circulated to American military personnel deployed across the globe. He described the soldiers' attitude in a dispatch: "They were just going on one more trip, and they didn't seem excited about it." Liebling fell into conversation with a private from Brooklyn. "These little books are a great thing," the soldier told him. "They take you away. I remember when my battalion was cut off on top of a hill at El Guettar, I read a whole book in one day. It was called 'Knight Without Armor.' This one I am reading now is called 'Candide.' It is kind of unusual, but I like it. I think the fellow who wrote it, Voltaire, used the same gag too often, though. The characters are always getting killed then turning out not to have been killed after all, and they tell their friends what happened to them in the meantime. I like the character in it called Pangloss."

The capacious range of the ASE list is suggested by the two books the infantryman mentions: *Knight Without Armour*, by the popular twentieth-century English novelist James Hilton (also the author of *Goodbye, Mr. Chips* and *Lost Horizon*), and *Candide*, the satire by Voltaire, the French Enlightenment writer. The soldier's favorite character, Pangloss, is the subject of Voltaire's ridicule for his incurably optimistic philosophy: "*Tout va pour le mieux dans le meilleur des mondes possibles*" [All is for the best in the best of all possible worlds]. Of course the readers of the ASEs were often in the midst of the worst rather than the best of all possible worlds, yet they drew obvious solace from the distractions reading provided. The catholic nature of the ASE list—the reluctance to censor, the lack of a party line—seems to me of a piece with the way the war was understood at the time, before a monolithic perspective took hold and prevented us from seeing this event in our history as a complex human experience compounded of frailty and ambiguity as well as courage and clarity.

The volume of books written about World War II is daunting, but I offer here a selection of works that might confirm some expectations and confound others or otherwise enrich understanding.

Readers looking for a one-volume historical survey of the war might try John Keegan's *The Second World War* (Viking) or Antony Beevor's *The Second World War* (Little, Brown). Rick Atkinson's Liberation Trilogy (Holt)—*An Army at Dawn: The War in North Africa, 1942–1943*; *The Day of Battle: The War in Sicily and Italy, 1943–1944*; *The Guns at Last Light: The War in Western Europe, 1944–1945*—chronicles the failures and successes of the U.S. Army as it made its challenging way from North Africa to Germany. Ian W. Toll tells the U.S. Navy's story of the Pacific Theater in a complementary trilogy: *Pacific Crucible: War at Sea in the Pacific, 1941–1942*; *The Conquering Tide: War in the Pacific Islands, 1942–1944*; *Twilight of the Gods: War in the Western Pacific, 1944–1945* (W. W. Norton).

The mythology of the war to which my book responds was born during the war itself, but it gathered renewed strength and coherence during the Reagan administration as a way of coming to terms with Vietnam. It then came into fullest flower around the time of the war's fiftieth anniversary in the books of Stephen Ambrose, especially *Band of Brothers: E Company, 506th Regiment, 101st Airborne from Normandy to Hitler's Eagle's Nest*; *D-Day: June 6, 1944: The Climactic Battle of World War II*; and *Citizen Soldiers: The U.S. Army from the Normandy Beaches to the Bulge to the Surrender of Germany, June 7, 1944 to May 7, 1945* (Simon & Schuster). (The HBO series based on *Band of Brothers* debuted in 2001, around the time that the events of 9/11 reenergized the myth.) Tom Brokaw's *The Greatest Generation* (Random House) coined a term that proved infectious. The theme of American "greatness" continues to characterize political rhetoric across the spectrum. It can be found in presidential addresses at Normandy, State of the Union addresses, and speeches delivered on various occasions. Paul Fussell offered one of the more incendiary responses to the idea of the "Good War" in *Wartime: Understanding and Behavior in the Second World War* (Oxford). Studs Terkel's *"The Good War": An Oral History of World War Two* (The New Press) presents a revelatory range of perspectives that refuse to be reduced to a single narrative.

Books by historians, journalists, and critics that contribute to an understanding of the war, the postwar period, and American myths more generally include Michael C. C. Adams, *The Best War Ever: America and World War II* (Johns Hopkins Univ. Press); M. Todd Bennett, *One World, Big Screen: Hollywood, the Allies, and World War II* (Univ. of North Carolina Press); Sheri Chinen Biesen, *Blackout: World War II and the Origins of Film Noir* (Johns Hopkins Univ. Press); David W. Blight, *American Oracle: The Civil War in the Civil Rights Era* (Harvard-Belknap); John Bodnar, *The "Good War" in American Memory* (Johns Hopkins Univ. Press); Sandra M. Bolzenius, *Glory in Their Spirit: How Four Black Women Took on the Army During World*

War II (Univ. of Illinois Press); Peter N. Carroll, *The Odyssey of the Abraham Lincoln Brigade: Americans in the Spanish Civil War* (Stanford Univ. Press); Thomas Doherty, *Hollywood and Hitler, 1933–1939* and *Projections of War: Hollywood, American Culture, and World War II* (Columbia Univ. Press); John W. Dower, *Cultures of War: Pearl Harbor, Hiroshima, 9-11, Iraq* (W. W. Norton); Richard Drinnon, *Facing West: The Metaphysics of Indian-Hating and Empire-Building* (Univ. of Oklahoma Press); Shelby Foote, *The Civil War* (Vintage); Charles Glass, *The Deserters: A Hidden History of World War II* (Penguin); Joseph C. Goulden, *The Best Years: 1945–1950* (Dover); Greg Grandin, *The End of the Myth: From the Frontier to the Border Wall in the Mind of America* (Metropolitan); David Hajdu, *The Ten-Cent Plague: The Great Comic-Book Scare and How it Changed America* (Picador); Mark Harris, *Five Came Back: A Story of Hollywood and the Second World War* (Penguin); Bradley W. Hart, *Hitler's American Friends: The Third Reich's Supporters in the United States* (Thomas Dunne); Linda Hervieux, *Forgotten: The Untold Story of D-Day's Black Heroes, at Home and at War* (Harper); Aaron Hiltner, *Taking Leave, Taking Liberties: American Troops on the World War II Home Front* (Univ. of Chicago Press); William I. Hitchcock, *The Bitter Road to Freedom: The Human Cost of Allied Victory in World War II Europe* (Simon & Schuster); Maria Höhn and Martin Klimke, *A Breath of Freedom: The Civil Rights Struggle, African American GIs, and Germany* (Palgrave); Stephen Kinzer, *The True Flag: Theodore Roosevelt, Mark Twain, and the Birth of American Empire* (Griffin); Rawn James Jr., *The Double V: How Wars, Protest, and Harry Truman Desegregated America's Military* (Bloomsbury); Jill Lepore, *The Secret History of Wonder Woman* (Vintage), Richard Lingeman, *The Noir Forties: The American People from Victory to Cold War* (Nation); James Naremore, *More than Night: Film Noir in Its Contexts* (Univ. of California Press); Mark Osteen, *Nightmare Alley: Film Noir and the American Dream* (Johns Hopkins Univ. Press); Mary Louise Roberts, *What Soldiers Do: Sex and the American GI in World War II France* (Univ. of Chicago Press) and *D-Day Through French Eyes: Normandy 1944* (Univ. of Chicago Press); Roy Scranton, *Total Mobilization: World War II and American Literature* (Univ. of Chicago Press); Scott Simmon, *The Invention of the Western Film: A Cultural History of the Genre's First Half-Century* (Cambridge); Richard Slotkin, *Regeneration Through Violence: The Mythology of the American Frontier, 1600–1860, The Fatal Environment: The Myth of the Frontier in the Age of Industrialization, 1800–1890*, and especially *Gunfighter Nation: The Myth of the Frontier in Twentieth-Century America* (Univ. of Oklahoma Press); and Jane Tompkins, *West Of Everything: The Inner Life of Westerns* (Oxford).

Several publications sponsored by the government help to reveal a time before the myth had been fixed, including John Dollard's study of Spanish Civil War veterans, *Fear in Battle* (originally published in *The Infantry Journal*), and *The American Soldier*, a multivolume study conducted by a team of sociologists led by Samuel A.

Stouffer. A number of the fascinating guidebooks and instructional pamphlets created for overseas service members have been recently reprinted: *Instructions for American Servicemen in Iraq During World War II* and *Instructions for American Servicemen in France During World War II* (Univ. of Chicago Press) and a series produced by the University of Oxford's Bodleian Library, which includes *Instructions for American Servicemen in Britain 1942*, *Instructions for American Servicemen in Australia 1942*, and *112 Gripes about the French*, as well as the 1962 *Pocket Guide to Vietnam*.

The following collections of letters and reportage offer a rich tapestry of experience on the home front and abroad: *The Good Fight Continues: World War II Letters from the Abraham Lincoln Brigade*, edited by Peter N. Carroll et al. (New York Univ. Press); Ernie Pyle's several books, including *Ernie Pyle in England* (1941), *Here Is Your War: Story of G.I. Joe* (1943), *Brave Men* (1944), and *Last Chapter* (1946); A. J. Liebling's dispatches, collected in *World War II Writings* (Library of America) and sampled in *Just Enough Liebling* (North Point); Virginia Cowles's *Looking for Trouble* (Faber & Faber), which also details its author's experience in the Spanish Civil War; John Steinbeck's *Once There Was a War* (Penguin Classics); Martha Gellhorn's *The Face of War* (Atlantic Monthly), which ranges from the Spanish Civil War to U.S. intervention in Central America; the journalist Eric Sevareid's personal history *Not So Wild a Dream* (Univ. of Missouri Press), also published as an ASE; Joel Sayre's look into a neglected theater of the war, *Persian Gulf Command* (Random House); W. C. Heinz's *When We Were One: Stories of World War II* (Da Capo); and John Hersey's *Into the Valley: Marines at Guadalcanal* (Bison), originally published as *Into the Valley: A Skirmish of the Marines* (Knopf), and *Hiroshima* (1946; rev. ed. 1985). The work of these journalists and many others can be found in the two-volume *Reporting World War II* (Library of America).

Wartime diaries and memoirs, often published only decades later, offer raw, unmediated responses to events. See the poet John Ciardi's *Saipan: The War Diary of John Ciardi* (Univ. of Arkansas Press) and Bert Stiles's *Serenade to the Big Bird* (W. W. Norton). (Stiles was killed in action in 1944, and his book was published posthumously.) Although sometimes based on notes or journals, memoirs are more often written at a greater remove, layering the reflections of age and experience over the immediacy of youth. Among the most incisive are E. B. Sledge, *With the Old Breed* (Random House); Samuel Hynes, *Flights of Passage* (Penguin); and Alvin Kernan, *Crossing the Line* (Naval Institute); all three are also available in *World War II Memoirs: The Pacific Theater* (Library of America). Other noteworthy memoirs or journals include Philip Ardery, *Bomber Pilot: A Memoir of World War II* (Univ. Press of Kentucky); Elmer Bendiner, *The Fall of Fortresses* (Silvertail); Harold L. Bond, *Return to Cassino: A Memoir of the Fight for Rome* (Doubleday); Victor Brombert, *Trains of Thought: From Paris to Omaha Beach, Memories of a Wartime Youth* (Anchor);

Charles R. Cawthon, *Other Clay: A Remembrance of the World War II Infantry* (Bison); Charles W. Dryden, *A-Train: Memoirs of a Tuskegee Airman* (Univ. of Alabama Press); Paul Fussell, *Doing Battle: The Making of a Skeptic* (Back Bay); J. Glenn Gray, *The Warriors: Reflections on Men in Battle* (Bison); Robert Kotlowitz, *Before Their Time* (Anchor); Robert Leckie, *Helmet for My Pillow: From Parris Island to the Pacific* (Bantam); Betty Ann Lussier, *The Intrepid Woman: Betty Lussier's Secret War, 1942–1945* (Naval Institute); Charles B. MacDonald, *Company Commander* (Burford); John Muirhead, *Those Who Fall* (Random House); Bill Mauldin, *Up Front* (W. W. Norton) and *Willie & Joe: Back Home* (Fantagraphics); Charlton Ogburn Jr., *The Marauders* (Overlook); Mary Lee Settle, *All the Brave Promises: Memories of Aircraft Woman 2nd Class 2146391* (Univ. of South Carolina Press); and the collection of firsthand accounts *And If I Perish: Frontline U.S. Army Nurses in World War II*, edited by Evelyn M. Monahan and Rosemary Neidel-Greenlee (Anchor).

Imaginative literature is equally important to anyone interested in questions of cultural memory. The war produced some widely celebrated novels, several of which are by now available in deluxe fiftieth-anniversary editions: Nelson Algren, *The Man with the Golden Arm* (Seven Stories); Joseph Heller, *Catch-22* (Simon & Schuster); James Jones, *From Here to Eternity*, *The Thin Red Line*, and *Whistle* (Modern Library); Norman Mailer, *The Naked and the Dead* (Picador); William Styron, *Sophie's Choice* (Vintage); Kurt Vonnegut, *Slaughterhouse-Five* (Random House); and Herman Wouk, *The Caine Mutiny* (Back Bay). Less heralded fiction, noir novels among them, offer invaluable perspectives on the war and its aftermath: Charlotte Armstrong, *Mischief* (available in the Library of America collection *Women Crime Writers: Four Suspense Novels of the 1950s*); Richard Brooks, *The Brick Foxhole* (Mysterious Press ebook); John Horne Burns, *The Gallery* (New York Review Books); Don Carpenter, *Hard Rain Falling* (New York Review Books); David Goodis, *Dark Passage*, *Nightfall*, and *The Burglar* (collected in the Library of America's *Five Noir Novels of the 1940s & 50s*); Chester Himes, *If He Hollers Let Him Go* (Da Capo); Dorothy B. Hughes, *In a Lonely Place* (New York Review Books); Sloan Wilson, *The Man in the Gray Flannel Suit* (Da Capo); and Charles Willeford, *Pick-Up*, available in *Omnibus I* (Orion). As is the case with "Grave Digger" Jones and "Coffin Ed" Johnson, the detectives of Himes's hardboiled Harlem novels, Ross Macdonald's Lew Archer was unmistakably shaped by his World War II service: see, for example, *The Way Some People Die*, *The Barbarous Coast*, *The Doomsters*, and *The Galton Case* (Vintage Crime/Black Lizard). World War II poets are far less widely known, but their diverse, powerfully rendered experiences are available in the anthology *Poets of World War II*, edited by Harvey Shapiro (Library of America).

The idea that each war is seen through the lens of other wars is central to this book. Fiction and nonfiction about Korea and Vietnam also shed light on World War II and the way it has been remembered. Fiction of the Korean War includes James A. Michener, *The Bridges at Toko-Ri* (Dial); James Salter, *The Hunters* (Vintage); and William Styron, *The Long March* (Vintage), and his posthumous short story collection *The Suicide Run: Five Tales of the Marine Corps* (Random House). These books might profitably be read with Bruce Cumings's history *The Korean War* (Modern Library). Essential Vietnam memoirs include Philip Caputo, *A Rumor of War* (Picador); Tim O'Brien, *If I Die in a Combat Zone, Box Me Up and Ship Me Home* (Mariner); and Tobias Wolff, *In Pharaoh's Army: Memories of the Lost War* (Vintage). William Styron's nonfiction writing on World War II, Korea, and Vietnam can be found in *This Quiet Dust and Other Writings* (Vintage). Stanley Karnow's *Vietnam: A History* (Penguin) remains a standard account. Other books on Vietnam that I found especially illuminating include Robert S. McNamara, *In Retrospect: The Tragedy and Lessons of Vietnam* (Vintage), and Neil Sheehan, *A Bright Shining Lie: John Paul Vann and America in Vietnam* (Vintage). Also recommended are Errol Morris's film documentary on McNamara, *The Fog of War* (2003); two collections of reportage: *Reporting Vietnam* and *Reporting Civil Rights* (Library of America); Michael Chabon's rather recent World War II novel *The Amazing Adventures of Kavalier and Clay* (Random House); and Ben Fountain's Iraq War novel *Billy Lynn's Long Halftime Walk* (Ecco).

Certain core texts have shaped my understanding of the United States in war and peace as well as of war transhistorically: James Baldwin, *Notes of a Native Son* (Beacon); Joan Didion, *Slouching Towards Bethlehem, The White Album* (FSG Classics), *After Henry*, and *South and West: From a Notebook* (Vintage); Frederick Douglass's speeches and writings, available in many editions, including *The Essential Douglass*, ed. Nicholas Buccola (Hackett), and *Frederick Douglass: Selected Speeches and Writings*, ed. Philip S. Foner and Yuval Taylor (Lawrence Hill); M. I. Finley, *The World of Odysseus* (New York Review Books); Ulysses S. Grant, *Personal Memoirs*, ed. Elizabeth D. Samet (Liveright); Abraham Lincoln's speeches and writings, available in *The Portable Abraham Lincoln*, ed. Andrew Delbanco (Penguin Classics), and *Speeches and Writings*, ed. Don E. Fehrenbacher (Library of America); Reinhold Niebuhr, *The Irony of American History*, available in an edition with a fine introduction by Andrew J. Bacevich (Univ. of Chicago Press); Alexis de Tocqueville, *Democracy in America* (Penguin Classics and many other editions); Virgil, *The Aeneid*, in Robert Fitzgerald's translation with his postscript about reading the poem in the Western Pacific (Anchor); Robert Penn Warren, *The Legacy of the Civil War* (Bison); and Robert Warshow's *The Immediate Experience: Movies, Comics, Theatre, and Other Aspects of Popular Culture* (Harvard Univ. Press).

When I mentioned to a Russian acquaintance that I was writing this book, she demanded, "What about everyone else's World War II?" The focus of this study is the United States, but here is a necessarily small collection of vital writing from other traditions: Vasily

Grossman's monumental novels *Life and Fate* and *Stalingrad* (New York Review Books) as well as his wartime reporting, collected in *A Writer at War: A Soviet Journalist with the Red Army, 1941–1945*, edited and translated by Antony Beevor (Vintage); Julien Gracq's novel of the Phony War, *Balcony in the Forest* (New York Review Books); Antoine de Saint-Exupéry's memoir about his participation in the Battle of France in 1940, *Flight to Arras* (Harcourt Brace); Simone Weil's *The Iliad or the Poem of Force*, trans. Mary McCarthy (New York Review Books); and, finally, five British books: Keith Douglas's *Alamein to Zem Zem* (Faber & Faber), Patrick Leigh Fermor's *Abducting a General: The Kreipe Operation and SOE in Crete* (John Murray), George MacDonald Fraser's *Quartered Safe Out Here* (Skyhorse), Penelope Fitzgerald's novel *Human Voices* (Mariner), and Evelyn Waugh's *The Sword of Honour Trilogy* (Everyman's Library).

The project of seeing the war anew would have been incomplete without an examination of visual media. Grant Wood and Jacob Lawrence, two painters whose works wrestled with transhistorical American themes, have been especially important. An overview of Wood's work can be found in Barbara Haskell's magnificent catalogue of the 2018 exhibit *Grant Wood: American Gothic and Other Fables* at the Whitney Museum of American Art in New York City. In 2000 the University of Washington Press and the Jacob Lawrence Catalogue Raisonné Project of Seattle published a beautiful two-volume set: *Jacob Lawrence: Paintings, Drawings, and Murals (1935–1999)* and *Over the Line: The Art and Life of Jacob Lawrence*.

In 1964, twenty years after the event, Liebling reprinted his article about crossing the English Channel in a collection called *Mollie and Other War Pieces*. He prefaced it with a characteristically wry observation about the movies: "We did get to France, as you must know if you have seen the Cinemepic called *The Longest Day*, in which with swashbuckling magnificence tricked out with little homely touches a glittering team Eisenhowered by Darryl Zanuck storms the Hun-infested shores . . . Everybody, of course, has his own D-Day." Film by its very nature tends to transform battles into choreographed spectacle, giving narrative sweep and coherence to the haphazard and fitful and relentless. But it is also the case that film (and now television) gives many of us our earliest and most powerful impressions of war.

In an important way, this book began in the movies I grew up watching, often with my father, in the days when nothing was "on demand" and when movies began at whatever point one happened to tune in. Thus, like the ancient epics, these war stories almost always began for me in medias res: *Wake Island* (1942), *Desperate Journey* (1942), *Sahara* (1943), *Five Graves to Cairo* (1943), *Destination Tokyo* (1943), *Thirty Seconds Over Tokyo* (1944), *They Were Expendable* (1945), *The Best Years of Our Lives* (1946), *Twelve O'Clock High* (1949), *The Desert Fox* (1951), *Flying Leathernecks* (1951), *The Caine Mutiny* (1954), *To Hell and Back* (1955), *The Bridge on the River Kwai* (1957), *Run Silent, Run Deep* (1958), *Patton* (1970).

Some of these films were of the "Cinemepic" variety lampooned by Liebling, but over the years this catalogue would be greatly expanded as a result of new reproduction technologies, visits to revival houses, and, much later, hours spent in the Library of Congress Motion Picture and Television Reading Room and in a screening room at the Museum of Modern Art in New York, watching not only movies about World War II but countless others that bear the sometimes almost invisible scars of American wars. I offer here only a sampling of hundreds of films, ranging from action to melodrama, from tragedy to comedy, from Western to noir: *The Birth of a Nation* (1915), *I Am a Fugitive from a Chain Gang* (1932), *Heroes for Sale* (1933), *Young Mr. Lincoln* (1939), *Gone with the Wind* (1939), *The Roaring Twenties* (1939), *Confessions of a Nazi Spy* (1939), *Sergeant York* (1941), *Cry 'Havoc'* (1943), *The Fallen Sparrow* (1943), *Hail the Conquering Hero* (1944), *The Fighting Sullivans* (1944), *Pride of the Marines* (1945), *Till the End of Time* (1946), *My Darling Clementine* (1946), *The Blue Dahlia* (1946), *The Strange Love of Martha Ivers* (1946), *Crack-Up* (1946), *Nobody Lives Forever* (1946), *Somewhere in the Night* (1946), *Deadline at Dawn* (1946), *High Wall* (1947), *Crossfire* (1947), *Boomerang!* (1947), *Desperate* (1947), *Ride the Pink Horse* (1947), *Daisy Kenyon* (1947), *Railroaded!* (1947), *Violence* (1947), *The Hucksters* (1947), *Homecoming* (1948), *Pitfall* (1948), *The Naked City* (1948), *Command Decision* (1948), *Act of Violence* (1948), *Brute Force* (1948), *Kiss the Blood Off My Hands* (1948), *Fort Apache* (1948), *The Crooked Way* (1949), *The Clay Pigeon* (1949), *Impact* (1949), *She Wore a Yellow Ribbon* (1949), *Rio Grande* (1950), *Try and Get Me* (1950), *Side Street* (1950), *In a Lonely Place* (1950), *Winchester '73* (1950), *Bright Victory* (1951), *The Steel Helmet* (1951), *Fort Defiance* (1951), *The Phenix City Story* (1951), *Horizons West* (1952), *The Sniper* (1952), *Sudden Fear* (1952), *Bend of the River* (1952), *Suddenly* (1954), *The Bridges at Toko-Ri* (1954), *The Man from Laramie* (1955), *Bad Day at Black Rock* (1955), *The Man in the Gray Flannel Suit* (1956), *Bitter Victory* (1957), *Men in War* (1957), *The Great Escape* (1963), *Saving Private Ryan* (1998).

ACKNOWLEDGMENTS

The person I most want to read this book no longer can. I write these words at my father's desk, and I knew World War II first as my father's war. In 1942, recently out of high school, Theodore Samet enlisted in the Army Air Forces. He served as an air traffic controller at a series of stateside bases before shipping out to India, where he spent his war at various airfields. I like best to imagine him in his control tower, a Keatsian "watcher of the skies," alert for the planes ferrying cargo to Chittagong or moving the wounded to Karachi. My asking him to tell me stories of those days and his invariable reply ("Who the hell remembers? It was a hundred years ago") constituted one of our oldest rituals. But the stories sometimes came, often at unexpected moments and more frequently in recent years, when he knew I was working on this book. My father always took a much more than dutiful interest in my work, and he would ask me questions about certain details as he read my books. It took him a long time to make his way through them, in part because he was a careful reader but chiefly because he was still working until the very last months of his life and thus never had the retiree's luxury of devoting himself to the reading he so enjoyed. I anticipated our discussions about this book, and it is my persistent sadness that he died before we could have them. *Looking for the Good War* is dedicated to him. Its writing has also been sustained by the love and fierce encouragement of my mother.

I am deeply grateful to the John Simon Guggenheim Memorial Foundation for a fellowship that supported much of my research and writing. The fellowship enabled me to spend many days in the screening room at the Museum of Modern Art's Film Study Center in New York City and at the Motion Picture, Broadcasting and

Recorded Sound Division of the Library of Congress, where my visits were graciously coordinated by Rosemary Hanes and where Dorinda Hartmann has a miraculous way with old and fragile material. I also had the great pleasure of doing research at the New York Public Library, and I am especially grateful for the expertise and kindness of Cheryl Beredo, Curator of the Manuscripts, Archives and Rare Books Division at the Library's Schomburg Center for Research in Black Culture. I thank E. T. Williams, whose mother's correspondence with family and friends at the Schomburg Center is such an extraordinary resource, for encouraging my use of the letters and for providing a biographical context for them. Early versions of passages in this book were first published in *Armed Forces & Society*, *The Dallas Morning News*, and *Foreign Policy*. Brief portions also originally appeared, in different form, in *The New York Times Book Review* and are published with the permission of *The New York Times*.

I have been fortunate over the years to have taught several colloquia on American culture and politics with Suzanne Nielsen and, more recently, a seminar on the literature of World War II with Elizabeth Lazzari. I have learned a great deal from both of these exceptional teachers. Other colleagues and friends listened to ideas, suggested books and films, or read parts of the manuscript. I am especially grateful to Max Adams, David Bromwich, Stephen Greenblatt, Steven Johnson, Adam Keller, Rosanna Warren, and Frank Wilkinson. I will not forget Frank's readiness to help during a difficult stage of revision. I am grateful to Kees FaesenKloet and Brian Smith for being willing to watch any movie, no matter how obscure, and to discuss it in detail. During a year of personal as well as communal loss, I have gained a deeper appreciation for their friendship as well as for that of Matthew Boethin, Jonathan Lewis, Karin Roffman, Anne Taranto, Nick Utzig, and Noriko Utzig. Karin and Nick were always ready to read material, often at short notice, and they responded with characteristic patience and insight. It is a very good feeling to have David Kuhn and Nate Muscato at Aevitas Creative Management in one's corner. Eric Chinski and Julia Ringo are marvelous, deeply thoughtful editors, and it is always such a delight to work with everyone at FSG.

The views expressed in this book do not reflect the official policy or position of the Department of the Army, the Department of Defense, or the U.S. Government.

Elizabeth D. Samet is the author of *No Man's Land: Preparing for War and Peace in Post-9/11 America; Soldier's Heart: Reading Literature Through Peace and War at West Point*, which won the Los Angeles Times Book Prize for Current Interest and was named one of the 100 Notable Books of 2007 by *The New York Times*; and *Willing Obedience: Citizens, Soldiers, and the Progress of Consent in America, 1776–1898*. Samet is the editor of *Leadership: Essential Writings by Our Greatest Thinkers, The Annotated Memoirs of Ulysses S. Grant*, and *World War II Memoirs: The Pacific Theater*. She is the recipient of a National Endowment for the Humanities Public Scholar Grant and the Hiett Prize in the Humanities, and she was awarded a Guggenheim Fellowship to support the research and writing of *Looking for the Good War*. She is a professor of English at West Point.